A World without Prisons

A World without Prisons

Alternatives to Incarceration throughout the World

Calvert R. Dodge
University of Maryland

LexingtonBooks
D.C. Heath and Company
Lexington, Massachusetts
Toronto

Library of Congress Cataloging in Publication Data

Dodge, Calvert R.
  A world without prisons.

  Includes indexes.
  1. Corrections. 2. Punishment. I. Title.
  HV8665.D57   364.6   78-24629
  ISBN 0-669-02706-5

Published simultaneously in Canada.

Printed in the United States of America.

International Standard Book Number: 0-669-02706-5

Library of Congress Catalog Card Number: 78-24629

To

Hugh Carey, Fay H. Knopp, Jerome Miller,
and William G. Nagel of the United States;
W. Breukelaar, H. Neelop, and A. Heijder of
the Netherlands; Thomas Mathiesen of
Norway and Hans v. Hofer of Sweden.

and to

E.E.M.

Contents

Contents

List of
Figures and Tables

Foreword

The punishment of criminals is an ancient and dismal rite. History is replete with examples of gruesome penalties inflicted by society on those who break its law. No country has been without its cunningly contrived methods of inflicting pain, and even the briefest recapitulation would chill the blood and remind us how mightily we have insisted on obedience to the law.

In that quest we have never scrupled to become savage. But if severe punishment of the offender is a repeated design in the tapestry of history, so too is the plea for understanding, forgiveness, and mercy. To think that the only appropriate response to the offender is the lash is to forget the many who have urged helping and healing instead. One need remember only the response of Jesus to the question of punishment or forgiveness. "How often should I forgive a brother who sins against me? Seven times?" "No," Jesus replied, "seventy times seven."

It is easy to come to believe that imprisonment is the natural punishment for criminal activity. Prisons seem always to have been with us. They appear to offer security to the public by removing the offender to a place so remote that he cannot reach them. To those who have been victimized by crime, the prison, oppressive and terrible to behold, suggests safety and security. Even for those who have never been robbed or hurt, the threat of crime is so repugnant that it elicits their approval for caging the lawbreaker.

The cage is something of an innovation historically. There were dungeons a thousand years ago, by and large the cages were used for persons of high rank or political prisoners or some special type of person. The common criminal was summarily hung, whipped, branded, mutilated, crushed by stones, or dealt with in some other direct and brutal fashion. Imprisonment would have been too costly a practice, and those who advocated it would surely have been considered mollycoddlers.

But with the Enlightenment in eighteenth-century Europe and America came the notion that a person who committed a crime was not necessarily in league with Satan. An offender could be saved, rehabilitated, and returned to the company of civil men and women. To accomplish this, reformers developed the penitentiary, that grim pile in which the penitent was supposed to pray, work, and discover if not an Edenic innocence, at least a willingness to live within the law. This process of self-discovery and repentance was urged by men who did not hesitate to invoke the most brutal disciplines in an effort to refine the spirit and bring it to a state of grace. More often than not, however, they merely broke the spirit. This was not accidental. Elam Lynds, the first warden of Sing Sing, contended that "reformation of the criminal could not possibly be effected until the spirit of the criminal was broken."[a]

Most people, secure in the knowledge that wrongdoers behind bars were paying their just debt to society, slept an untroubled sleep.

Penitentiaries, even from the beginning, proved to be the most imperfect of institutions. Not long after they were established, citizens who gained some understanding of what went on behind the walls formed organizations to improve them. They sought to make prisons humane and caring institutions from which an inmate might emerge after three, ten, or fifteen years with a new willingness to stay on the safe side of the law. All in vain; the penitentiaries proved to be unimprovable.

Even today prison improvement seems to elude even the most ardent reformers. Thus within a year of its opening, the Metropolitan Correctional Center in New York City, whose modern design delighted architectural critics, was found by a federal court to be abusing the rights of its inmates. The nature of the prison confounds the best intentions of both citizens and correctional authorities. Strive as they may, they cannot make the prison less than it is: cages to hold the young, the poor, and, increasingly, the minorities.

Secure confinement is regrettably necessary for some offenders—those so violent and assaultive that to put them in the community is to put the community in peril. But such lawbreakers are in the minority. Most criminal acts are crimes against property. Those who commit them deserve the censure of society. They may require punishment of some sort, but it is not likely that they require imprisonment. Incarceration of the nondangerous is inappropriate for a number of reasons. First, prisons do not reform such inmates; indeed such reform as is possible may come more readily through other means. Second, prisons are among the costliest institutions in the world to build, operate, and maintain. To punish by imprisonment then is to punish the public as well. Third, prison criminalizes many inmates far beyond their condition before incarceration. Fourth, brutalizing an offender through caging somehow subtly makes all of us more brutal. A society that uses violent means of assuring tranquility finds that tranquility strangely elusive.

If prisons are not the answer, what is? There are many answers, and some of them are discussed in this volume. They have in common an attempt to find punishments more effective, humane, and economical than routine incarceration. The search for such alternatives has become increasingly important because the demand for more imprisonment as the cure-all for crime has become strident. This is true of a number of countries; it is

---

[a]Ronald L. Goldfarb and Linda R. Singer, *After Conviction* (New York: Simon and Schuster, 1973), p. 37.

especially true of the United States. Politicians are running for election with pledges of toughness on offenders. Police insist that there is little purpose in catching thieves if they are not punished, and for the police punishment is equated with imprisonment. The press and the public in general have become most insistent on putting offenders of every type in prison.

Judges, reflecting the fearful mood of the public, have become more cautious; they have given fewer probationary sentences and have lengthened the term of sentences that they have awarded. At the other end of the correctional spectrum, paroling authorities have asked that more time be served before parole be granted.

All this caution, based on the ill-founded notion that more time in prison will somehow mean less crime, has filled American prisons to overflowing. So overcrowded are these institutions that in many states inmates are doubly and triply bunked, confined in tents, trailers, warehouses, ships, and a host of unsuitable facilities. Inmates have won a number of lawsuits protesting these conditions, and many correctional systems have been found to deny prisoners their most basic human rights.

To provide new prisons for people presently confined as well as for growing prison populations would cost this country $1 billion a year for the next decade, according to the head of the American Correctional Association. Already under construction or in the planning stage are 900 new prisons and jails. The objective appears to be to continue to expand prison construction in order to accommodate an increasingly larger percentage of the nation's total population. Today that population stands at the highest level in its history with more than one-half million men, women, and children behind bars.

If the search for alternatives to imprisonment was imperative in the past, it is doubly imperative today, if only because of the financial burden that building more prisons would impose. Every encouragement must be given to exploring criminal justice sanctions that seek to deal appropriately with offenders but do not require secure confinement.

Three new approaches, found primarily in England, Holland, and the Scandinavian countries, bear great promise. They are the use of community service orders, now frequently given in England; day fines, penalties based on both the gravity of the offense and the financial income of the offender, now given in Sweden and other countries; and restitution to victims, now in practice in many countries and to a limited extent in the United States. These criminal justice sanctions deserve the most careful scrutiny and testing, for they have the possibility of satisfying the needs of a modern society: they enact a penalty for breaking the law but one that is not so severe that it impairs the ability of the offender to function, and they require that society and the victim be compensated for the injury sustained.

It should not be assumed that these are entirely new notions. On the contrary, they have their roots in early Western history. *Wergeld*, for example, described in King Alfred's laws in ninth-century England, is money compensation given in cases of homicide to the kin of the person slain. Such a money tribute was required in order to avoid a protracted blood feud. Some payments, called *bots*, were made for cases of personal injury. Fines called *wites* were paid to kings in addition to compensation to the victims and their families. Forced service to the state for an offender is not a new concept by any means. But its translation into the modern community service order in lieu of imprisonment certainly is.

There are, of course, other approaches to dealing with offenders that are in keeping with modern society. It is wise to keep in mind that punishment is not a static matter. It is a changing and developing societal response. What we develop and institutionalize today, therefore, may be inappropriate years hence. The future must find its own solutions to society's deviants, and certainly it will do so.

The warning to heed is that in our effort to find appropriate punishment, we should not be lured by technology into cures that may be worse than the illness. Drugs and shock therapies, as applied to offenders in an effort to rehabilitate them, demand the most rigorous controls. Perhaps they are beyond the pale. The optimal punishment for a civilized society is that which departs least from the normal conduct of life in all its characteristics. It is this plus the development of understanding and tolerance that should be our steadfast goal.

Hackensack, New Jersey   *Milton G. Rector*
June 30, 1979   President
                    The National Council on Crime and Delinquency

Preface

In today's world many approaches to incarceration and rehabilitation may be found. Each of these approaches was developed to aid citizens found guilty of crimes to either "pay" for their act or to be "cured" so that they could reenter the community as law abiders.

Each nation has existing systems of prisons and correctional institutions for one or more of the following reasons: (1) to deter criminal acts; (2) to safeguard the public from the criminal; (3) to resocialize or rehabilitate the convicted person.

To deter criminal acts? Incarceration appears not to deter. Throughout the world criminal statistics indicate that the harsher the penalty, the greater the chance of recidivism.

To safeguard the public from the criminal? Research during the past fifty years indicates that only a temporary safeguard appears plausible.

To resocialize or rehabilitate convicted citizens? To many of the penal system's critics this reason for incarceration has also proved invalid.

Volumes have been written, an abundance of empirical research has been made and reported, and the common sense of simple economics as well as social and psychological reasoning have all emphasized that prisons are not needed. Yet prisons continue to exist, and plans and budgets for prison construction abound in many countries today. There are "facts" that support each cause related to corrections. Those in favor of prison abolition have a set of facts supporting the demise of the prison system. Those in favor of supporting change within the system have an equally substantive set of facts. There are many other schools of thought that fall on the continuum from larger and stronger prisons to abolition of them. This book may be useful in supporting the abolitionists' cause. It may also foster change within existing systems. Its appeal is dependent on the reader's frame of reference.

It is, most of all, an idea book suggesting alternatives to incarceration that are being used or implemented in several nations outside the United States. It is addressed to those who are interested in changing what many consider an outmoded, useless, economically wasteful corrections system—a system that has embedded itself in the social and political systems of many of the nations of the world.

This book is also addressed to members of the bar, the judicial system, the correction systems, community and business leaders, and others who have the power to instigate social change.

Several of the alternatives described in this volume are spelled out in considerable detail in order to provide the reader with a more complete picture of the alternatives so that replication of them in another community can be made. Many references are included from which readers may gather additional information.

A World without Prisons is not a book containing theories nor is it a report of empirical research proving this or that particular program. The alternatives described in these pages may help support a new direction in corrections that has already been developing—toward new concern for the victim, the accused, and the convicted, as well as for the citizen who must pay the price of whatever system is used. The theme contained in these pages suggests a new order in corrections. The new order is based on greater public concern and support of more desirable and humane systems for correcting man's socially unacceptable behavior. The new order must focus on involvement and caring for others. In an age of technological advancement we must do everything possible to avoid building a world of automatons. In the field of corrections this can be translated into involvement of the convicted, the participants in the judicial system, the general public, and even the victim of crime. The victim must be helped to understand this principle of caring for the accused and for others even while under the strain of the particular traumatic circumstances surrounding his own experience as a crime victim.

Criminality is a concern of most of us in varying degrees. To some it is simply a matter of our safety needs. To others it is philosophical. Today with a dramatic increase in the level of interest that many individuals and nations have demonstrated toward the problems of crime and incarceration, there is a correspondingly increased demand for ideas and suggestions about what can or should be done. This increased interest exists for a variety of reasons. The relatively high probability that each of us may become involved, like it or not, in some aspect of criminality is one reason for this new interest. Terrorism, aircraft hijacking, vandalism, mugging, theft, fraud, and the myriad of other types of crimes appear to be coming to roost upon the doorsteps of the average citizen. In the United States alone there will probably be more than 5 million major criminal acts committed each year through the 1980s. These figures will continue to rise until major changes in our social system alter the situation in some positive manner. Each of us stands an ever increasing possibility of being involved even when we may abhor involvement. To some of us the questions to which we address ourselves will be focused on the social, technological, and environmental changes that may be at the root of crime. To others the focus of involvement may be on the religious and moral aspects of criminality. To others it may simply be a matter of making demands on governmental organizations to take some sort of action about crime. Other nations are experiencing an upswing in criminality and are also examining their systems of justice and methods of penal sanction. There are many indications, as are discussed in this volume, that we are entering into an age of prison and corrections reformation unsurpassed in the past. The key to this reformation appears to be the interest and involvement of lay citizens in certain countries. It is the interest of the ordinary citizen that is so vital in changing a gigantic machine, the corrections machine.

In any approach to involvement in the area of crime or corrections the most vital question concerns our own beliefs, values, and attitudes toward other people. Most of us, too often, give only lip service to concern. This book is for people who desire to go beyond lip service and to become involved. New ideas require involvement. Like seeds, these ideas require dissemination in fertile ground and nurturing in order to grow and develop. Some of these ideas may not develop to any great extent or usefulness while others, given the necessary citizen involvement, may grow into remarkable success programs ushering in the new order in corrections and care. Changing an outmoded and useless correction system will take many years—perhaps many decades—but the need for the change is clearly evident.

In reviewing the alternatives described in this volume, the reader may keep in mind that it took only a few people to create the now antiquated Philadelphia and Auburn systems of prisons which were copied by many nations during the past two-hundred years. It requires only one or two people to decide to make changes. This process of change demands that some action be taken, that someone become involved. The purpopse of this book is to foster that process.

Stuttgart, Germany   *Calvert R. Dodge*
June 30, 1979

Acknowledgments

Each contributor has provided valuable assistance to the development of this book, and I express my thanks and gratitude to all those who have shared materials with me for the readers of this book:

> To the many corrections system administrators and community leaders who made arrangements for me to visit prisons, police departments, and alternative facilities and who arranged for me to interview clients, prisoners, officials, and other representatives especially in the Federal Republic of Germany, South Korea, and the United Kingdom.
>
> To Hansjorg Albrecht of the Max Planck Institute of Germany, and to Paul Cavadino of NACRO, London, England, Milton Rector of the National Council on Crime and Delinquency, United States,
>
> To Erik J. Besier and Alfred Heijder of the Netherlands,
>
> To Jerry Bergman for his special assistance and encouragement,
>
> To Sue Bateman, Headquarters European Communication, United States Army, for her editing and typing assistance,
>
> To the many others who have helped make this book possible,

I express my gratitude.

Part I
Overview

Creo que la vida de un hombre por desgraciado que sea, vale
mas que todo cuanto pueda gastarse.

*I think that a man's life, no matter how wretched he may be, is
worthier than all that has to be spent.*

Francisco Franco de Blas, "Formacion Penitenciaria del Coronel Montesinos y su Celebre
Sistema," in *Revista de Estudios Penitenciarios*, Madrid, Direcciòn General de Prisionea, año
18, no. 159 (October-December, 1962):101.

1 Historical Perspective

Developing institutions for enforcing the laws of society is a relatively modern practice. Confinement before the seventeenth century was simply a form of detention, and no other reason to justify its existence was needed. Before this period and dating back to the use of the Code of Hammurabi, designed by King Hammurabi of Babylon in the eighteenth century B.C., the punishment for crime included restitution, exile, and a wide variety of methods of corporal and capital punishment.[1] The ruling principle of law was an eye for an eye and a tooth for a tooth. The chopping block was in vogue for cutting off fingers, hands, and heads, as befitted the crime. Other formal laws included the Mosaic law and the legal codes of the Roman empire. Often tribal groups handled law offenders as they saw fit, and examples of taboos that motivated retaliatory action by these clans or tribes in preliterate society included murder, incest, and theft of food or property. The Teutonic tribes of northwestern Europe extracted money from lawbreakers at the beginning of the Christian era.

Modern criminal justice is perhaps more closely related to the time when the royal house of an area assumed control over administration of laws. Under these circumstances compensation was paid to the king instead of to the wronged person or his family. This movement of the crown into the patterns of tribal society during the twelfth century ushered in the establishment of systems of punishment. Thus the seeds for the development of prisons as we know them today were sown in the soil of punishment on behalf of the individual wronged and, later, on behalf of society which had also been wronged. There seems to be no clear-cut philosophy or rationalization for the establishment of the punishment concept by the societies of the twelfth century. Prisons existed at that time solely for prisoners awaiting trial or punishment and were not considered institutions where confinement itself would be considered punishment. It was not until the sixteenth century that such places of detention were to be considered a form of punishment. One of the first such institutions was Bridewell, a house for correcting law offenders opened in London in 1557.[2] Banishment was another form of punishment. From 1597 to 1776 England transported over a hundred thousand criminals to America. England also sent criminals to Australia and France, and other countries shipped prisoners to penal colonies on islands or isolated parts of colonies.

During the eighteenth century and especially after the American revolution, systems of punishment were being questioned. In the latter part of the eighteenth century social theorists including Beccaria, Rousseau, Blackstone, and Montesquieu were arguing against the old systems of brutal punishment, banishment, and other forms of dehumanization. William Penn, founder of Pennsylvania, initiated attempts to change his state's punishment system favoring something less severe than a copy of English brutality. In 1785 William Paley publicly advocated the concept of solitary imprisonment.[3] In the United States it was the Quakers in Philadelphia who are credited with beginning a movement in penal reform that was to spread to many other parts of the world. The argument of the Quakers, a strong sect of the Christian religion led by Penn, suggested that convicted criminals had affronted both God and society. These criminals should be removed from the public stocks and pillaries that stood in almost every community and placed in singular private prison cells where they could reflect on their misbehavior and improve their spiritual condition. If the prisoner could read, a Bible would be the only reading material provided. A spokesman for the Quaker group suggested:

> The reformation of a criminal can never be effected by a public punishment. . . . Experience proves, that public punishments have increased propensities to crimes. A man who has lost his self-respect at a whipping post, has nothing valuable to lose to society. Pain has begotten insensibility to the whip, and shame to infamy. Added to his old habits of vice, he probably feels a spirit of revenge against the whole community whose laws have inflicted his punishment upon him and hence he is stimulated to add to the number and enormity of his outrages upon society.[4]

The Philadelphia group's proposal was considered fairly innovative. The suggestion was to incorporate this new model into a social punishment system that had already received support in the Great Law of Pennsylvania written by Penn, enacted in 1682, which directed that "every county within the province of Pennsylvania and territories thereunto belonging shall . . . build or cause to be built in the most convenient place in each respective county a sufficient house for restraint, labor, and punishment of all such persons as thereunto be committed by law."[5] While the wording of this law and similar such laws may have carried with them some intention of the people's responsibility for the care of other humans, the actual use of such institutions was, from the beginning of their construction, more of an incorporation of the combined banishment-punishment principle. Much of the world's prisons adopting the Philadelphia or similar models of imprisonment became dumping grounds for the accused and untried, the mentally incompetent, the debtor, and a host of other types of offenders. To this day these prisons appear, in many cases, to be housing the accused, the misdemeanants, the felons, all under the same roof, all subject to indiscriminate socialization or punishment methods as if all were simply archenemies of society.

The Philadelphia Society for Alleviating the Miseries of Public Prisons was created in 1787.[6] The society believed that the punishment should not destroy the offender physically or mentally. This society included some influential citizens and was one of the more powerful groups responsible for developing a new penology and for the invention of the penitentiary concept. It was groups such as this that demanded of government some rationalization, some justification, of prisons as they were. A new age had been born with a clearly humanitarian intent. During the nearly two hundred years of penal evolution since then, the rationalization for imprisonment has become even more vague.

The penitentiary idea became popular, and between 1800 and 1850 New York, New Jersey, Massachusetts, and Connecticut were following Pennsylvania's lead and building their own model prisons. Considerable amounts of money were being spent for the construction of these fortress-like structures, whose outer walls were often three feet thick. Europeans were also building prisons similar to these models. The Dartmoor prison in England was built in 1809 and cost 66,815 pounds—a huge outlay for such a structure. The utopian idea, at least in terms of punishment, was exemplified in the construction of these stabilizers of society. Some leaders of law and justice saw them as "laboratories committed to the improvement of all mankind."[7]

These penitentiaries were said to have been designed to accomplish the goals of social planners who attributed crime to a harmful home environment, a lack of work skills, or ignorance as to what was right and what was wrong on the part of the criminal. The architects of these new and innovative prison units designed them to minimize the prisoners' chances of being injured, to provide adequate education and opportunity to learn work skills, and to ensure that ample biblical teaching would be provided. Various states pursued these goals in what they considered to be the appropriate manner.

The Pennsylvania system was developed on the theory that solitary confinement accompanied by bench labor within one's cell would accomplish these several aims. In this solitary cell the offender was denied all contact, all communication, with the outside world except that provided by and incorporated within biblical scriptures, religious tracts, and visits from the clergy or selected citizens of unquestioned religious fervor. The design of the prison was aimed at this goal and this solitary experience. Walls between cells were thick; cells were somewhat large, and each was equipped with some sort of crude plumbing fixture (usually a pail with cover) and water. In the cell was a workbench, and tools were furnished for the particular duty assigned to the prisoner. In addition, each cell had a small private exercise area. Theoretically the design accomplished its purposes, including the elimination of external influencs, promotion of work, and opportunity for private thought to accomplish penitence, introspection, and the accumulation of religious knowledge. Time did not improve this approach. During the month of July 1896, almost one hundred years after the penitentiary was developed and many years after the development of the Philadelphia concept for prisons, little had changed. Oscar Wilde summarized this general conclusion when he petitioned the prison governor in England for some changes of routine:

> The petitioner has been subject to the fearful system of solitary celular confinement: without human intercourse of any kind: without writing materials whose use might help to distract the mind: without suitable or sufficient books . . . condemned to absolute silence: cut off from knowledge of the external world and the movements of life; leading an existence composed of bitter degradation and terrible hardships, hideous in its recurring monotony of dreary task and sickening privation. . . . This tomb for those who are not yet dead.[8]

Eastern State Penitentiary was built with this single man-single cell idea incorporated in its design. A product of Quaker thinking and planning, it was a gloomy fortress of stone. Each convict was locked in a separate cell and confined there for the length of his sentence, working at what were considered by prison officials to be useful trades. This design was to allow the inmate a chance to come to terms with his inner self, his Maker, and to gain a more religious outlook for the future.

A second theory was developing at about the same time as the Quakers' innovation. This theory differed from the approach of the Quakers in that inmates were allowed to work together. Perhaps a theory of rehabilitation helped generate this new theory; perhaps economics played a major role in its development. The program for the prison provided work situations in which prisoners could work outside their cells in workshops during the day. Sometimes the prisoners could even work outside the prison groups on road and building construction and other projects where larger groups of laborers were needed. This "model" prison was first built in Auburn, New York, and was opened in 1819. Sing Sing prison in New York was built several years later along the same design. While inmates slept in separate cells, they were moved into workshops or road gangs during the day, eating together in a common dining facility. The whip was used abundantly by prison guards, and they enforced a policy of absolute silence among the convicts. From about 1835 until the middle 1950s nearly all prisons and reformatories built in the United States and many other countries were based on this general prison design in 1819. High walls, guard towers, multiple story blocks of cells, with new buildings built rather randomly around the original structure, were standard features of construction for the Auburn prison concept. These structures exist today, although many of the routines of the 1880s have changed. Both the Philadelphia and the Auburn systems were copied by other nations. Arguments for or against either system depended on which philosophy was involved. If the philosophy was a case of pure economics, relative values of the two systems were argued on the basis of dollars returned to the government in the form of prison labor for dollars spent. If it was a case of prison reform the arguments would revolve around isolation or communality as a means of rehabilitation. To those demanding retaliation, the arguments concerned the degree of harshness that one system had over the other. Eventually these arguments were replaced by the philosophy of recidivism and the effect that prisons had on prisoners in terms of the chances of their returning to prison, that is, of becoming recidivist. Comparisons of the worth of prison systems today center around the criterion of recidivism.

When Alexis de Tocqueville and Gustave de Beaumont visited the United States to investigate these rival prison systems in 1831, they made the following observation in part.

> The Philadelphia system, being that which produces the deepest impressions on the soul of the convict, must effect more reformation than that of Auburn. The latter, however, is perhaps more conformable to the habits of man in society, and on this account effects a greater number of reformations which might be called "legal", inasmuch as they produce the external fulfillment of social obligations. If those be so, the Philadelphia system produces more honest men, and that of New York more obedient citizens.[9]

Arguments about which system alleviates crime, reduces recidivism, or serves the best rehabilitative function have continued to this day. The rivalry between the systems, however, is not as visible as it was in the late 1880s. The Auburn system, Sing Sing being one example, became the model for almost every maximum security prison built in the United States, and both the Philadelphia system and Auburn systems became the models for many of the prisons built in Europe. The Auburn system reflected the Puritan theory of human nature. In many of the nations using these systems or combinations, the restrictions are no longer so evident. Silence, isolation, and the whip are no longer the general rule although they have not been entirely eliminated. In most of these types of prisons custody and control remain foremost on the minds of staff and serve as heavy influences when changes are to be effected. Resocialization programs within walls of these types of prisons continues to have a heavy shroud of custody interfering with its progress. In Europe the custody-control concept appears to be stronger than in the United States, and recent outbreaks of terrorism as well as political unrest have served only to reemphasize this control and custody viewpoint.

During the period of the development of the Philadelphia and Auburn prison systems many theories have evolved that were intended to support the idea of the penitentiary. It appears that society was presented with a system of imprisonment before it was presented with an argument for a prison system. Justification now had to be made for it. To some it was evident that our prison system had become society's white elephant and even more justification for its existence was necessary. Today the arguments for imprisonment usually include one or more of the following:

1. Imprisonment deters others from committing crimes; it makes the potential perpetrator of a crime think twice.
2. Imprisonment provides the means by which criminals may repay society for the damage done to society or to its individual members.
3. Imprisonment provides a place where the idle, the vagrants, those who do not contribute to society's well-being may find labor and thus they may become beneficial to society and to themselves. The original vagrancy laws of England developed in 1849 were for the purpose of accumulating a labor force for the upper class manufacturers of the country.
4. Prisons are essential so that wrongdoers may be punished and, at the same time, make peace with their God for their antisocial or anti-God-like acts.
5. Imprisonment is simply a hospital for the socially sick person and serves to cure him.
6. Prisons exist in order that the process of rehabilitation or resocialization can be most efficiently accomplished by society.
7. Prisons exist in order to protect society from people who are violent or destructive.
8. Imprisonment is necessary in order to protect the criminal from becoming brutalized by his fellowman in an eye-for-an-eye attitude.

The reasons for continued support of imprisonment and for corrections in general, in which some part of the system will include imprisonment, can be further divided into retaliation, exploitation, humanism, and treatment. Retaliation is the oldest justification for the development of the corrections system. Man reacted to acts against him by counteracts. Capital and corporal punishments are a crude refinement of this concept. During the time of King Henry VIII executions were the rule rather than the exception, and the annual average of executions in the London area amounted to about three hundred.[10] These executions were usually for crimes against property. In France pickpockets were publicly executed to deter pickpocketing, but this practice had to be stopped. It seemed that during the executions, while large crowds were gathered in the city or town square to witness the execution, pickpocketing in the audience increased to a great extent. By the middle of the nineteenth century the death penalty was beginning to disappear from many law books, although in the United States it continued into the 1960s and beyond. Whipping and flogging have survived much longer. The whip was abolished as a legal means of punishment in England in 1948, but it remains a legal form of punishment in many other countries today.

Exploitation of prisoners has almost always been considered a justifiable means of punishing and correcting them. Even the modern systems of corrections that employ restitution as a part of the correcting process may find themselves accused of exploiting the prisoner. Before and during the time of the Roman Empire criminals were exploited as a labor force in quarries, in agriculture, and in road construction. In modern times this exploitation has been extended to include manufacturing. One of the first state prisons in the United States was located in a Connecticut mine.[11] Galley slaves in the Middle Ages and, more recently, chain gangs are examples of this correcting process. Vagrancy laws of 1849 in England, which set the trend for vagrancy laws in many Western nations, were said to be brought about by the demand for cheap labor rather than by any wrong-doing on the part of the vagrant. The Auburn system supported the use of labor in this exploitative manner. In Germany and other European countries agreements are made between manufacturer and prison officials whereby prisoners do the manufacturer's labor for a small compensation. At the present time the pay for prison labor is far below minimum standards, and in many instances the payment is only enough for the prisoner to accumulate cigarette and stationery money or shaving materials. This exploitative reason for corrections, however, is diminishing in popularity, and in some cases, where prisoners are required to work at such labor, much higher compensation is granted. This is especially true in the Scandinavian countries.

Humanism as a reason for corrections existence probably stems from moral and ethical reasoning extracted from religious doctrine. This is probably true in Christian, Buddhist, and other nations where religious philosophies have influenced social conduct to a great extent. Reformation of prisons and the correcting process have been especially motivated by the concepts of Christianity including compassion and charity. Many prison educational programs, prison libraries, and even prison recreational programs were originally developed with a central purpose of teaching religious doctrine and concepts as applied in society. Following this religious effort further, humanitarianism in prisons is indicated by the development of medical services, the allowance of visits from relatives, and the tolerence of correspondence between prisoner and family. Later in the history of prisons, crafts and hobbies and other activities were introduced, often with humanism as the motivating factor. Most corrections system reformers before World War II applied the concepts of humanism to their efforts at prison reform rather than to the development of effective treatment programs.

Treatment has probably been the most recent and rapidly expanding reason for the justification of corrections as it exists today. Most of the theories of social theorists, sociologists, criminologists, and behaviorists are attempts to provide a cause for criminality and to provide treatment after the cause has been identified. Beginning more generally during the late nineteenth century these theories may fall within some general class of reasoning as to the cause of crime such as biological, psychological, sociological, and environmental. Some theories explained that the cause of crime is a misshapen cranium. Others claimed that bodily structure was related to criminality. With the popularity of Freudian theory a multiplicity of theories emerged that were concerned with the psychological causes of criminality. Gall, a leading brain anatomist of his time, ushered in the new age of corrections in terms of this treatment concept. His demand for individualization of punishment received considerable support from other scientists and especially from representatives in the field of psychiatry. During the last fifty years considerable influence has been exerted on the corrections systems in various parts of the world as a result of this focus on treatment. Legal systems have been challenged, and judges have been confronted with concepts such as moral insanity while the concept of "the same punishment for the same crime" was changing. Revisions of laws to accommodate this treatment concept have been slow in coming, especially in terms of the individualization concept. Revisions of laws have been greatly expanded since World War II, and changes in penal codes and citizen involvement today reflect this new era and its direction.

Alongside these reasons for the existence of prisons is a fairly new force, a demand for abolition of prisons by an influential segment of the population. While this group is small and most of its members are located in the United States, it is growing at a comparatively rapid rate. The seemingly normal system of corrections and imprisonment is now being challenged, and the arguments for abolition are many. Part of the efforts of the abolitionist centers around the argument that a new public viewpoint about imprisonment must be developed. This viewpoint is that imprisonment is abnormal and represents an idiosyncracy of civilization. The viewpoint also suggests that once this point of abnormality is accepted, then the several reasons for imprisonment begin to lose their validity. Then and only then will theorists, reformers, abolitionists, governments, and the general public come to grips with the problem and begin to solve it. Until recently mankind was so enveloped in the idea that imprisonment was a natural phenomenon, a normal part of civilization, that the concept of prisons, per se, was never seriously questioned. This attitude, it appears, is beginning to change as we enter the twenty-first century.

Types of Correctional Institutions

Once justification legitimized the construction of prisons, it was only a matter of time for the construction of offshoots of the Philadelphia and Auburn systems and their European counterparts. In the evolution of the prison system, seven major types of institutions were developed. They included maximum security prisons, minimum security prisons, minimum security correctional centers, special institutions for women, youth correction centers, institutions for juveniles, and reception and classification centers. A brief description of these institutions will provide some basis for understanding the differences and similarities as well as the purposes of each.

Maximum Security Prisons

A maximum security prison is built to incorporate maximum supervision, control, and surveillance of inmates. As mentioned in the description of the Philadelphia system, the building design and the prison program revolve around security and minimal outside activity or treatment programs. Trust or trustworthiness on the inmate's part is not expected, and mistrust is assumed. Any social activity or social well-being of the prisoner is viewed from the standpoint of its interference with prison security. Thick walls, double steel fences, electronic sensing devices, and the positioning of flood lights all epitomize a modern maximum security institution's victory of external control over internal treatment or reform. Privacy is abolished. Doors have grilles for the custodian to observe the prisoner. Toilets are unscreened. Showers are taken under strict supervision. All activity is designed in terms of its relationship to custody. Even eating utensils may be denied to inmates in some of these institutions. Outside intrusions are also guarded against through the use of special devices built to prevent physical contact with visitors. Communication with visiting relatives may be limited to a phone system in the visiting room, and before and after the visit the prisoner is usually stripped, and his body crevices are thoroughly searched for contraband. Movement of prisoners within prison walls is limited and is always under supervision by guards, often with the assistance of closed circuit television. Maximum security prisons uphold their tradition for taking away much and giving little.

Imprisonment in a maximum security prison usually means that the person

no longer has an occupational or personal framework.

is denied total freedom.

is denied social, sexual, and family relationships.

is denied most communication outlets with others from his home area or elsewhere.

is deprived of any ability to organize.

is provided a mixed set of regulations. If it appears to someone in power that a regulation was broken, further loss of liberty, extension of sentence, or other penalties may result. Interpretation is often a matter of the mood of a guard or other prison staff member.

lives in a cloud of uncertainty with regard to rights in prison, parole hearings, date of release, and many other significant items of information.

is denied civil rights, voting, due process, legal assistance, privacy, and similar rights.

lives in a system wherein might is often right, where idleness, loneliness, and boredom become normal and unalterable parts of life.

is usually located in a rural area many miles from his home.

While these factors occur with any type of incarceration, they are usually most pronounced in systems of maximum security.[12]

Medium Security Prisons

A medium security prison is the result of developments in the social and behavioral sciences since 1900 and the increasing value placed on education, the work ethic, and changes in technology. Probation and parole, which were begun earlier than this, provided data indicating that different people convicted of different or same crimes could be handled differently, and that age, family, and other background were determining factors in the success of programs other than incarceration in a maximum security prison. The medium security prison developed to an even greater extent after 1950, and over 50 pecent of the medium security institutions in the United States were built after this year. The Netherlands, Sweden, and Denmark, as well as several other countries, were experimenting with medium security prisons during the early 1950s. More intensive correctional services are usually permissible in these institutions. A larger range of opportunities is provided inmates, but security remains a priority with staff members. Most of these institutions have walls, fences, and some form of electronic device for the control of gates, doors, and surveillance. The design of these institutions is focused on confinement under observation. In many cases observation or guard towers and armed guards remain to characterize these institutions as cages.

Internal security is similar to that in maximum security prisons but less strict. Head counting is a matter of routine. The buildings are separated into schools, housing, industrial shops, and recreation facilities. Usually a gate or set of gates exists that separates the movement of traffic and controls movement from one area to another.

Some innovations in the medium security field have been encouraging. A different design, which includes a combination of small cottages housing twelve to sixteen persons, and improved treatment programs have displaced some of the emphasis on security and control. These are exceptions, however, to the general picture of medium security institutions in most countries.

Minimum Security Correctional Centers

The minimum security correctional center does not rely on secure buildings, high walls, fences, and similar security measures for control of inmates. Most minimum security correctional centers are relatively open, and custody is more a product of selection and classification than of structure and security. In this category are drug rehabilitation centers, forestry camps, farms, educational centers, work-apprenticeship centers, and similar facilities. In Canada many of these centers are called resource centers.

The minimum security facility is economically useful to society in that its primary purpose in most cases is either to prepare persons for work in the community or actually use assigned persons for work that benefits the state or community. Lumbering, road and dam construction, farming, forest fire fighting, forest park maintenance, and state building maintenance are often performed by incarcerated persons assigned to the minimum security units of a state. The needs of the offenders are usually secondary, but these facilities are more therapeutic than closed security units. Usually there is some separation of older inmates from youthful inmates, a control system relies more on trust than on walls and guns, and there is more general freedom of movement. The sleeping units may include cottages or dormitories holding eight to twenty-four beds, and sometimes there are even private bedrooms. Schools, vocational training programs, libraries, chapels, and other types of support facilities and programs are built around the living units. Sometimes this design is like a campus or village. Often inmates work in family-type teams alternating their cooking, cleaning, washing, and other routine duties with one another. More recently minimum security correctional centers have been located in cities and towns and have included renovated houses, hotels, motels, and apartment units. In these environments prisoners are taught to use support activities normally located in the neighborhood. Often contracts are made with local vocational schools and other agencies for training and education.

Institutions for Women

There are generally about thirty times more men than women confined to correctional institutions. Often the facilities for women consist of makeshift temporary housing areas as if the prison and institutional administrators are expecting the problems of women prisoners to be solved by their disappearance from the system. The development of prison programs for women has remained a problem for most prison wardens. Often the women were housed in a segregated part of a maximum or medium security prison. Since the theory was that mixing women with men in prisons would be the first step to catastrophe, prison wardens often locked the women in their cells. A progressive step came when women were allowed out of cells and into day rooms where they could play cards, sew, or watch television. Some form of educational opportunity for women was introduced along with occasional counseling services. The number of women prisoners kept increasing especially during the last three decades. This has necessitated the changes in theory and action concerning incarcerated females. In some cases women's correctional centers have been constructed, and these have included small family-type cottages, landscaped yards, attractive support facilities, and work areas. Security has been minimal and has been maintained without walls or fences in many facilities. Living rooms, dining areas, and individual rooms in these cottages underline the expectation of correction facility administrators and others that most offenders can be expected to behave like human beings in positive environments. Experiences of staffs in institutions where this principle has been predominant indicate that these expectations are usually met by more than 90 percent of the women assigned to them. While this village design has been adopted by several states in America and by one or two other nations, the majority of penal facilities for women are far less accommodating.

Women's facilities (as well as men's facilities) for incarceration differ widely in each nation. They are often reflections of irrational theories and ideas of governments, correctional facility administrators, and social theorists in the various nations.

Incarcerated mothers are separated from their children, and in general, visits with their children are not allowed or are permitted rarely. This and separation from other relatives is a severe deprivation. Recently there have been some exceptions to this model. A facility in Frankfort, Germany, for example allows the female offender to keep a newly or recently born child through a lengthy nurturing period and beyond in many cases in order to ensure the child's and mother's physical and emotional health. When a woman is assigned to a prison many miles from her home, the distance often diminishes the prospects of visits between her and her children or between her and other relatives.

Often women, like men, in prison, attempt to form some sort of informal inmate organization. This informal organization may have many reasons for its existence; these reasons may include easing loneliness, regaining some kind of social status, identifying with a viable role, restoring ego that has been damaged considerably, and easing guilt, fear, anxiety, and embarrassment. The establishment of such informal societies usually destroys much of the effects of any environmental control efforts made by the staff. These counterforces felt in almost any prison or institutional environment have been particularly destructive in women's institutions. Often the inmate organizations are so threatening to the administration that steps are taken to intervene and manipulate the institutional environment. These inmate groups are sometimes referred to as therapeutic in nature, but they often serve the administration better by keeping inmates orderly. Most women prisoners are not mature in terms of dealing with survival in a prison setting, and this immaturity often works against them in prisons.

Women's correctional institutions as separate units are costly. For a variety of reasons legislators are reluctant to vote large sums of money for construction of facilities for women. The women's facility in Purdy, Washington, is an exceptionally well designed and well operated, campuslike facility that many states and nations would like to copy. Duplicates of the Purdy model are costly, and it is not likely that many of these model women's prisons will be constructed in the next twenty years.

Youth Correction Centers

Reformatories for youths were developed after the creation of the penitentiary concept. The reformatory idea was transformed into actual buildings
during the middle 1800s. The Lyman Boys' School in Westborough, Massachusetts, was opened in 1846. The New York State Agricultural and Industrial School opened in 1849. In 1853 the Maine Boys Training Center was
opened. By 1870 youth reformatories had been opened in more than a
dozen states, in Canada, and in several northern European nations. The
basis for the establishment of these reformatories was that rehabilitation of
the young criminal depended on teaching him right from wrong. Often
teaching or training was primarily an emphasis on correct behavior, formal
education, and, where possible, some vocational and academic training. A
youth who was given a work skill could follow the right path in life,
according to early corrections theorists.

Buildings for reformatories range from the old renovated maximum
security prison, which has been converted to a reformatory, to more
modern designs incorporating the cottage and village concepts. The term
reformatory is being replaced in some nations and states with names such as
youth correction center or youth training center in attempts to depict a more
humanitarian approach on the part of corrections administrators. Security
at these centers may be similar to that followed in maximum security institutions or that of the minimum security types. The academic and vocational
training programs are emphasized, and often there are apprenticeship
programs whereby some inmates may work for and earn first apprenticeship certificates. In many countries apprenticeship programs involve elaborate shop equipment and a master craftsman as trainer. In Bavaria, Germany, for example, at the Youth Institution near Munich some apprenticeship programs such as electrical equipment repair, woodcraft, metalcraft,
and toolmaking each have room for about twenty students in their yearlong
programs. The institution has about seven hundred youths incarcerated.
The net result is that most youths incarcerated in the institution never have
the opportunity to earn their work-skill apprenticeship certificate. This
same ratio of vocational training opportunities to number of incarcerated
youths exists in most youth institutions in the United States and in other
nations.

Youth institutions have been the focus of behaviorists, and there are
usually many more supplemental programs available in these youth centers
than at the adult correctional institutions. These programs include counseling,
therapeutic groups, psychological services, and social training programs. All
these supplemental programs are designed to help modify the youth's behavior.
Some youth institutions are designed, in building and in program, to
accommodate only youths who have passed through a screening process

that has qualified them for the particular rehabilitative methods emphasized at the institution. While several of these youth correction centers in the United States and other nations have emphasized the therapeutic treatment concept, others have held to the vocational training concept as originally conceived by the founders of the reformatory movement. Others have maintained some of the ideas originated in the 1800s about strict discipline and order. Between 1900 and 1960 reformatories often were supervised by retired military personnel. Today the youths assigned to these institutions may not have to stand at flag-raising ceremonies with the superintendent sitting on a white horse before them, but the daily routine may include many of the artifacts of that age. As recently as 1969 whistles were used to tell the youths when to stand and when to sit in the dining hall and at other events, and the use of the cat-o'-nine-tails was a common practice in the Arizona prison system in America. Some youth institutions differ from adult maximum and medium security prisons only in the ages of the committed. This age varies but generally ranges from sixteen to about thirty years of age.

Youth correction centers often hold their populations for reasons that diminish the value of the original idea behind the construction of such centers. They are simply detention or holding facilities for youths awaiting assignment to some other system of placement. Sometimes they are used to house youths who need a foster home. In other cases these institutions hold youths who have problems that are primarily situational and who could benefit to a greater extent from some other community service closer to home. In many cases mentally retarded youths are consigned to these institutions simply because there are no other facilities with room to accommodate them. In cases where community involvement in youth resocialization has taken effect, the large youth institution is often operating far below normal capacity. In other instances where the number of walkaways or escapees has increased, the staff and administration become involved with elaborate methods of control, and the element of trust is virtually extinguished.

While many youth institutions have wire fences, walls, and gates, many others have been designed and built along the village or college campus design. These open centers provide a test and challenge to the youths consigned to them, especially those young people with an impulse to escape the frustrations of life by running away. Centers located in rural areas may also provide the youths with temporary relief from pressures at home. Many youth institutions also provide sophisticated and well-staffed vocational, educational, and life-skill or social-skill training to a majority of youths in the institution. This kind of training is generally not available to youths outside the institution. The small group therapy concept has been especially productive in youth training centers. Guidance is usually injected by qualified staff members, but much of the interaction and communication has been left to the members of each group.

While the youth training center was a useful alternative to the high-walled penitentiary of the past, it often involves large numbers of youths in custody situations that are not conducive to positive rehabilitative efforts. Security and control is often more important to that administration than any rehabilitative efforts. Vocational and academic programs may be haphazard and may serve only as a part of the overall control methods of the institution. Often only a small number of youths can be accommodated in vocational training programs, and the remainder of the population must be kept busy in work that will not benefit them vocationally or academically. Clearly the dilemmas developed by the youth correction institution are complex, and sincere efforts have sometimes been made to solve them. Many of the alternative programs which have been provided to some youths ordinarily assigned to youth correctional institutions have proven far superior to those of the standard institutions. Clearly these alternatives need to be supported and expanded to provide for many more youths.

Institutions for Juveniles

Child dependency is a universal problem, and each nation seeks to solve this problem differently. In the early part of the nineteenth century homes for runaways were established in Europe and in the United States. Early reformers saw the necessity of removing delinquent children from jails where they were often easy prey for older, more hardened criminals. Often the homes for youths were not much better than adult penitentiaries, and security and control became the criteria on which staff members were hired or fired. There was little regard for the youths who were committed to these homes. Eventually warehousing of children became the purpose of many juvenile institutions. Large old buildings with dormitories or individual locked rooms, generally poor diet, and inadequately trained staffs were the standard for these institutions. During the early 1900s the cottage concept for housing youth gained recognition. This concept included the use of small cottages housing twelve to twenty-four youths, a husband and wife team as house parents, and a family-type routine. Today this model is the predominant type of institution for juveniles. Cottages may be spread over many acres of land. There is usually an attached apartment for the permanent house parents, although with changing civil service laws and changing shift work this concept is not as popular as it once was. Cottage life may include dining family style in the cottage, school or work routines during the day, formal recreational programs, and informal entertainment in the cottage. Visits to town, public parks, movies, shopping centers, and other types of outside activities are also part of the routine for the young people.

Security is not a primary concern of the staff assigned to cottage management. Grilles, fences, walls, and other security devices are seen much less often at these institutions. Gymnasiums, schools, swimming pools, and often a working farm or ranch may be attached to these institutions.

Walkaways are frequent and sometimes cause considerable public concern.

In past years, especially before World War II, these juvenile institutions were located in rural areas. Often agricultural training was the only vocational education available. The pressures of the city were lessened, and there was time for the youth to come to grips with some of his problems with the help of nurturing and available adults. Theorists believed that this agricultural setting was ideal for the city child as well as for the rural delinquent. It was an escape from the environment that originally contributed to the child's misbehavior or antisocial attitude. Modern theorists suggest that the child must learn to cope with his own environment rather than to escape it. Because of this theory and for economical reasons, several juvenile institutions have been constructed in urban settings. More experience with these urban juvenile correction centers will disclose the value of this particular theory. In the meantime alternative programs for juveniles have centered around the idea of reintegrating the juvenile with his family or close relatives; other programs have concentrated on the small group development concept, in which the youth is confronted with the problem of establishing a new set of values, beliefs, and attitudes in a family setting.

Reception and Classification Centers

Reception and classification centers are a more recent addition to the corrections systems networks in most countries. As each nation or state acquired additional institutions for its criminals and delinquents, some type of agency was required to serve as a central control of the incoming population. Later this central control concept evolved into what is known today as a reception and classification center. Often these centers may be located at one of the prisons. The center is usually secured with fences or walls. Traffic control is highly evident, security devices are numerous, and the design and construction is depressing and considered regressive rehabilitative design. Contact between persons passing through the reception and classification center and the facility staff is at a minimum and sometimes even forbidden. Barbed wire, electronic surveillance devices, double gate systems, iron doors, and a minimum of activity at these centers are characteristic of most reception centers today. It is a no-man's-land between the sentencing process and the actual correcting process. It is its own society where security and control remain foremost in the minds of the staff. The staff is never acquainted with the incoming prisoners except in cases of repeaters. As a result, each incoming person is treated with a minimum of trust and a maximum of suspicion.

While there are exceptions to this bleak description, most reception and classification centers fit this dark picture. Exceptions like the Reception and Medical Center at Lake Butler, Florida, serve as excellent models but are not often duplicated. More often these centers resemble the diagnostic center at Montgomery, Alabama. At Lake Butler a variety of recreational, self-improvement, and other activities are available, along with maximum contact between staff and committed persons. The facility is campuslike and tends to provide a sign of hope for the incarcerated person. At Montgomery the inmate spends his entire diagnostic period, which lasts from three to six weeks or longer, in confinement except during interviewing and testing periods. A minimum of contact between staff and inmates is permitted.

Penologists and others who have researched this reception and classification process have concluded that it is often humiliating and degrading but that in any case, it should not take more than four or five days to accomplish. Improvement of these centers is generally related to the overall management policies of the state or nation's corrections system, and in this context it becomes difficult to change any one part of the incarceration process where the entire system is traditional and ingrained in the political woodwork of the society. Where the system is less political and more concerned with efficiency and people-centered programs, these reception and classification centers often reflect this humanistic approach in their day-to-day operations.

The Future of Corrections and Institutions

Several states and nations appear to be moving toward a breakthrough in corrections. In the United States more than a decade of intensive experimentation and research in the field of corrections is beginning to show signs of some success. In Sweden, the Netherlands, England, and Canada changes in criminal codes and corrections procedures have signaled the new era. Community involvement in corrections, especially alternate programs, is at an all-time high in numbers of programs and in numbers of volunteer citizens actually working in these programs.

But the pressures of tradition are not easily lifted. Deeply rooted in society are sometimes ancient beliefs and fears about deviants and how they should be corrected. Often society operates to alleviate its problems in what may be labeled a pendulum effect. When the philosophy and operational climate of a society is liberal, it may welcome the closing of prisons and new alternatives to corrections. At another time, such as that following the outburst of terrorism in Europe in the late 1970s, the pendulum effect of society's attitudes is most evidenced by public support of anticriminal laws that are much more restrictive and conservative. The public may even support laws that restrict the movement of the general public and laws that call for search-without-warrant or other questionable laws as it did in Germany during 1978 and 1979.

Alternatives to prison, in any case, are often too much threatening to existing elements of society. Corrections systems are always the target, and corrections administrators are being asked to give up offenders to other, often untested, community treatment programs. This is often the case when there is no widespread change in public attitude about how offenders should be handled. Often only small vociferous segments of the population may make it appear that all of society is demanding immediate change. Corrections administrators usually justify requests to legislators for larger budgets and are granted these requests by legislators. The arguments for alternatives by less powerful groups often go unheard by tradition-bound leaders. The net result of this struggle between the status quo traditionalists and the abolitionists or community treatment supporters is an extremely slow movement of modernization of corrections systems. Only when a large segment of the population demands change will change come about. In Spain during the spring of 1978 the public was demanding changes in the corrections system after reports of cruel and inhuman punishment in prisons became general knowledge. When no action was made by the Spanish government, the public took the situation in hand and dragged the corrections department director into the street and shot him. Of course, no nation wants change brought about in this manner. Instead the public must be made an integral part of whatever change is desired, and their wishes must be heard.

One of the goals of any future corrections system must be the development of programs that aid the offender to permanently identify with noncriminal persons. This goal, if pursued, should lead society away from the traditional philosophy and approach to the design of corrections institutions and the development of programs. This will mean a dismantling of large prisons and the use of small units within the community close to the offender's home. There are many ramifications of the concept of moving rehabilitation to the offender's neighborhood. Communication with family, neighbors, and social services can be much more direct. A graduated release program can be implemented in which correctional staff, the offender, and community resource people interact closely to aid the offender in gradually assuming command of his own life in his own community. This method of reintegrating the person into society may help eliminate extended contacts with corrections in the usual parole officer-ex-offender relationship. A step-by-step reintegration program will help to treat the ex-offender's problems one at a time, using a combination of community resources to solve these problems. In this way the actual release date will be a step in the total process of reintegration with most of the normal problems such as a job, a place to live, and financial and social assistance already solved. This gradual reintegration program is a sharp contrast to the release from prison of most offenders today. Often it is a suit of clothes, $25 or $50, and a bus ticket to the place where steps leading to incarceration began. This is a highly traumatic episode and often contributes to the return of paroled or released offenders to prison within six or eight months after discharge.

Small units for incarceration located in the city where most offenders are convicted will also attract a number of more qualified and often much more professional staff who are within easy traveling distance to the unit.

Links between future prisons and the community may take on designs hardly acceptable in today's prisons. Small units may be ideally located to operate small manufacturing services or to be associated with manufacturers in the neighborhood to allow maximum industrial training in meaningful skills for those incarcerated. Wages for incarcerated offenders are being adjusted upward in several countries and are already almost comparable to wages paid outside prison for comparable labor. Much of these earnings can be set aside in a savings account, and controls in withdrawals may help the inmate to use the money carefully with the help of prison or community budget advisors. In addition to better prospects for learning a trade and earning and saving money, the inmate will have opportunities to associate himself with local religious and social groups, therapeutic groups, clubs, and recreational organizations. Association with these programs will not be temporary, since many of these memberships may continue after the inmate is released.

Staffs of small prisons will perform multiple roles. There will be a greater emphasis on family-type operations, and this means that staffs will be treatment oriented. Custody will remain important, but the emphasis will change from security to resocialization. Most of the decisions concerning the prisoner's life will be made by staff members who are well acquainted with the offender, and these decisions may be made in small groups with the inmate participating in the decision-making process. In this environment separation by age will no longer be emphasized. Mature offenders can be helpful to younger inmates who are influenced to a great extent by members of their peer groups.

These examples of innovations will help the discharged ex-offender identify with and function satisfactorily in society. The aim is to help the offender establish an anticriminal pattern of life and to live it alongside noncriminals. The enhancement of self-esteem, a satisfactory job experience, comfortable living conditions, the development of several friendships, and other types of social life can contribute to this pattern. Members of small custodial treatment units may function as a vital part of this life-style development procedure.

Under these circumstances there is no room for prisons as they are today in many countries, nor should money be wasted on large security and custodial prisons in the future.

The social system of a country is reflected in its correctional system. In countries where the public has been brought into the corrections picture, there is usually good support for improving resocialization methods. This has been exemplified in the case of Sweden's correctional process, where aggressiveness toward the lawbreaker has changed from punitive or retaliatory to treatment or humanistic. In the Netherlands this common interest in re-socializing law offenders has also been extremely helpful in reducing the task of justice departments and corrections agencies. A commonality of purpose and goals has helped build public support for corrections reform and public involvement in the correcting process itself. Other countries are taking a much closer look at successful alternatives since they may mean the reduction of federal or state budgets, higher success rates of those released, and the improvement of treatment programs accomplished by smaller staffs located in the offender's home community. The sharing of this knowledge and experience may help other nations advance their own corrections technology.

Notes

1. Don C. Gibbons, *Society, Crime, and Criminal Careers: An Introduction to Criminology,* 3d ed. (Englewood Cliffs, N.J.: Prentice-Hall, 1977), p. 466.

2. Robert M. Carter et al., *Correctional Institutions* (New York: J.B. Lippincott Co., 1972), p. 36.

3. Harry E. Barnes and N.K. Teeters, *New Horizons in Criminology* (Englewood Cliffs, N.J.: Prentice-Hall, 1951), p. 412.

4. Carter et al., *Correctional Institutions,* p. 37.

5. Calvert R. Dodge, *A Nation without Prisons* (Lexington, Mass.: Lexington Books, D.C. Heath and Co., 1975), p. 4.

6. Dartmoor Prison, "Information on Dartmoor Prison," mimeographed (Dartmoor, England, 1977).

7. Harry E. Barnes, *The Story of Punishment* (Boston: The Stratford Co., 1930), chap. 6.

8. H. Montgomery Hyde. *Oscar Wilde: The Aftermath* (New York: Farrar, Straus and Co., 1963), p. 71.

9. Gustave de Beaumont and Alexis de Tocqueville, *On the Penitentiary System in the United States and Its Application in France,* forword by H.R. Lantz (Carbondale, Ill.: Southern Illinois University Press, 1964), p. 48.

10. Dartmoor Prison, "The History of Dartmoor Prison," mimeographed (Dartmoor, England, 1977).

11. Gibbons, *Society, Crime, and Criminal Careers,* pp. 466-467. For a complete picture of American Corrections see, U.S. Department of Justice, *Major Institutions Corrections Task Force Progress Report,* National Advisory Commission on Criminal Justice Standards and Goals, (Washington, D.C.: U.S. Government Printing Office, May 1972), and *Progress Report* (Gov. Pub. No. 30378, June, 1973).

12. Dodge, *A Nation without Prisons.* See chapter 1 for additional descriptions of types of prisons.

2 Prison Management In A Climate of Change

Alternatives to prison and abolishment of prisons have become popular themes for crusades by various groups in several nations. Several alternatives that have been successfully developed have given credence to the alternative crusade. The success of programs that have been applied to delinquent youths in the state of Massachusetts since the abolishment of correctional institutions for youths in January 1972 gave credence to the abolishment crusade.[1] The new trend in criminal laws in Finland, Sweden, the Netherlands, Canada, and other countries, including the United States, and continued pressures for prison reform in various countries by significant segments of the population give hope that there is a climate for change in the prison systems of the world.[2] Crime rates, however, appear to be increasing. Resistance to prison abolishment, therefore, is also strong. Legislative bodies have voted greater amounts of money for prison construction, prison staff recruitment and training, and prison programs than ever before in the history of the world's prison systems. The corrections systems remain the primary means by which society attempts to correct its deviants in order to maintain social order. These corrective bodies are an important part of society and its governing powers. Corrections systems reflect the ideology of a nation, although they often lag behind rapidly changing philosophies. One reason for this lag is the uniqueness of the prison system itself. It is usually isolated physically and often politically from the nation; many of its administrators and inmates may have entered the system during periods of popularity of old ideologies; and the response of correctional institutions to current political philosophies is traditionally slow. A result of this lag is the emergence of a highly nonproductive government bureaucracy in many countries that serves neither a problem-solving nor a regulatory function as these concepts apply to social deviates. Old value systems may be adhered to in corrections systems simply because changes in the status quo of the system are upsetting. Contributing to this status quo stance taken by many prison administrators is the prison population itself. Prison authorities operate on the basis that they have been given a mandate to stamp out criminal behavior. Prisoners may operate under a different value system and often use every possible resource to resist this process. They organize and operate a separate society within prison walls.

Status quo management may be justified when the value systems of administrators and prisoners are constantly on a collision course. The value of this system when viewed from a larger perspective may be even more questionable. Often prisoners socialized under temporarily popular ideological political systems become, in their time of freedom, the stalwarts of society's new ideological position. Menachem Begin of Israel, a former terrorist, Mahatma and Indira Gandhi of India, Anwar Sadat of Egypt, Jomo Kenyatta of Kenya are but a few representatives.

In a changing society and changing ideologies the debate concerning the value of prisons continues. At one time the debate revolved around the classical criminal laws of the 1800s in which punishment was to counterbalance the pleasure of the crime. The debate continued during the period of positivist thought at the beginning of the twentieth century. Positivism suggests that crime is a natural phenomenon produced by several factors, biological and environmental. The debate continues today with new theories interspersed with the old.

While these debates concerning the corrective process continue, the prison system continues to grow. Moratoriums on prison construction are rare even when the most reputable of public organizations call for them. In the United States these organizations include the National Advisory Commission on Criminal Justice Standards and Goals, the National Council on Crime and Delinquency,[3] and other powerful representatives of prison reform. As of January 1, 1979, however, American prisons and jails were overflowing with approximately 250,000 prisoners. It is apparent that any crusade for alternatives to prisons or for their abolishment will require continuous and strong reinforcement.

One argument in any debate about prison changes centers around the social value of prisons. Does the institution of imprisonment profit society in terms of deterrence, safety, or rehabilitation? A preponderance of evidence has been accumulated that supports the contention that prisons are unprofitable in terms of these criteria. When a society invests in some segment of its operation, it usually requires evidence of social profit. People are willing to be taxed for education if education appears to be socially profitable. A country's technological, scientific, or cultural advance is supported as long as these efforts appear to demonstrate their worth. When profits are less likely, there is a correspondingly greater resistance to underwrite their existence, as is the case in some welfare and social service programs. Penitentiary systems at the time of their creation two hundred years ago quickly demonstrated themselves as socially nonprofitable. Today criminologists and penologists suggest that in these terms prisons are bankrupt. Nevertheless heavy investment is continually being poured into prison systems which are accused of having no socially redeeming value. This vast network of walls, wire, and cages grows, seemingly propped up by mythical justification for its existence. Its existence refutes the argument that social bankruptcy is justification for dissolution.

In order to examine the question of prison systems' existence we may take a variety of theories and appropriately research them. We may relate these theories to politics, to economics, to public concern, and to other propositions. The core of this particular discussion centers around prison management and control and is based on a survey of prison wardens, superintendents, and justice department administrators in North America and northern Europe. A central revelation of the survey was that the prison system is a society distinct from the social system surrounding it. Over thirty years ago Tannenbaum suggested that the discipline and social order suggested by the larger society have been difficult to administer in the micro society because prisons are social systems with their own codes of right and wrong.[4] This statement was validated by a majority of those responding to this survey. In addition, the survey of prison managers and others revealed two prime elements that support prison existence, growth, and power in communities. The first of these elements is the established criminal laws of a nation. The second element is the economic investment. Those who argue for abolition and alternatives must reckon with these two elements in any crusade for change.

The first powerful element on the side of prisons is that they represent an established system for reimplanting society's moral fiber into the minds and behavior of deviants. Criminal laws which are a result of rule making fortify this system of correction. Crime is a social and political phenomenon. Whatever their origin, criminal laws are finalized only when penal sanction is affixed. Penitentiaries have been seen as the most efficient means of carrying out these sanctions. The sources of criminal laws have little bearing on the administration of penal sanctions. Criminal laws originate from a number of sources, including religious dogma, a political factions ideology, the whim and fancy of special interest groups reflecting cultural differences, clashes in social values and social conflict. They may be created to replace or rebuild decaying informal norms. Sources of laws are inconsequential in determining systems of sanctions. The sanctions, however, should be uniform, and prisons appear to the public to provide uniform sanction. In this context corrections administrators and prison managers may be viewed as a powerful arm of the state. Criminal laws take time to change, and often police, the courts, and the corrections systems become more powerful because new laws are added to rather than replace old laws. The result is that nations often create overcriminalization, since many of the laws apply to a long list of social behavior that has no victims. The administration of penal sanction remains entrusted in the hands of prison systems. This power is not easily dissolved.

The second element that buttresses the power of the prison and corrections systems is the economic investment in the enterprise of penal sanctioning. As socially unprofitable as the prison system may appear, money is continually provided in larger amounts each year for its support and expansion. In America alone the costs of keeping the corrections system operating is estimated to be over $1 billion a year, and this figure does not include new construction. Predictions indicate that between 1979 and 1989 capital improvements alone will cost well over $1 billion a year at present inflation rates. The taxpayer will be asked to support the government in order to hold about 450,000 institutionalized offenders including adult felons, juveniles, and misdemeanants. This money will also be spent, in part, to process approximately 1 million new admissions. It will also be used to pay the salaries of 160,000 correctional staff members, the majority of whom have no real connection with treatment or resocialization concepts in the modern sense of the word. Comparative investment figures apply to England and Germany but not to Scandanavian countries. The cost of building a penal institution has been estimated at anywhere from $22,000 to $30,000 per bed. Confining a person in an institution costs between $400 and $800 a month depending on the extent of services provided to the incarcerated person and the wages paid to inmates who work in prison or associated industries. Corrections budget figures may increase by 200 percent or more in the next ten years. The per capita cost for custodial treatment may exceed the average annual income of a nation's residents at this rate. Although prisoners often do much of the work in a prison such as cooking, dining hall care, farming, construction, and laundry and valet services for staff with little or no compensation, there appears to be a major change in this concept. Prisoners in some countries now receive the standard minimum wage for the particular labor performed. This policy is becoming popular with the consequence that costs of maintaining prisoners will skyrocket. Yet the present investment in buildings, staffs, and programs is considered by many to be too great a public investment to abandon. In the United States over 900 penal facilities are being considered for construction or already under construction. The average cost of these prisons will approximate $6.7 million per facility, or $24,000 per bed.[5] These concrete and steel cages will add even greater substance to the theory that the economical investment in prisons forbids consideration of their dissolution. The power that this investment gives to prison managers is formidable in contrast to the arguments presented by citizens demanding alternatives or abolishment.

These two elements of support, the law and economical investment, give the prison system as it is today a considerable lead in the battle between those favoring the status quo and those favoring change in it.

A third element that penetrated the many reports from wardens, justice department administrations, and others in the survey made by this author is the efficient or appropriate use of authority and control within the prison system itself. This concept of control has the effect of preserving the status quo while giving the appearance that procedures for penal sanction, deterrence, safety, and rehabilitation are being conducted properly. These factors are usually the most important ones when any group or population segment examines the system. As long as prisons appear to be carrying out their prescribed purposes, justification for their continued existence is relatively easy. Convicted criminals are placed in prisons for the public's safety. If escapes are few, then the prison system is successful by this criteria. We also expect that once in prison, convicts must not upset the equilibrium of prison organization; they must conform. If there are no riots, no prison murders, and comparative peace among prisoners and prison staffs, the public is more easily satisfied that the system is being managed with the proper amount of authority and control. Arguments concerning a prison's role in deterring crime or rehabilitating criminals can be made less useful in appraising a prison's value, since there are so many other variables that may enter into these arguments.

In addition to security and peace within prisons the public is also concerned with cost. Efficient use of prisoners in labor that contributes to the prison's existence is usually well received by taxpayers. Today, as more rights are being given prisoners and as such concepts as minimum wages comparable to union scales penetrates the prison system, managers of prisons may be confronted with heavy increases in their budgets. These increases may tip the scale of economic worth of prisons, lending weight to the abolitionist cause. The exercise of even greater controls and authority may be called for to prevent this wage increase from undermining the system. During the entire history of the penitentiary system since the first models were constructed in New York, Pennsylvania, England and other nations, and through all the philosophical, sociological, biological, and psychological models of prisoner care and treatment, one central theme has remained dominant in prison management: control and security. Even when prisoners have been so well organized that they, in fact, operated the prison, it was important for the system to appear to be under control.

This control was exercised in many ways. Prisoners had most, if not all, of their constitutional rights taken away from them. The right to correspond with relatives or friends was severely curtailed or not tolerated, and when tolerated, censorship was extreme. No detrimental news about life within the microcosm was ever released. When the public interest in prisons and prison management began to increase, the press releases from a prison were usually prepared by the warden and his assistant. Public communications such as interviews and spontaneous statements by prison officials were almost nonexistent prior to 1950. Public concern was often only aroused by events such as riots and strikes and then was only temporary. Disclosures about atrocities within prison walls have become more common in the last two decades, when representatives of the press and others began to follow up leads given by eyewitnesses. In a southern U.S. prison it was disclosed that during the 1960s prison administrators and staff were involved in murdering prisoners by flagellation, starvation, and other means and burying them in the prison graveyard or farm with falsified death certificates. The stories were on front pages of newspapers, on television and radio broadcasts but became old quickly and served little purpose for the abolitionists and alternatives crusaders. Riots often become the only means by which prisoners can broadcast their grievances to the outside world. The public, however, generally falls back into complacency once the "fires" have been extinguished and managers have control of the situation. Operation of prison systems are once again left to the experts. The day-to-day operation of a prison is generally a dull subject, and the public seldom inquires into present plans and operations or long-range goals and objectives. Prison management in essence, epitomizes the concept of "incestual dialogue" wherein prison associations, probation and parole organizations, sympathetic legislators, sociologists, psychologists, or others may continue a dialogue that applauds the system or justifies its existence.

A prison system survives and grows on the bedrock principle of control. Control means keeping all the residents (a recent term) or inmates within the confines of the institution until they are paroled, discharged, executed, or until they die. This task of control is a twenty-four-hour-a-day job, and the responsibility rests on the warden or superintendent's shoulders. Every day is a distinct period in which anything might happen, and alertness of the staff is paramount. Treatment programs are often tolerated and reformists' arguments heard, but authority and control remain the bulwark of prison management. All else is secondary.

When persons are hired as prison employees, it is often difficult for them to understand that incarceration is itself a form of punishment and that prisons are not places where punishment is given. In contemporary prisons there are a substantial number of employees who seek to satisfy their own sadistic or voyeuristic appetites. They would have enjoyed the job more so during the time of Henry V of England when over 260 crimes were punishable by death. Regimentation of inmates, strict and orderly plans for living under resolute rule with ample room for corporal punishment remain parts of most prison management systems. Authority for these punishments and this regimentation is often given to guards and other caretakers whose only qualification for their job is that they are twenty-one years of age or older, in good health, and have some schooling. Authority and control are also invested in a wide variety of personality types. In one system prison staffs may have been appointed for political favors accomplished. In another system civil service examinations must be taken and interviews conducted. Whatever qualifications are necessary to enter the system, remaining in the system rests to a considerable extent on the ability to exercise control over others. Rules of operation, in some cases, may date back to the creation of the Philadelphia, Auburn, and Elmira models in the United States or earlier. More recently some changes in management style and procedures have occurred. Despite these changes, however, the major portion of prisons in Europe, the United States, South America, and most of the rest of the world are managed under the old rules. Corporal punishment, twenty-four-hour lockups for as many as 50 percent or more of the prison population, punitive treatment, regimentation, slave labor, use of prisoners in psychological and medical experimentation, denial of legal rights, and other seemingly inhumane methods prevail. With few exceptions the power of the warden is upheld without fear of outside inquiries. Many of the prison administrators are experienced and able persons, and many are sympathetic to the crusades for alternatives, resocialization, and even abolishment. Nevertheless, prisons are designed, funded, and constructed to maintain security, and prison managers function well when this atmosphere is maintained.

The Present Climate

While prisons are separate microcosms and they enjoy a considerable immunity from public pressure, the influence of the public cannot be totally discounted. In time prison systems begin to reflect to some extent the changing attitudes of the larger society. In a punitive society prisons emphasize punitive measures. In a lenient society prisons are less punitive. Upon the death of Generalissimo Franco in the middle 1970s the government of Spain began to change from one of harshness to one of liberality under King Juan Carlos. The populations of concentration camps for homosexuals and other persons convicted of victimless crimes began to decrease. The prison system lagged behind in moving toward humanistic goals, and reports of inhumane prison treatment brought the concern of some Spanish citizens to a feverish pitch. The shooting of the corrections director in March 1978 signified that the Spanish people demanded some changes toward humane treatment of prisoners, although the method to accomplish this change was not so humane. Political and social scientists in other countries have convinced some corrections leaders of the necessity of incorporating new management methods into the system. The period between 1950 and 1979 in the United States, Canada, and other countries has been showered with a variety of resocialization concepts that have been used in many prisons. These methods have ranged from work release programs to aversion therapy and from small psychologically oriented group programs to programs of shock therapy. It has been a period in which a zigzag course has been followed in an attempt to discover how best to resocialize prisoners within the confines of a prison. Many of these programs of treatment were doomed to failure, and often the military or authoritarian model of prison management once again emerged as the safest model. This model supports an informal organizational structure of prisoners in a pyramid structure of authority, with the older and more sophisticated or tougher prisoners ruling. Traditional roles are sustained and the powers of the rulers supported. Management of this kind of prison is based largely on the maintenance of the delicate balance between the informal organization of prisoners and the formal powers of the prison staff. Tampering with this balance creates conflict and leads to explosion. The use of steel and concrete cages, cells and blocks of cells, alleys and electronic devices is mandatory to maintain control of the flow of human energy in this microcosm. Corruption, terror, power politics, informal prisoner-led government are maintained in this model.

There appears to be enough evidence today to substantiate the idea that a climate for change exists in the prison system and in the handling of convicted persons. The seeds for this climate of change took root in the early 1950s. It was at this time that arguments concerning the constitutional rights of prisoners began to increase. Prison microcosms were to incorporate some of the elements of the free society. Prisoners were to be given choices and were to be enlisted along with prison staffs to help create a viable progressive institution. The concept was attempted in Hawaii and in Sweden and in several other states and countries. Practices such as selling privileges to inmates and holding prisoner-conducted kangaroo courts were to be eliminated. Control and management through force and fear were to be abandoned. Old inmate leaders were no longer to be allowed to rule or to establish rules. Instead inmate councils and formal groups with inmate representation from all strata of prisoner society were to be enlisted to assist in the development of programs in prisons. This approach was revolutionary and brought with it many problems. It exposed the dependency of management on inmate organization. Many prison managers manipulated the prisoner organization to fit their management pattern and style. A treatment model for prison programming also began to develop during the early 1950s. Often the treatment segment of prison staffs tended to threaten prison management, and inmates took advantage of this development to add to the confusion. Over fifty riots occurred in U.S. prisons between 1950 and 1953.[6] The transitional period from tightly governed and custody-oriented prisons to prisons founded on some democratic or treatment model fostered an epidemic of crisis, especially in America but also in several other countries. The result of this crisis was political and public clamor for a stronger emphasis on authority and control over prisoners. This was welcomed by prison managers. Most of them took the natural course of reassuming dictatorial powers and restoring tight authority and control over their institutions. Security, custody, and traditional programs including the reestablishment of prisoner organization in the institution deeply wounded the revolutionary concept of treatment. Clearly the climate during the 1950s was hostile to the revolution favoring treatment. Reformists, alternative supporters, and abolitionists were without arms for their crusade. Support for the changes was almost nonexistent in the prison systems themselves.

The decade of the 1960s ushered in another chapter in the development of the seeds of change planted by the early modern reformists of the 1950s. Civil service in many nations and states had now established more uniformity in describing prison managers' positions and staff and line jobs in prisons. Some upgrading of prison management was inevitable. Some politically appointed administrators, however, remained in the system because of the grandfather clauses allowing them to keep their position until retirement. Training of prison staffs was becoming more sophisticated although the theme of security and control remained at the core. Accused citizens, prisoners, and others were beginning to challenge the laws of the nations, and partisans, including reformers and others, became a part of this steadily increasing voice for change. The U.S. Supreme Court made several decisions regarding the constitutional rights of accused persons. Rules regarding mail censorship, lawyer assistance, work, church, and treatment opportunities began to affect the system. In the United States the Safe Streets Act of Congress, the creation of the Law Enforcement Assistance Administration, and other national and state legislative acts placed a greater focus on prisons, law enforcement procedures, and the laws themselves. Demand for treatment programs in prisons had now become popularized through research and theory, and the display by news media, writers, and others of the horrors of prison management appeared to antiquate the old way. Varieties of institutional management that incorporated treatment and resocialization in some form of democratic process had now become popular. The new penology of the 1960s in theory, at least, was to be humanitarian with emphasis on treatment and care. Alfred Schnur in his book *The New Penology: Fact or Fiction?* suggested that the new penology of the 1960s existed mainly on paper and in textbooks, and he underlined his theory by citing examples such as the ratio of twenty-three psychiatrists to treat 165,000 inmates. If treatment in this instance was given equally, each prisoner would receive about a minute and twenty seconds of therapy a month. Elmer Johnson, another analyzer of the new penology, suggested that social work professionals having at least a master's degree existed in only fourteen states.[7] Often the definitions and labels given treatment programs and employees responsible for these programs in prisons were ambiguous. Treatment personnel were often without authority and often attempted to play their roles as caring persons while adhering to the principles of control that were more likely to be noticed and approved by institution managers.[8]

During the 1960s the treatment and rehabilitation cause became more clear, and the justification for the existence of prisons on the old traditional grounds began to dissipate. This climate of change penetrated the general society. Prison administration was being challenged, the old ways were criticized, and the laws were being reappraised and changed in support of this new attitude. Several European nations were beginning to outdistance the United States in developing the treatment model. In many prisons the tug-of-war between custodial types and treatment types of personnel spilled into public view. They often served to split both prisoners and staff in pro-treatment and antitreatment groups. These splits more often reinforced the view of prison managers that the authoritarian-punitive model for prison management would emerge the victor. Prison disturbances during the 1960s and early 1970s appeared to differ from those of the early 1950s. Generally the more recent upheavals in prisons reflected the views of prisoners that their particular institution had not changed but was continuing the old penology of punishment and custody. Abuse of power by prison managers was a part of this battle theme. Racial discrimination and other types of discrimination, many of which reflected viewpoints of the general society, also served as causes for prison disturbances in the United States. The Netherlands and other countries were witnessing prison disturbances over problems such as firearms carried by prison guards, poor food, crowding of prisoners in small cells, and other complaints.

The climate for change during the 1970s is essentially the same as it was during the 1960s. In some nations where a period of liberalization exists, a corresponding liberalization may occur in penal institutions. But in this freer environment crimes of violence and predation may increase as they have in the United States, Spain, and Italy. Public response may include a demand for strengthening the structure of the prison system and laws to protect society. Discipline is respected, and managers who rule with a stronger hand are often encouraged. In other countries where a liberal and caring attitude exists but where crimes of violence have not increased even when crime in general may have increased, the treatment model for prisons is upheld. This is the case in Sweden, the Netherlands, and Denmark. Alternative programs and even prison abolishment are given wider berth in these nations.

These combinations of events, reassertion of constitutional rights, demand for objective treatment without discrimination, humanistic handling of incarcerated persons, and changes in public law and attitude have ushered in the climate for change. These events have occurred within the last thirty years and have profoundly altered several prison systems. Even where management is conducted in the context of old military or authoritarian models, the prison environment is changing. Modifications may include some movement away from punitive repressiveness in closed and security-bound institutions to facilities that are democratically operated with treatment being the only concern of the staff and inmate. In the Netherlands the old models of prisons have been greatly modified and used only for a small number of incorrigibles. In Sweden prison managers have the advantage of widespread public support. Pride in the Swedish correctional system is expressed almost universally by the general public. This pride stems from several sources. A Swedish criminal or prisoner, for example, remains a Swedish citizen meriting respect, continues to be a member of the community, and is never regarded as an outcast. Treatment programs, open institutions, and community involvement are also integral parts of the Swedish system. Respect for one another is an attitude of the Swedish people that permeates the prison management system. The cornerstone of this management is based on a humanitarian and egalitarian model of human conduct. In countries where racial and ethnic populations confront each other, this attitude may be more difficult to find.

The input of social scientists, managerial consultants, and performance evaluators during the past three decades has had a generally positive effect in staff training and on the design and construction of prisons, although much of the effort has gone to more efficient development of the institution rather than to the program for inmates. Fundamental problems of management remain mostly unsolved. The issues that remain with the present corrections systems of America, Canada, most western European nations, Australia, New Zealand, and several other nations include the following:

1. Identification and association with a clear and fully supported set of goals and objectives on which to operate.
2. Development of a sophisticated but realistic program of employee selection and training.
3. Programs of treatment that are publicly acknowledged and supported.
4. Program planning leading to a maximum of community involvement which includes the recognition that there is a possibility of prison dissolution.
5. A recognition of the importance of prisoner involvement in prison organization and management with a corresponding use of this involvement.

Respondents to the survey made by this author indicated that several models of prison management have emerged or are now emerging in the present climate of change. These models represent a continuum from authoritarian to participatory models. There are, for example, few if any prisons in the United States under strict authoritarian control that do not allow the inmates some choice in several aspects of daily living, for example, selection of movies to attend. There are no so-called open prisons that do not reserve many decisions for management. Leaves from an open prison, for example, are not left up to prisoner committees although in some cases their advice is given consideration.

Some decisions are not now within the powers of prison management and probably will not be in the decades to come. Legislative bodies still control funding which provides wages, food, hospital care, and counseling or therapeutic services. It would not be possible for inmates to decide to double their own wages, food allotment, hospital care, and counseling or therapeutic services. Since the Attica riots in the United States, the hunger strikes in The Netherlands and other types of prisoner protests in the early 1970s, prisoner influence in legislative decisions appears to have increased.

Management models in which authority and control emanated from the warden appear to be giving way to models in which an increased amount of reliance is being placed on the senior staff members with decision making influenced by the input of all staff members. Military models of management also exist today, especially in South America, Africa, and Asia. They also exist in some prison systems in Europe and North America. Evolution of these systems into a participatory model will predictably, continue at a very slow rate.

Fortress styles of construction are giving way in some countries to economic pressures rather than to reformist pressure. Smaller facilities with less emphasis on walls and steel fences require less initial construction budgeting and appear to be acceptable for prisoners needing less than maximum security facilities. This trend is continuing in several nations. In addition to economics two other variables relate to both the construction of prisons and their management:

1. *Structural:* The greater the structure and the more the controls and restrictions imposed on individuals, the greater will be the gap between the prisoner and his controllers. As a consequence of this gap treatment or rehabilitation efforts are correspondingly reduced.
2. *Numbers of prisoners:* The greater the number of inmates placed in a confined situation, the more difficult it is to communicate with them and to exercise authority and control. Consequently staffs have limited input into the internal workings of an institution and a correspondingly higher reliance on inmate organization. In institutions where there are only two or three staff members in charge of fifty or a hundred inmates it would be naive to expect those staff members to exercise any meaningful authority. "The cons run the joint" is not just an old saying but a factual and appropriate statement applicable to many prison communities today.

The net result of the present systems of management in many prisons to-is that treatment and resocialization is generally not the end result of a stay in prison. Imprisonment in many cases is simply a struggle for survival. In the research reported by Thomas P. Wilson, participatory management practices are strongly associated with prisoner cooperation, yet the participatory management model continues to pose obstacles to the power and control that many prison managers appear to require in order to manage.[9]

Future Models

Materials accumulated in this author's research as well as research by others is not encouraging for the reformers or abolitionist crusaders. The penitentiary system of many nations continues to survive and grow entrenched in a political, economical, and philosophical environment that tolerates its existence or accepts its growth. Most of the suggested models of management embrace old philosophical concepts. The viewpoint that many prisoners must now have treatment in open institutional settings often necessitates that systems of authority and control, in the more secure prisons for hard-core prisoners, must be greater than in the past. The identifiable styles of management that will dominate the penology of the remaining two decades in the twentieth century include authoritarian, humanitarian, corporate management, treatment, and reintegrative models that will be either prison or community administered.

Several combinations and modifications of these models have been suggested by prison authorities, but these models form the core of future prison management. Each model may be judged by "its ability to reproduce or to predict the behavioral characteristics such as stability, oscillation, growth and other attributes of the system."[10] In the case of prison authority and control these characteristics would relate to satisfactory detention and rehabilitation of residents in prison.

The authoritarian model continues to dominate most systems of incarceration in which maximum security is a viable reason for the existence of the system.

The humanitarian model encompasses several forms of cooperation between management and staff and between staff and residents. In this model the patterns of communication are emphasized and embrace a wide variety of systems including upward and downward (vertical) communication and horizontal communication. Prisoners are looked on as respected citizens and treated as such. This model appears to persist in Sweden and Denmark.

The corporate management model requires much of the staff accountability and performance measurement of similar models in industry. Grievance and program recommendation procedures for inmates serve as a checks-and-balance system for management. Legislators view the results of these procedures seriously and may vote to provide greater or lesser funds based on their results. The results, however, may simply imply that each dollar is used to its maximum in prison management and operation. Factors such as the effectiveness of rehabilitation or the rate of recidivism may be incidental. The Illinois prison system is an example of this model.

The treatment model may include some of the operational aspects of other models, but the emphasis is on treatment, and members of the staff who are responsible for treatment programs have a much larger voice in the operation of the institution. The Oregon and Washington penitentiary systems are examples of this model. The treatment model may include ad hoc committees of prisoners and staff to work on specific issues. These differ from the inmate councils in the authoritarian model that tend to create heated confrontation and staff-prisoner strife rather than solve problems that are mutually recognized as problems. In the humanitarian and treatment models an ombudsman may be used as a regular part of the management process.

The reintegrative model has as its central goal a system of operation in which there are several steps toward release that a prisoner must experience. These are designed to reintegrate him into society with some feeling that he can be successful. The first step may include staying at a maximum or medium security prison, then a minimum security institution, then a prerelease institution, and finally an open institution as close to his home as possible where he may begin a program of job finding, development of social relations, and family reintegration and acceptance.

Each of these models may have other names and may include aspects of complementary or contradictory models. A caste-prescriptive model, for example, simply characterizes the bureaucratic and machinelike prison in which staff and inmate behavior is subject to many rules and there is a caste system, a sharply defined hierarchy in which all staff enjoy some authority over those in the lower caste group, the inmates.[11] Another model is the happy-family-collaborative system in which management is structured around some sort of familial relationship or partnership of all inmates and staff members. This relationship is considered in the hummanitarian model. A formal bargaining model which may appear in Europe more than in the United States or Canada includes the concept of managing and operating the prison according to agreements or contracts developed between prisoners and management in union-style bargaining sessions.

A survey by Nagel reported in 1973 reaffirms the data accumulated and reported in this discussion concerning new models of management. In Nagel's report there is an almost absolute emphasis on control in the plans and operations of the twenty-six jails and adult detention centers visited by the survey committee.[12] Confinement remains the foundation and control remains the means by which confinement is assured.

The five models suggested in this discussion fall within two major categories: prisons that maximize inmate participation in management decisions and those that maximize authority within a framework of due process and justice.

The old authority model will become even more authoritarian in prisons housing predatory offenders. The difference will be that this authoritarian model will be confronted with the problems of due process rights for the inmates and restraints on the actions of the staff. The corporate model, which includes the concept of justice, and the treatment models will emphasize staff-inmate relationships, a corrections ombudsman, staff-inmate committees, inmate profit-sharing industry, open institutional files, and a very demanding due process procedure.

Security will remain the primary business of the prison of the future. Escapes, disorder, and contraband will continue to be major problems of this security. Security staff will continue to be recognized as primary to effective management. The concept of divide and rule serves as a sound security principle and supplements the idea of small group models of treatment. This format of small numbers of prisoners in small facilities will be supported for security reasons in the future. The consequence of organizing prison systems in small units will be the decentralization of the facility's organizational structure. Typical authoritarian hierarchies of management may have to give way to a system in which staff members working directly with small unit management will also be working in close organizational proximity to top levels of management.[13]

The continually rising costs of constructing large prison complexes may be the one factor that will tip the balance of corrections toward alternatives. Dependency on communities for resocialization efforts has been stressed in the United States, Canada, England, Sweden, the Netherlands, and other nations. The most efficiently managed and financially economical type of facility in the community is small in size and small in numbers of staff and residents. Old models of authority and control, under these circumstances, must give way to more cooperative management of resocialization of a nation's social deviates. While this idea may have considerable support, changes toward greater community control in the resocialization process and a reduction of the size of the prison's bureaucratic system will not be accomplished easily nor in periods of increased crime incidence.

Too little funding is provided for correcting the corrections business. Alternatives often appear to be as inefficient and as costly as prisons. Often the community becomes involved in the corrections process only to make the system even less workable. There is a constant fear among penologists that society is losing control of its deterrent and safety capabilities. This fear is even greater during periods of crimes of violence and terrorism. The public tends to support the present system and even an enlargement of it to accomplish peace and restore order and a feeling of safety among society. Imprisonment then may become even more repressive than it was.

With these perspectives in mind the climate for change depends largely on variables that may not be controlled either by advocates of alternatives and abolishment or by advocates of incarceration and controlled environments. These variables include economics, future legal definitions and laws, and the kinds of behavior of segments of the population in terms of relative threat to society's security.

Unless there are positive improvements in these variables, prison systems of the future may be smaller in terms of facilities, programs may be more varied, staffs better trained, and treatment emphasized, but management based on the old models suggested in this discussion will survive. There is clearly much to be accomplished by those who advocate alternatives and abolition if their crusades are to succeed.

Notes

1. Andrew Rutherford, "The Dissolution of the Training Schools in Massachusetts," in *A Nation without Prisons,* ed., Calvert R. Dodge, (Lexington, Mass: Lexington Books, D.C. Heath and Co., 1975), p. 61; Anttila Inker: "A New Trend in Criminal Law in Finland," in *Criminology bet ween the Rule of Law and the Outlaws,* ed. C.W.G. Jaspers, (Deventer, Netherlands: Kluver Co., 1976), p. 145; and Norval Morris, "Lessons from the Adult Correctional System of Sweden," in *Correctional Problems and Prospects,* ed. David Peterson and Charles W. Thomas, (Englewood Cliffs, N.J.: Prentice-Hall, 1975), p. 283.

2. H.W.R. Beerling, "An Outline of Dutch Criminal Procedure," in *Anglo-American Law Review* 5.1 (1976):50.

3. Calvert R. Dodge, ed., *A Nation without Prisons,* (Lexington, Mass.: Lexington Books, D.C. Heath and Co., 1975), p. 31; and Mark Morris, F. Knopp, eds., *Instead of Prisons,* National Council on Crime and Delinquency Policy Statement by Milton Rector et al., (Syracuse, N.Y.: Prison Research Project Education Action, 1976), p. 64.

4. Louis P. Carney, *Introduction to Correctional Science,* (New York: McGraw-Hill, 1974).

5. Mark Morris and F. Knopp, eds., *Instead of Prisons,* pp. 56, 59.

6. Richard McLeery, "Correctional Administration and Political Change," (Paper presented at Annual Meeting of the American Political Science Association, Washington, D.C., September 5-8, 1962) *Correctional Problems and Prospects,* Petersen and Thomas, (Englewood Cliffs, N.J.: Prentice-Hall, 1975), p. 159.

7. Don C. Gibbons, *Society, Crime, and Criminal Careers,* 3rd Ed. (Englewood Cliffs, N.J.: Prentice-Hall, 1977), pp. 58, 98, 494, 495.

8. McLeery, "Correctional Administration and Political Change," p. 157.

9. Thomas P. Wilson, "Patterns of Management and Adaptations to Organizational Roles: A Study of Prison Inmates," *American Journal of Sociology* 74, no. 2 (1968):146, reprinted in *Correctional Institutions,* ed. Robert M. Carter, (New York: J.B. Lippincott Co., 1972), p. 252.

10. J.W. Forrester, *Industrial Dynamics,* (Cambridge, Mass.: M.I.T. Press, 1971), p. 76.

11. Andrew Rutherford, "Formal Bargaining in Prison: In Search of a New Organizational Model,"*Yale Review of Law and Social Action* 2 (1971), p. 143.

12. William Nagel, *The New Red Barn: A Critical Look at the Modern American Prison* (Philadelphia: American Foundation, Institute of Corrections, 1973), pp. 17, 57, 80.

13. Roy E. Gerard and R.H. Levinson, *Functional Units: A Different Approach in Parole,* U.S. Bureau of Prisons, Gov. Printing Ser. Washington, D.C., 1974, pp. 5-8.

The following notes cite respondents to a general survey on prison management made in the U.S. in 1974 and in Europe in 1978:

J.J. Enomoto, California Corrections Department, letter to author, survey response.

Alex Wilson, Colorado State Penitentiary, survey response.

Calvin Auger, Iowa State Reformatory, survey response.

Charles J. Holmes, Bureau of Corrections, Kentucky, survey response.

Harold C. Hansen, Bruce W. McManus, Minnesota State Prison Administration, survey response.

James C. Fike, State of Illinois Prison Administration, survey response.

William L. Kime, Michigan Department of Corrections, survey response.

H.C. Cupp, Oregon State Penitentiary, survey response.

Samuel W. Smith, Utah State Prison Administration, survey response.

Donald R. Johns, Department of Social and Health Services, Seattle, Washington, survey response.

Inmate-Staff Relations pamphlet published by National Institute of Law Enforcement and Criminal Justice Research Center, Washington, D.C. and provided author in response to survey, 1974.

Prevention of Violence in Correctional Institutions, Nat. Instit. of Law Enforcement and Criminal Justice Research Center, survey response, 1974.

Inmate Disipline, ibid, 1974.

Legal Services, Redressing Prisoner Grievances, ibid., 1974.

Designing a Correctional Facility by Consultative Process, ibid.

Non-Judicial Remedies of Redressing Prisoner Grievances, ibid.

Note: During 1978 and 1979 inquiry-responses were received from twenty-five European correction system authorities representing twelve different countries.

Part II
Alternatives

3 Australia and New Zealand

Within the last twenty years Australia and New Zealand have followed somewhat similar courses in their development of progressive prison alternatives. In each of these countries there are several jurisdictions and within each jurisdiction there are several courts. Court options for prison alternatives are not universal in these various jurisdictions or courts since local laws as well as administrative and judicial programs and policies differ. This fact appears to be a continual problem since it places the process of choosing the appropriate sentence of incarceration or choice of alternative on the shoulders of the judges. Few sentences are fixed by law, and judges must continually weigh a multitude of factors before deciding what seems to them to be the most appropriate and beneficial sentence. We shall examine the systems of alternatives of each separately.

Australia

Australia with its population of some 13 million people is divided into eight central state jurisdictions. The laws of this southern Pacific continent consist of the common law developed over several centuries in England and later in Australia and various statutes enacted by the Australian Parliament. The courts of Australia consist of the Court of Appeal, the Supreme Court, and the various Magistrate Courts. All courts exercise both criminal and civil jurisdiction. Trials may be heard either by a judge or by a judge and jury.

The prison system of Australia originally designed to protect the public and to deter crime, has failed in its' rehabilitation efforts. Recidivists rates are as high in this country as in the United States and Europe, averaging 60 to 80 percent during the first twelve months of parole.

Both high cost of keeping a person in prison as well as poor results of prison confinement have helped motivate various groups to find less costly prison alternatives. Most of the alternatives used in Australia today appear to be ideas that came from England or from New Zealand. While research data does not indicate which of these alternatives may be more effective in this nation's rehabilitative efforts, these alternatives are usually much less costly than imprisonment. Most of them also involve the community members and appear to approach rehabilitation from a more humanistic philosophy.

The general trend in Australia, as it is in several other nations, is to give alternatives a try. The philosophy fostering this trend is that most offenders may be categorized as nondangerous to the community, and placing these offenders into the prison subculture may serve to increase rather than to decrease their chances of acting out antisocial attitudes when they are released. Alternatives to prison would appear to be the most logical route to take for these offenders. Some of these alternatives are briefly described.

Fines

The most common "sentence" imposed even when traffic offenses are not considered is the monetary fine. For minor offenses the fine is the only sanction available in most Australian courts. The fine is also becoming more readily used even when the court has power to sentence the offender to incarceration. Sometimes the fine is a part of the inclusive sentence, and the use of the fine may increase as the idea of making the offender pay restitution grows. The fine, as a sentence, has an early history in both civil and criminal cases, and in early England the fine was imposed as a sum due the king for the trial costs and for the offender's injury to the state. In one recent year about 96 percent of England's convicted offenders had some type of fine imposed on them.[1] In Australia imposition of fines is common, and often it is used in conjunction with probation or victim compensation. To avoid imprisoning offenders who have defaulted on fine payments, Australia has devised a government-funded criminal compensation program. The state of Tasmania most recently adopted this program in 1976. Amounts may reach up to $10,000. In addition, Tasmanian victims who assist police officers in the line of duty and are injured may be insured for an unlimited amount under this program.

The purpose of the victim compensation insurance fund is to suggest that both the state and the offender have a responsibility to make good any wrong done to the victim. This concept appears to be useful and to be gaining in popularity since irresponsible behavior is often a part of the criminal's profile. Courts have the power to delay payment of the fine, to seize the offender's property to help pay the fine or garnishee or attach the offender's earnings, and to work in other ways toward settlement of the fine while keeping the offender in the community.

The Suspended Sentence

As they do in England and in several other countries, Australian courts have the power to suspend a sentence. A sentence is given such as a one-year to three-year term. It is not placed into action by the court providing the offender does not violate any of the orders given to him by the court and which accompany the sentence. Often such a suspended sentence is accompanied by an order of probation or a bond imposition. Several Australian states have legislation allowing courts to use this type of sentence while others have abolished this legislation. A suspended sentence continues to be used primarily for first offenders and for less serious offenses. If the court feels that the offender probably will not commit additional crimes, this sentence remains as an appropriate alternative.

The Split Sentence

Australia also uses the split sentence which originated in the state of Queensland but is also used in Tasmania. It is a form of sentence often referred to in the United States as shock parole in which the offender does serve some time in prison but is released on recognizance before the sentence is completed. The difference between the recently introduced shock parole program in the United States and the split sentence in Australia is the time period in prison. In the United States this period amounts to only a month or two, while in Australia it may be a period of years.

Australian courts also use the deferred sentence whereby the sentence is not given until the court has observed the conduct of the convicted person for a period of time. Power to use this sentence is limited, and it is not used very often.

Each of these sentences is usually accompanied by a set of orders that may include directives to the offender to replace stolen or damaged property of the victim, to compensate the victim for injury or property, to comply with other directives that may even include suggested living accommodations and other personal conduct orders.

Conditional Discharge

In Australia conditional discharges are often used by the courts to allow the offender to go free of imprisonment provided that he lives up to a set of directives that the court has suggested. If these orders are followed and he does not commit further offenses during a set period of time, the sentence is eliminated. Often the orders that accompany a conditional discharge include a bond, probation under supervision, and conduct orders. In most Australian states probation is usually limited to three years or less. Minimum sentences range from six months in Queensland, for example, to one year in Victoria and Western Australia. While probation, suspended sentence, and conditional discharge differ from one another in some minor ways in Australia, they are similar to those in England and other countries and are described in more detail in other parts of this volume.

Part-Time Incarceration or
Periodic Detention

Periodic detention is one of Australia's more recent approaches to prison alternatives. Originating in New Zealand in the early 1960s, it has been adopted by several countries including the United States and some European nations.[2] Its goal is to provide an incentive for the offender while, at the same time, serving as a deterrent to further criminal action. The sentences of this type may be accompanied by some type of fine or probationary period, and there also may be additions to the sentence, including a period of part-time or periodic detention. Periodic or part-time detention is also known as weekend detention since the sentence usually includes a period of time in which the offender must work at some facility and live there over weekends. It was first introduced into the Australian penal sanction programs with the introduction of the Weekend Detention Act of 1970 in Queensland and with the Periodic Detention of Prisoners Act in New South Wales in 1970.[3]

Periodic detention and similar sentences involving short periods of prisoner incarceration can be considered both deterrent and punitive, but other goals that accompany such a sentence may differ. One example of this may be the desire of the court to approach the offender's alcoholic or mental problem. Periodic detention may allow the court to provide this service and also to incorporate a guarantee with it that insures the offender's attendance at rehabilitative sessions. In periodic or part-time detention the punitive measure is present, but the weekend or part-time idea may also be used purely for the convenience of the government. Thus a goal of periodic detention may be to reduce full-time prison populations. Another goal may be to enable the offender to maintain his job, family, and social relationships or to continue schooling or an apprenticeship. Its rehabilitative aims are likely to be considered more often by the courts since a large number of offenders who receive part-time or periodic detention probably would not have received normal sentences of incarceration.

Periodic detention usually includes orders for the offender to appear at the center for discussion group or other resocialization counseling two evenings each week. On weekends the offender checks into the center, usually on a Friday evening at seven or eight o'clock. His period of detention ends on Sunday at about four or five in the afternoon. Offenders are usually exempted from attending the center during Christmas and Easter weekends.

Offenders who qualify for periodic detention are eighteen years of age and over and have not served a sentence of imprisonment. The court must also be made aware of the offender's family conditions and be satisfied that his social and housing accommodations will not jeopardize the beneficial effects of part-time or weekend incarceration. As recently as 1976 offenders sentenced to this type of prison alternative have included those who were convicted of offenses against the person (about 20 percent), drug offenders (9 percent), minor offenses against the person (11 percent), and driving or traffic offenses (55 percent). Other persons receiving this type of sentence have included persons who were convicted of assault, robbery, fraud, break-ins, and breach of recognizance.

Usually periodic or weekend sentences average three months, but about 12 to 15 percent of the offenders sentenced to this program have received the maximum sentence of twelve months. About 86 percent of persons sentenced to periodic detention successfully complete their sentence. Research information to date has not uncovered any significant data concerning the effectiveness of the periodic detention program compared with nonsentencing or some other type of sentencing.

Periodic detention has an economic advantage over incarceration and has certain other advantages. In addition to a minimum disruption of the offender's home life, the program allows the convicted person to continue his employment or look for employment, attend school, or work for his own development in other ways. In addition, weekly work periods in the detention program provide more organized examples of working situations, a chance to get feedback about personal conduct, and a way to come into contact with programs that may help change attitude. These programs include work with pensioners, public park programs, hospitals, schools, and similar humanistic programs. Often the world of the offender has been one of association with machines and other nonhuman elements where compassion and empathy may not be involved. Periodic detention also reminds the offender of his deviation from some normal set of behavior, and in this way it may serve to change the attitude and behavior of the offender. The long-term detrimental effects of prison associations are minimized in this type of program, and the counseling sessions and group meetings can be used to help the offender over the various hurdles of readjustment on a week-by-week basis.

Work Release

Another form of part-time incarceration is work release. This alternative becomes available only after a prison sentence has begun. Work release cannot be used as a part of the court sentence in Australia. After the offender begins his prison term, custody administrators may determine that he is a good risk for work release. The offender may continue his regular job if he has one or may be employed with the aid of persons in the prison system or social welfare system. At the end of each work day the offender must return to the prison until the next work day. The program of work release has been broadened in recent years to allow certain prisoners time to be with their families, to attend school, or to take care of other matters that would be helpful to their own resocialization.[4]

To qualify for assignment to this program, the offender and his family are interviewed, his personal life is investigated, his job record is examined, and his criminal and prison record are also considered. The period of observation of candidates for the program may be as much as ninety days before approval is granted. If work is obtained for the participant, it is usually carefully selected in order to increase the probability that this employment will become the offender's permanent career after release from custody.[5] There are several varieties of the work release program in Australia. The Australian state of New South Wales, for example, adopted a new version of the work release concept in 1976. The offender remains at home in this program but is required to participate in a scheduled job in a prison near his home or at some other assigned location. This job usually begins at three-thirty or four o'clock in the afternoon and ends at midnight. This time period is selected since it is usually the time period when most crimes are committed. The goals of this variety of the work release program include the occupation of the offender's time when he might ordinarily be likely to commit a crime. Home and the prison or other work location are the basic locations for persons in this program. These restrictions are changed later, so that the offender is allowed time to be away from home and prison for social life and to conduct other legitimate business. Less than fifteen persons were participating in this program in late 1976, but the experiment shows considerable promise.

Attendance Center Alternatives

An alternative to incarceration utilized in Australia that has been increasing support and development in England and one or two other countries is the attendance center scheme. This alternative may be used by the courts and can be used when the offender is subject to a term in prison for up to a year. Persons convicted of more serious crimes or crimes of violent assault are usually not eligible for this particular alternative.

Attendance centers have been developed that can accommodate as many as forty or fifty offenders, but no ideal number has been determined. The offender must agree to the terms of this program. A decision to sentence a convicted person to the attendance center program is usually based on his past criminal records, family background, employment, and his place of residence. This last criteria is important, since the distance between the participant's home and the attendance center may be an important consideration if attendance is to continue on a regular basis. The sentence usually stipulates that the offender must attend the center for eighteen hours each week. This time is usually proportioned into various activities as follows: two evening during each week are used for job skill training and unpaid work at the center as well as for group or individual counseling. A portion of or all of each weekend during the sentence is devoted to service consisting of unpaid work at schools, hospitals, homes for handicapped persons, park and playground renovation, and work with local service clubs in programs to benefit the general public or particular persons in need of assistance. Along with this commitment is the threat of a severe penalty for breaking the terms of the commitment, which include arriving on time for any program or work, staying away from alcohol, contributing to peaceful conclusions of group meetings, and other rules. Usually the penalty for infractions includes a return to court and often a sentence to a regular full-time period of incarceration for up to twelve additional months. If the offender sentenced to the attendance center program commits a crime during his period of commitment, he is usually liable for the additional prison sentence.

The state of Victoria had developed two of these attendance centers by 1977, and each center had a full-time staff consisting of a director, a welfare supervisor, a program director, and a receptionist-bookkeeper. The attendance center concept appears to be constructive and gaining in public support. Expansion and the development of the program in other areas of Australia continues to develop. Research is not adequate to substantiate any special claim for the program at this time, in terms of its ability to affect recidivism rates or to deter crime.

Work Order Alternatives

The work order has become a very popular alternative to imprisonment in Australia, as it has in England in recent years. It was first introduced in Tasmania in early 1972 and was later adopted by the court system of the Australian Capital territory.[6] Actually this alternative, often called a Community Service Order, is a more realistic alternative in that actual incarceration in an institution of any kind is neither required nor accompanies any part of the order. The main ingredient of this alternative is a requirement that the offender work out a stipulated number of hours in the service of some specified public project, usually with other offenders and rehabilitative personnel. The Probation of Offenders Act of 1973 authorized this type of sentence in Tasmania but indicated that the work be carried out on any day except Saturday. Courts are now authorized to order the work be done at any time or on any day of the week. The offender must agree to the terms of this assignment.

Usually a work order is limited to 200 work hours. The courts also maintain the power under this act to fine the offender, to order imprisonment for up to ninety days, or to increase the number of hours of work providing that the number of work hours does not exceed 200 (twenty-five days). Offenders are required to attend classes in work or job skill instruction, apprenticeship programs, counseling sessions, and all other activities as a special work order committee may suggest.

Work order committees usually consist of a labor union member, a community public project representative, and the chief or principal probation officer. The committee has the task of recommending a program of work and counseling that may best help the offender. Usually the work chosen for the offender is useful to the community and does not contribute to the unemployment of someone else. Work may consist of assisting at a local hospital, old people's homes, children's programs, community centers, parks and public gardens, or programs of a similar nature.[7]

Costs of this alternative are very low and average about $5 per week per assigned offender. The cost of accommodating the same offender in a prison would usually amount to about thirty-five times as much as the work order commitment. In Tasmania, the program also allows the offender to maintain a normal job, stay with his family, maintain a better degree of self-esteem and at the same time contribute to the community and increase his sense of pride in himself for having paid for his crime in a recognized, accepted and constructive manner.

Usually vandals, misdemeanants, traffic violators, and similar offenders are eligible for the community work order sentence, but the success of the program indicates possibilities for expansion to include other types of offenders.

Often a work order may be given to a first-time offender who may not ordinarily receive a prison sentence. In addition, work orders are often assigned along with a period of probation. Because of these attachments, the work order is not as realistic an alternative as it could be. Perhaps as the community work order program becomes a distinctly separate program from probation and is applied to other than low-risk or no-risk offenders, its real potential and value will become clearer.

Probation and Parole

Probation is a period of time that the offender serves free from imprisonment but under the supervision of an officer of the court. Parole is time spent under the guidance of a custodial officer after an early release from prison. Usually parole can continue until the offender's full prison sentence has expired. These two types of noncustodial commitments are common in Australia as well as in many other countries. They are not considered realistic alternatives in any innovative sense of the word by many of their critics. This viewpoint is emphasized especially by such groups as the Prison Research Education Action Project of New York, funded by the New York State Council of Churches.[8] This group has suggested that both programs are failures and provide a system of continual harrassment rather than help for offenders. Parole is usually based on the recommendation of a parole board, and critics have suggested that these boards are too often made up of middle-class people who must make biased judgments about lower-class, minority people committed to prison.

Probation is usually given by a court when a judge is searching for some program to keep tabs on the offender while at the same time not actually placing him under lock and key. The objectivity of these court decisions is often missing, since the judge may be influenced by lawyers, investigative officers, and others who are eligible to report to the court on the everyday conduct of the convicted person.

The various Australian states have approached both probation and parole very differently. Discrepancies in the use of parole has been exemplified, for example, by statistics of 1974 from Australian parole boards. New South Wales paroled 41.27 persons per 100,000 population; Victoria, on the other hand, paroled only 24.68 persons per 100,000 population while South Australia paroled only 8.84 persons per 100,000, and Tasmania paroled 7.52 persons per 100,000.[9] The difference between 41 persons and 7 persons per 100,000 population is not a result of the use of some other alternative but possibly a difference in the attitudes and beliefs of parole board members in these states. Clearly parole programs appear to be in need of considerable research to determine their real worth. The same could be said of probation programs in Australia as well as in other countries. High parole rates and high probation rates are no indication of low prison populations in Australia, as our research has discovered.[10]

All the programs described here will be affected by future trends in crime rates, research results, economics, and other factors. If recidivism is a major consideration in gathering support for any prison alternative, then factors such as the costs of periodic detention compared with the costs of imprisonment will be extremely relevant. In Australia it costs about $125 dollars per day to keep an offender in maximum confinement. Periodic detention only costs about $3 to $5 per day. If both programs produce the same rates of recidivism, it would appear that there would be public demand for the alternative. Yet the mood of the people must also be considered, and if this mood is vengeful, then these comparisons may be irrelevant. Legislative bodies and public officials must consider all factors before decisions to change traditional programs can be made. We may make similar comparisons between other programs previously described and, depending on who is evaluating the data, come up with arguments supporting either of the alternatives being compared. There appears to be a need for considerable research based on widely accepted goals, of each of these programs.

New Zealand

With a population of over 3 million people, New Zealand is the largest English-speaking neighbor of Australia in the far eastern Pacific area. The two nations do not maintain close political or governmental ties, but their justice department operations are similar. Like its neighbor, New Zealand has adopted many of the common laws and statutes of the United Kingdom. In addition, the nation is guided by laws of the New Zealand Parliament and various regulations and bylaws and other subordinate types of legislature. Its hierarchy of courts includes the Court of Appeal, the Supreme Court, and various Magistrate Courts. All these courts exercise both civil and criminal jurisdiction. Trials may be by a judge or by a judge and jury.

The range of court sentences is similar to those in Australia and includes the fine for minor infractions of the law and prison sentences for more serious convictions. The courts may also discharge the offender without entering a conviction; they may convict and discharge an offender or order him to return to court for sentencing should he be found guilty of further violation of the law. Preventive detention may also be imposed on persistent sex offenders. Prison sentencing of mental incompetents who have committed criminal acts has been abolished, and the law has been changed to provide for corrective training for these offenders.

The fine is the most common penal sanction imposed even when traffic offenses are not considered. The fine is the only sanction available to courts in cases of minor offenses. Often New Zealand courts, like Australian courts, use this sanction instead of inprisonment for more serious cases. Short sentences in prison are not considered very useful rehabilitative measures. The New Zealand Criminal Justice Act of 1967 has limited the use of sentences of less than six months in prison to cases where, in the opinion of the court, there is no other appropriate alternative. Fines are paid 97 to 98 percent of the time.

Work Release

New Zealand has used the work release concept since the enactment of the Penal Institutions Amendment Act of 1961. Prison inmates in this program may be released during the day to work in private employment, but as in the

Australian scheme, they must return to their prison accommodations in the evening. Persons involved in this program must contribute part of their wages toward the cost of prison accommodations and their meals at the prison. An additional portion of their wages may be withheld in order to clear up any fine imposed on them by the courts. The balance of the wage earnings may be used to assist their dependents or to be placed in their own savings account. Work release was first conceived and developed in the United States in 1913, but new variations of the program have helped introduce new methods of operation and have included counseling programs and other approaches in the last ten years.[11] In England the program received encouragement with the establishment of the first hostels for outworkers and prerelease units near certain prisons. Comparable programs have since developed in France, Sweden, Belgium, Norway, and Australia. Work release may be considered a secondary type of prison alternative in that it is available only after the offender has served a period of time in prison, often several years. The program is available only to administrators of custody programs and not to courts as an alternative of the first instance, that is, in place of custodial care and before any type of custodial care is imposed.

Probation and Probation Hostels

Probation continues to be a popular means of sentencing in New Zealand, as it does in Australia. Case histories of the offenders are provided to the court prior to sentencing. All penal measures short of imprisonment are usually handled by the New Zealand probation departments.[12] Probation officers usually require that the offender report to his office each week and follow a set of orders developed by the court.

The probation hostel is designed to provide a calm living accommodation for offenders in cases where home conditions may be inadequate or may even contribute toward the offender's criminal behavior. They are also provided when there is no permanent home for the offender. Many of the hostels are operated by churches. Often these hostels help the offender locate work, improve his education, and work out personal problems. Small hostels modeled on the small family home idea are usually the ideal type of accommodation but are more expensive to operate.

Periodic Detention

The periodic detention concept originated in New Zealand in 1962. The objective of the program is to provide a form of detention that allows the convicted person to remain at home the majority of the time. Similar programs have been established in Australia and in the United Kingdom. The original plan was to use the program with young people only. By 1973, however, periodic detention was extended to include adult offenders, some with long criminal records. Periodic detention was written into law with an amendment to the Criminal Justice Act of 1954 and became effective November 28, 1962. A subsequent amendment to the act in 1966 made the sentence of periodic detention applicable also to adults. J.L. Robson, Secretary of Justice in 1963, initiated and directed the development of this pioneer program of treatment.[13] Originally eligibility for periodic sentencing limited participants to youths between fifteen and twenty years of age without records of having been previously sentenced to some detention center or hostel training or to imprisonment for one month or more. A background report is usually developed by a probation officer, and this report must include a medical examination to indicate the participant's suitability for work and exercise during the program. The sentence to periodic detention must include information such as the number of periods in each week on which the offender must report to the center, the first day and time he is to report, and the duration of the sentence. No single, continuous period of custody may exceed sixty hours. The offender must agree to participation in the program. As in the Australian program, detainees may work on a wide variety of community programs or at the center itself. The work done must not affect the employment of regular employees in any of the agencies, and offenders are not entitled to any remuneration for the work. In some programs of this type remuneration is provided and used for room and board for the offender.

Advisory Committees were incorporated into the program early in its history and have functioned well in many ways. These committees consist of representatives from the court, business and industry, labor groups, and other lay people. The committee assists the development of each center by advising in items such as staff appointments, work programs, and general policy matters. The committee serves as a very effective link between the community and the judicial system in this rehabilitative program. Wardens for these centers have included ex-naval officers, ex-army majors, ministers of religion, and ex-police constables.[14] Each center has been able to develop its own unique approach.

Detainees usually arrive at the center by 7 p.m. on Fridays and begin a routine that includes cleaning, cooking, maintenance, and group discussions. On Saturday the day begins with early breakfast and then a regular work day, beginning at 8 a.m., which may consist of work at the center or at a hospital, an elderly person's home, a public park, or other project. During the week detainees may attend one or two evening sessions from 7 to 9:30 p.m. Educational classes have included basic English and mathematics, and some centers have incorporated field trips to the mountains, boat-building projects, and dramatics. On Saturday nights detainees may participate in sport and recreational activities and may attend a movie, returning to the center on their own. Often the warden's wife is in charge of the kitchen, and one or two participants are assigned to assist her in the preparation of food.

Research has indicated that the rate of recidivism for persons who experienced detention of this sort is about 33 percent when the risk period is two years. The 67 percent success rate in one study suggests that the program has considerable merit when compared with other more costly programs which are often less successful. Other studies have indicated that approximately 64 percent of the total sample remained free of further convictions during a two-year period, despite the fact that many of the subjects in the sample had originally been convicted of serious offenses prior to sentencing to periodic detention.[15]

By 1978 some two thousand detainees were actively involved in the periodic detention program and were assisting a wide range of groups and institutions as well as individuals. Projects now include home care for the handicapped and elderly, health camp maintenance, beach and park cleanup and repair, ground maintenance, and renovation of Maori tribe village buildings.

In addition to these described alternatives New Zealand also gives prison administrators the power to assign offenders from parole and work release programs to prerelease and postrelease centers.

Probation statistics for 1977 have indicated that of 6,778 probationers in New Zealand only 1,565 committed breaches of parole or new offenses during a one-year period of study. The ages of offenders in New Zealand are comparable to most other countries, in that almost two-thirds of all those convicted are under twenty-five years. The ratio of prisoners per 100,000 population is about 150 compared with 250 prisoners per 100,000 population in the United States and 21 prisoners per 100,000 population in the Netherlands. The daily average of prisoners during 1977 was 2,707 males and 113 females in New Zealand prisons, lockups, and jails.[16]

Conclusions

Alternatives to prison in Australia and in New Zealand may be compared with similar programs in the United Kingdom. Several of these alternatives and especially periodic detention are demonstrating that innovative programs may someday replace long terms of incarceration for many of the citizens of these nations. In a perusal of research material concerned with the effects that these alternatives have on recidivism, evidence was not sufficient to justify making any great claims for any of these programs. Evidence that does warrant continued support for programs such as periodic detention and other particularly well-managed alternatives is that they cost less than full-time imprisonment, and the rates of recidivism for participants in these programs are usually not any greater than those of their prison population counterparts.

Prior to 1960 Australia and New Zealand had little to offer the offender other than imprisonment and parole. In the last twenty years remarkable progress has been made with the introduction of a variety of alternatives in both countries. There is every indication that these programs will continue and that pure alternatives, which are not tied to the prison system such as parole, may be introduced. Both countries are currently suffering from overcrowding of prisons and rising crime rates. The incentives for the invention and development of alternatives to incarceration appear to be lower costs to the taxpayers, comparable if not better results when compared with prison results, and a more humanistic approach to the resocialization of society's deviants.

Notes

1. Home Office, The Sentence of the Court, London, Government Home Office, Her Majesty's Stationery Office, 1970, p. 4.

2. R. Te Punga, "Periodic Detention" in *Proceedings of the Seventh National Conference of the Australian Crime Prevention and After-Care Council,* Canberra, Australia, 1973, p. G1.

3. Ivan Potas, "Alternatives to Imprisonment" *Crime and Justice Journal,* ed. D. Biles, (Canberra, Australia: Australian Institute of Criminology, 1977), p. 119.

4. Ibid., p. 120.

5. Ibid., p. 125, see also E. Barnett, "Release to Work," *Proceedings of the Seventh National Conference of the Australian Crime Prevention and Correction and After-Care Council,* 1973, p. J2.

6. I. Potas, "Alternatives to Imprisonment," p. 122.

7. Ibid., p. 123.

8. Mark Morris and F.H. Knopp, eds., *Instead of Prisons,* Prison Research Education Project, (New York: New York Council of Churches, 1976).

9. I. Potas, "Alternatives to Imprisonment," p. 130, see also *Canberra Times,* 13 July 1976, Cost figures have been updated to predicted levels of the 1979-1980 U.S. dollar.

10. A.R. Shearer, *Penal Policy in New Zealand,* (Wellington, New Zealand: Government Printer, 1970), p. 4.

11. M.B. Hoare, C.R. Bevan, and W.D. Simpson, "Alternatives to Imprisonment and Progessive Variations in Current Practise," *Australian and New Zealand Journal of Criminology* 5 (March 1972):29.

12. Shearer, *Penal Policy in New Zealand,* p. 5.

13. New Zealand Department of Justice, *Periodic Detention in New Zealand,* Research Series Pamphlet No. 4 (Wellington, New Zealand: Research Section, Government Printer, 1973), pp. 5, 6.

14. Ibid., p. 9.

15. Ibid., p. 24.

16. New Zealand Government, Report of the Department of Justice for the Year ending 31 March 1978 (Wellington, New Zealand: E.C. Keating, Government Printer, 1978), p. 18. See also J.L. Robson, "Penal Policy in New Zealand," *Australian and New Zealand Journal of Criminology* 4 (December 1971):195-206; Sheila Varne, "Saturday Work: A Real Alternative? *Australian and New Zealand Journal of Criminology* 9 (June 1976):95-103; Peter Prisgrove, "Periodic Detention: A Critical Examination," *Australian and New Zealand Journal of Criminology* 6 (1973):147-157; R.W. Drinkwater, "Alternatives to Imprisonment, *Australian and New Zealand Journal of Criminology* 2 (December 1969):217-230; T.C. Waring, "Community Involvement in the Corrective Process," *Australian and New Zealand Journel of Criminology* 2 (December 1969):232-237; New Zealand Year Book, "Justice, Law and Order and Public Safety," (Wellington, New Zealand: Government Printer, 1977), Pamphlet sections 8, 8A.

4 Canada

Today Canada's leaders in judicial reform are preparing for the 1980s. Significant changes are taking place in the organization, management, and operation of the corrections system. These changes have been developing since the early 1960s, but the most notable changes have taken place during 1977 and 1978.[1] Amendments to Canada's Criminal Code, which opened the way for the courts to order convicted offenders to make restitution to their victims or perform community work in lieu of imprisonment, set a precedent for the country, and each province has developed plans or is carrying out programs today that underline this and other types of alternatives to incarceration.

At the present time Canada has about thirty thousand prisoners in its prisons and jails throughout the country.[2] It costs an average of $40 per day to maintain a prisoner in these units. The total yearly cost of this lockup system is over $400 million a year.[3] Through innovative approaches to prison alternatives, Canada is well on its way to changing this picture. The hard facts of high costs have helped stimulate the country's budgeters and correctional people toward greater support for other more efficient ideas. Probation supervision, for example, only costs about $3 per day per probationer.[4] Community-based resource center programs average about $16 per day per person, and community correctional centers, which include bed and food, cost about $24 per day.[5] The Community Services (work) order program costs a little over $2 per day per inmate.[6] Even with inflation causing an increasingly upward trend in costs per person, the comparisons are so dramatic that they must be carefully examined as alternatives to the typical prison system. During the middle 1970s Canada began to make the changes in its corrections system to accommodate the thinking of many of its most prominent leaders in the justice sector, as well as in the other branches of government. The Law Reform Commission of Canada made proposals which included allowing petty thieves, vandals, and other minor criminals to pay for their crimes by restoring or replacing the property they stole or damaged or by doing some kind of work for the community. These methods would be considered punishment enough, and it would spare the prisoner a prison sentence and all its consequences (loss of job, absence from family, learning new criminal behavior from fellow prisoners, for example).[7] The many new approaches to resocialization of convicted persons in Canadian prison reforms and law changes, plus new alternatives to prison, appear to indicate that Canada, with its diverse populations, is attempting to test the best rehabilitative programs and to incorporate usable ideas into its ongoing and progressive view of its corrections system. Canadian corrections has also taken the position that criminal justice problems cannot be isolated from the community itself and that criminal justice solutions are in part also the problem of the community.[8] It is the community, the Canadian society, that defines acceptable modes of social behavior; it is the community that labels deviance. It is also the community that has the most effective resources in manpower and facilities that can contribute to the solution of the problem of useful corrections. During the late 1970s Canada increased the involvement of volunteers to assist convicted persons. Options for a variety of work for volunteers also increased, and community acceptance of volunteers' working in corrections became more widespread.[9] The seventies have seen the changing of an old concept with regard to social outcasts from that of "do not touch" to "touch often."

In 1977 in British Columbia, for example, the first full-time institutional position for a volunteer coordinator was filled to coordinate and develop volunteer activities in several of the province's institutions.[10] Options for volunteers to work in pretrial services (particularly in custody remand), youth detention centers, community correctional centers, and custody facilities were increasing significantly. Where no volunteer coordinator exists, the local corrections personnel have assumed the task of gathering volunteers and helping them to work with convicted persons. Some programs have also been initiated by community organizations. Under these circumstances assistance from volunteer programs of the corrections branch has been given in the form of orientation materials, financial assistance, and the payment of tuition for relevant training courses. New materials have been printed, and in general, the Canadian Volunteer Program has won national support for the concept of citizen involvement injustice.[11]

The alternative programs are not necessarily restricted to the provinces under which they are explained. But the separation of these programs by province suggests that alternative ideas may differ from area to area because of several factors, some of which may include the structure of the system in an area, the diversity of the population, the available resources, distances between segments of population, and financial resources. An idea for working with convicted persons in one area may be adaptable to another area and may be altered and used according to resources available. This blending and sampling concept provides a flexible method of working with people, a concept not nearly as acceptable in a rigid corrections approach.

The Federal Penitentiary System

In their search to find effective ways to help resocialize offenders, Canadian penal authorities have introduced new methods of working with inmates in institutions. One example of this concept is the Living Unit Program which has been gradually introduced into the penitentiary system since a pilot program was developed in 1969.[12] The core idea of the Living Unit Program includes a living unit enclosure where inmates sleep. A canteen stocked with small items that inmates may purchase, a living room where inmates can gather, a hall for inmate meetings, and offices for the living unit's institutional personnel are parts of this unit. Within the unit the staff members and inmates work together to solve individual and collective problems of everyday life at the institution. In so doing inmates learn what is appropriate and applicable to life outside the institution. They learn to identify problems, analyze them, and suggest solutions. They find out what is and is not feasible as well as acceptable. They also learn that restrictions are a part of any societal or communal life, necessary for social order, and not an invention of those in power (either in their own family, the institution, or the community). The aim of cooperative problem solving is to demonstrate that to achieve common goals, in penal institutions as in society, the interest of individuals must take second place to those of the group. The ability to deal with minor privileges and offenses requires inmates to deal with themselves, to be their own arbiters. When an inmate joins his peers in a discussion of his actions, he cannot attribute his reward or punishment to favoritism or victimization by prison authorities. The Living Unit Program is an enlightening experience in which the inmate learns to consider the consequences of his acts and the possible effect on other people. He also has the opportunity, perhaps for the first time, to learn how to deal with problems constructively. Early research provided ample evidence that Living Unit members had less resentment of authority and less tension within themselves; thus this program must be considered a feasible change in a positive direction. While the Living Unit Program is not considered an alternative to prison, its concept should not be lost by those focusing on alternatives. Even if the concept had never been used in alternative programs, those persons who have experienced the Living Unit Program may be excellent risks to be considered for alternative programs. Fortunately, the Living Unit idea is more widely used than discussed here, especially in the halfway house alternative in Canada and in other countries.

Citizen Participation

Some ten thousand citizens participate as volunteers in Canada's federal penitentiary programs. Most of these programs relate to life outside prison walls. These citizen volunteers provide an important link or contact with society. Individual volunteers, service clubs, social agencies, religious groups, and private industry, as well as other special interest groups, have been involved since 1965. All these volunteer groups serve as potentially valuable sources for developing innovative alternatives to prison.

One of the major problems of the old version of federal penitentiary programs was the forbidding of inmates to ever have leave from the institution. When parole or discharge was finally given, the inmate received a suit of clothes (prison-made) and a little money; he had no job and diminished prospects of finding a job, no prearranged living accommodations, few friends, weakened family ties, and very low morale. Offenders were also confronted with a world that had changed considerably during their confinement. These factors thwarted even the most determined efforts of the discharged person to lead a constructive resocialized life outside of prison. In the 1950s changes began taking place, leading to Canadian parole as it is known today and, predictably, to evolving changes including the possibility that parole will someday be replaced by an alternative means of reentry into society for former inmates. In the 1950s a few Canadian inmates, nearing their release after serving long terms, were permitted to go into the community on a daily basis to work and adjust to a free society. In 1960 and 1961 the Penitentiary Act of the federal government took additional steps to to improve offenders' chances of "making it on the outs" (succeeding outside of prison walls). This change was implemented by the Temporary Absence Clause, which was introduced into the act.

The Temporary Absence Clause is a provision whereby an inmate of a federal penal institution may obtain leave of absence for limited periods of time for medical, humanitarian, and rehabilitative reasons.[13] It may be granted with or without escort. It may range from the usual one day to fifteen days. Thus an inmate may obtain medical help that is not provided within the institution. He may obtain leave for home visits because of a family member's illness or death, school graduations, or unusual family hardships. The rehabilitative temporary absence leave is granted for interviews with prospective employers and landlords, attendance at lectures, functions related to an inmate's special studies, family visits, and individual and group participation in sports, art, music, and drama activities in nearby communities. Temporary absence, as would be the case, is granted to inmates who meet strict requirements in terms of the nature of offense, length of confinement, behavior during incarceration, and similar criteria. But the seeds of constructive alternatives may be found in such a program. Usually inmates who have served at least six months since their last admission may qualify for temporary absence while inmates serving life sentences or those affiliated with organized crime must serve at least three years before qualifying for temporary absence. Habitual criminals and dangerous criminals are further restricted from temporary absence.

Still another concept that is a part of this pattern of allowing federal prisoners time away from the prison is day parole.[14] Day parole is a program whereby inmates may leave confinement prior to full parole or discharge to undertake employment or education or training not available in the institutions. Day parolees must abide by rules set by the National Parole Board, and they are supervised by staff members attached to the National Parole Board. They must return to an institution at a time specified by the parole board, and this particular alternative fits the general concepts of work release.

Along with several other nations Canada in 1968 introduced the halfway house concept for its federal prisoners. The pilot project was first introduced in Montreal and was entitled the Community Correctional Center.[15] Since 1969 other centers have been opened in urban areas throughout the nation. Classified as a minimum security institution, the Community Correctional Center provides accommodation for a small group of carefully selected inmates on day parole, to determine their suitability for return to society. When there is difficulty adjusting to the outside community, the case is reviewed to determine the problem. Aptitude testing and evaluation are provided to help in the readjustment period and search for work. The Community Correctional Center staff maintains close working relationships with a myriad of public and private social service and business people, civic organizations, religious groups, public and private law enforcement and education agencies. Requirements for acceptance into a Community Correctional Center include the inmate's needs for additional job training, counseling, his personal problems, and the location of his family. Screening of inmates is done by the Canadian Penitentiary System and National Parole Board staff members, and final authorization comes from the National Parole Board. Informal meetings are held with people who will be involved with the inmate's new role in the community, including his family, local police, possible employers, and clergy. Canada is aware of the use of inappropriate titles, as are other nations involved in major reformation movements, and titles such as the Community Correctional Center carry the usual stigma. Ontario province, for example, uses the title Community Resource Center, and this center has most of the Community Correctional Center's ideas and operational procedures but without the stigma of the word corrections attached to it. This appears to be a trend in American, Canadian, Dutch, and Scandinavian penal programs. These title discrepancies may appear insignificant at first sight, but in the process of the prisoner's search for a new life, titles of places where he sleeps and eats and other ascribed labels become highly significant and may definitely be a part of the total motivating or nonmotivating influences on his behavior.

Federal penitentiary systems usually do not set the pace of a nation's reformation movements. Usually ideas are put into action on a small scale within some particular community or by a particular community and then

are copied in various modified forms by county, state, or province and
finally may be adopted nationwide. It is with this thought that we now ex-
plore several of the provincial programs of Canada.

Ontario

Ontario's new era in prisoner rehabilitation was established during 1977 and
1978. The new dimensions at the beginning of this era included Institutional
Temporary Absence Programs (TAP), and Institutional Industrial and
Community Residential Training Programs, and Community Resource
Center Programs, both of which included the temporary absence
provision.[16] In a number of communities across the province the development of life skills courses and the involvement of volunteers in programs in
institutions had been established by the latter part of 1978.

The Temporary Absence Program has been considered a major
breakthrough in progressive development of alternatives to prison. It actually began in August 1969.[17] The program is not suitable for what may be
considered hard-core criminal or incorrigible prisoners, and some inmates
are not interested in it and others are not sufficiently motivated to take part
in the program. The program offsets the ill effects and the harm of isolation
and encourages response to trust. It can promote or reawaken a sense of
family and community responsibility, and it is available to a considerable
segment of the total number of sentenced persons. Until the mid 1970s a
temporary absence of from one to fifteen days could be granted on
humanitarian grounds, for purposes of related rehabilitation, and for job
interviews, family problems, and similar situations. Provisions for extended
temporary absence, beyond the fifteen-day period, were approved at this
time, and sentenced persons were able to participate in industrial employment programs and to reside in more open community settings where working, earning, and learning possibilities were greater.

The Temporary Absence Program is presented to persons when they are
first admitted to an institution. If a person is interested, he makes an application and his request is reviewed by a panel of counselors and administrators. Additional community investigations may follow. When a
person is selected, he is given the conditions and terms of the program. Persons who have committed crimes involving violence, brutality, or arson, who
have habitually used or trafficked in drugs, who have a long history of
alcoholism, who have committed a sexual offense, or who have escaped or
attempted to escape are usually not eligible for the program, but this is not
an absolute rule. The Ontario Ministry of Correctional Services, which
oversees such programs, accepts the philosophy that this gradual reintegration into society is a practical and essential aspect of correctional program-

ming but also acknowledges its responsibility to insure public safety. Thus conditions of suspension, withdrawal, revocation, and further institutional or court sanctions are made very clear to persons whose applications are approved.

Wherever possible, when the Temporary Absence Program involves an employer, an institutional representative, ideally from the probation or parole staff, will visit the prospective employer and arrange for him to sign an agreement form and to discuss the payment procedure. Periodic visits are made to the place of employment to see how the assigned person is progressing. Many employers have supported the program by providing jobs for sentenced persons on the basis of their skills and training regardless of their criminal record. They allow inmates to adjust to a working situation and assist them when problems arise. In some cases the Temporary Absence Program has allowed the sentenced person to continue the job he had at the time of sentence without any interruption or an interruption of only a few days. While the prerogative for this kind of arrangement is left to the employer, more is being done to communicate with the employer and to provide him with information that would help him decide in favor of the convicted person. He would then notify the superintendent of the nearest institution or the coordinator of the Temporary Absence Program in the Ministry of Corrections that he wanted to continue the employment of the convicted person.

The development of the Temporary Absence Program has allowed sentenced persons a great deal of latitude in their search for jobs. They may visit the potential employer's office for assessment tests and interviews and arrange their work schedules in such a way that they are able to take advantage of shift work and overtime when it is available. In these situations standard wages must be paid, and the sentenced person must meet all contractual agreements. Employers involved in the Temporary Absence Program play a key role in the rehabilitation of the offender by allowing him to earn money for his family and by imposing responsibilities that will be essential and vital to his readjustment to society after release.

The Temporary Absence Program is also used for educational programming at all educational levels, and sentenced persons who have been accepted in the program have been able to participate in their own education in secondary schools, community colleges, and universities. Generally the arrangements and rules follow the same pattern as for employment.

The Temporary Absence Program has received good publicity, positive and enthusiastic response of employers and inmates, and is presently reaching about 20 percent of Ontario's eight thousand adult institutional inmates.

While the Temporary Absence Program involves the sentenced person who is most likely to survive in such a program, the Industrial Employment

Temporary Absence Program was developed for persons considered too high a risk for such freedom. This program also involves the assistance and participation of private industrial concerns but is much more closely supervised, and the programs operate within the confines of minimum security institutions such as Guelph and Maplehurst Correctional Centers in Ontario. These industrial programs enable a large range of long-term inmates, who would not otherwise be considered equipped or eligible for normal employment or educational Temporary Absence Programs, to participate. While employed in these programs the sentenced person is in a relatively open setting under direct supervision, and his work is evaluated by managers, foremen, and supervisors of the private industrial segment of society. The sentenced person is housed and supervised in normal institutional facilities at night.

Ontario's Community Residential Training Temporary Absence Program and its Community Resource Centers are somewhat similar to U.S. programs of halfway houses. They provide a place to stay, to work in the community, to obtain assistance in social, physical, or psychological problems, and to participate in community affairs. Of over eighty thousand applications for participation in the Temporary Absence Program made between 1969 and 1979, about fifty thousand were approved. According to the Ontario Ministry of Corrections about 99 percent of all approved applicants completed the program without recourse to further institutional or court sanctions for a violation of conditions or for further offenses.[18] The low failure rate is attributed to careful screening and the desire and capacity on the part of the vast majority of those approved for the program to participate successfully. The part that employers take and the active participation of helpful community resource people are also considered very important contributing factors. Employers pay standard wages, give advance notice of overtime work, report problems and suggestions, make required payroll deductions, and aid the success of the program in other ways. The sentenced participant is made aware of his participation is many ways, including the deduction of money for his room and board at the institution to which he is attached.

Community Resource Centers

Ontario's Community Resource Centers usually accommodate from seven to eighteen sentenced persons. They provide a live-in environment in the community from which the participant may begin the process of returning to the community by working at gainful employment or attending educational upgrading courses while serving a sentence. These centers are located in rural as well as urban areas, several are bilingual, and at present one is for women. In addition, several mobile centers are used in the more remote areas of northern Ontario. These are used for those native persons who cut timber for the pulp and paper industries.

Each resident of a Community Resource Center who earns an income pays a maximum of $35 a week to his center for room and board. He also contributes to his community by paying taxes, by supporting his family, and, in some cases, by making restitution to the victim of his offense. Ontario's Ministry of Corrections, however, has full legal responsibility for the participant's safety and health, as well as for the safety of the public.

Although no one is excluded from consideration for the Community Resource Center program, an assessment committee at each institution will not normally recommend a person who has committed crimes as noted in the Temporary Absence Program.[18] The application may be made solely on the initiative of the inmate, or the staff may recommend that he consider making an application. In the application the person must indicate whether he has obtained employment or has been accepted in a community educational program and, if not, where he would like to seek work or further education. He must also indicate what he thinks the Community Resource Program will do for him if he is accepted. If there are contradictions or contraindications to his acceptance, and he acknowledges his awareness of them, he may explain his actions or past record and give an indication of the progress he has made. Local law enforcement agencies are also consulted for their opinions on the applicant's suitability for the program. The program allows the sentenced person to establish himself in the community prior to the completion of his sentence. It permits employers, educators, and other members of the community to play a part in the resocializing process, and the Community Resource Center provides an evironment that, for motivated individuals, is more conducive to rehabilitation than an institutional setting.

Residents of the Community Resource Center Program work or attend school, usually during the day, and return to the center each evening. Meals are generally family-style, with the residents sharing many of the chores. All center staffs attempt to make positive use of peer group pressure with respect to behavior in the house and use of leisure time. Group discussions and therapeutic programs are features of most Resource Center programs, and these are supplemented by individual counseling according to each participant's needs. Staff members at the Community Resource Centers gradually build a list of employers and educational facilities that are willing to cooperate with the center. Many residents of the centers are lacking in such basic life skills as assessing their own employment potential, seeking employment, handling the job interview, relating to fellow employees, and maintaining good working habits. At least one staff member at each center has been trained to give counseling in these and other personal skills.

Residents of the Community Resource Centers may apply for a weekend leave, which must be approved by both the center staff and the superintendent of the parent institution. In 1978 there were twenty-one Community Resource Centers in operation in Ontario.

Community Work Order

Legislative provisions in the mid 1970s provided Canadian judges with the provisions of the Community Work Order. The Community Work Order is a broad and varied plan for providing alternatives to incarceration and perhaps is the purest form of alternative as we know the meaning of the term since a person committed to the Community Work Order may not even enter a penal institution.[19] For most of the history of law in Canada, judges most frequently used one option or a combination of basic options in the sentencing of an offender—imprisonment, a fine, or a term of probation. Imprisonment is often seen as being inappropriate or too severe a punishment for certain types of crimes, and the costs to the taxpayer have become prohibitive. (In some cases costs of imprisonment were estimated at $50 per day during the late 1970s.) Fines do not affect all people equally. For those with substantial incomes, fines may have little more than a nuisance value, yet the same monetary penalty might cause severe hardship to a person without a job or with a limited income. Probation, which has long been the mainstay of community corrections, offers the offender the chance to abide by the accepted rules of society without the stigma of going to prison. The individual on probation may receive assistance with his therapy, his education, his home situation, his employment, his relationship with others, or training for a career. Probation orders, however, have usually required the offender to repay society for his antisocial behavior, either in terms of loss of freedom or through restitution of some form or other.[20] Probation, in addition, carries the stigma of police surveillance. A Community Work Order provides an alternative. A judge may, after having satisfied himself of the suitability of the offender for such a program and the existence of appropriate work, stipulate that the sentenced person will spend a specified number of hours working for the benefit of the community.

In October 1977 seven pilot projects were announced that opened the doors to a greatly increased use of Community Work Orders. These seven projects were designed to provide a variety of operational models in both rural and urban siutations and to provide the basis for further expansion of the program. The operation of the various projects incorporated such groups as the Quinte Community-Oriented Sentencing Committee in Belleville, Ontario; the Probation-Parole Services local office in Oshawa;

the Peterborough Volunteer Bureau; the John Howard Society; the St. Leonard Society; and a native Indian organization.

An offender who receives a sentence of the Community Work Order alternative may be required to participate in working with handicapped people, repairing damage that he may have done in the community, coaching a sports team, cleaning a park, or helping a city build a public dock. These examples indicate that the types of opportunities for use of Community Work Orders can be considerable and depend on the innovative thinking of judges and their advisors, community leaders, and a wide variety of other persons interested in either community development or prisoner rehabilitation. Community Work Orders are aimed at work projects that will be of tangible benefit to the community. Accepting the responsibility for other people's needs is seen, by the project's participants, as a means of helping the sentenced person discover his own strengths and abilities and to gain self-assurance. Thus far a number of offenders have continued as volunteers in their work order placement after the terms of the order were satisfied. Failure to complete an assignment is considered a breach of probation and in some cases results in the offender's return to court.

The church has begun to take a more active role in supporting alternatives to incarceration and alternative means of rehabilitation for the incarcerated. Beginning in late 1976 the National Community Education Program of the Church Council on Justice and Corrections began distributing thousands of packets of information to businessmen, young people's groups, radio, television, community and educational organizations, and others to help people understand the idea of alternatives and to help citizens become involved with convicted offenders.[21] This program and another program entitled Correctional Volunteers in Action and similar programs are designed to provide opportunities for volunteers to assist as life skill instructors, group discussion leaders, job locators, family service assistants, vocational counselors, and literacy teachers.[22] While these programs are not alternatives in themselves, they tend to generate ideas and programs which, in turn, often develop into alternative programs or projects. A life skill instructor helps teach the offender how to seek employment, manage his personal affairs, and organize daily routines.

British Columbia

In the British Columbia correctional system, alternatives have taken the form of community correctional centers, community-based residential centers, various probation and attendance programs, as well as the Community Service Order Program. The Community Service Order Program is similar to Ontario's Community Work Order Program, and both have been

modeled after the British Community Work Service Program which has
been operating successfully in Great Britain since 1972.[23] It was originally
developed as an alternative to short prison terms for adult offenders.
Volunteer organizations provide tasks for the work service, and the probation officer reports to the court on the offender's suitability for the program
and on the availability of these tasks. The court issues either a standard probation order, with a clause for community service, or a special community
work service order; it specifies the number of hours of service (from 20 to
240) to be performed and a period not exceeding twelve months for completion of the tasks assigned. The offender is then ordered by the court to
report to a probation office for assignment to a probation officer. During
his work order, he is supervised by a probation officer or by a member of
the voluntary cooperating agency. If the offender breaches the service
order, he is first given a warning. If the breach continues, he may be fined
or returned to court, where the order is revoked and he is resentenced. This
option for the program gives it great clout. In Great Britain the program has
received general approval from the public, the probation services, and offenders themselves, and this public support is also increasing in the Canadian province of British Columbia. The concept itself was originally introduced in British Columbia by various, generally small, courts and probation officers as an informal program for young offenders, either with a formal probation order or as a part of a voluntary diversion program. Lack of
organization and manpower prevented early growth of the program. During
the years 1970 to 1974 the British Columbia Corrections Association Bien-
nial Institute, the British Columbia Task Force on Correctional Services
and Facilities, and the Five-Year Plan Committee of the Corrections Branch
all identified the need for a formalized alternative program in the
province.[24] In 1975 a pilot program was developed for nine centers in the
province which was to be implemented with the cooperation of probation
officers, Justice Council coordinators, and community volunteer groups. A
Community Service supervisor was hired for each of the centers, and in
1975 the program was formally implemented in these centers.

Following the success of the pilot programs, legislative action was made
to change the Criminal Code and the Juvenile Delinquents Act to provide a
completely official approach to the program. In one year alone some three
thousand offenders entered the program.

Since the program's development to provide alternatives to incarceration for both adult and juvenile offenders, juvenile cases account for 55.7
percent of the cases and adult cases account for the remaining 44.3 percent.
Eighty-eight percent of the cases are male, and native Indians account for 9
percent of the total cases in the program.

The most common offenses for which admissions are made are theft
under $200 and breaking and entering. About one-third of the participants

are admitted by a probation officer inquiry, and most of these are by a verbal rather than written agreement. Of the two-thirds admitted by the court, most are by a standard probation order rather than a special Community Service Probation Order. Table 4-1 indicates other offenses of participants in this program.

In British Columbia almost all the program participants are assigned work for the community rather than for the victim. Supervision of two-thirds of the work is performed by community volunteer group members. Half the orders are for work in a community or service agency, and about 36 percent of the orders are for work on community recreation facilities and park development. The average number of hours assigned per work order is approximately thirty-seven.

The success of the program is registered in the completion of almost 94 percent of work assigned and in the positive comments by 76 percent of the evaluators. The offenders are usually between eighteen and twenty-five years of age. British Columbia is also involved in a program similar to Ontario's Temporary Absence Program. In addition, British Columbia has developed the Attendance Program, which is designed for juveniles in need of supervision but not incarceration. In cases where the community and other agencies are unable to supply support services, or where the available services are insufficient or unsuitable, the Corrections Branch uses the Attendance Program as one of its alternatives. There are three categories of the program: (1) Daily attendance, whereby the juvenile attends school

Table 4-1
Offenses Committed by Community Service Order Participants in British Columbia

Offense	Percentage of Participants Committing Offense (N = 1,459)
Causing a disturbance	1.4
Public mischief	1.9
Impaired driving (intoxicated, etc.)	2.0
Theft over $200	5.4
Theft under $200	27.3
Breaking and entering	22.3
Possession of stolen property	3.9
Mischief	8.5
Breach of the Narcotic Control Act for possession	6.7
Breach of the Government Liquor Act	3.7
Breach of the Motor Vehicle Act	1.4

Source: *The Community Service Order Program: The British Columbia Experience,* Ministry of the Attorney General, Victoria, British Columbia, Canada, July 1977. Reprinted with permission.

or work during the day and then reports to a center where specific activities (recreation, counseling) may be provided. (2) Weekend attendance, whereby the probationer must attend and reside at a center from Friday evening to Sunday afternoon until succesful graduation. (3) A full residence attendance program, whereby the probationer must reside at the center during weekdays and weekends. These programs are alternatives to full incarceration; they maintain a community approach with community facilities and offer the court the option of ordering supervision in structured settings of a specific kind of program for offenders unable to or unwilling to respond to home or normal community supervision. The actual program varies from educational training, recreation, and community service activities to involvement in wilderness programs such as Outward Bound,[24] a wilderness program structured to build self-confidence and trust in young people. The Corrections Branch operates the staffs, funds the program, and maintains a close relationship with schools, child welfare agencies, employers, mental health programs, and other community resources to foster complete involvement in the probationer's progress.

In the latter part of the 1970s British Columbia began expanding its alternative programs and increasing community involvement. Efforts are continually being made to decrease the size of prisons or correctional institutions in favor of alternative programs. The central center, known as the Lower Mainland Regional Correctional Center, has a population of five hundred to six hundred persons, but the other seven centers have an average of seventy to eighty persons. British Columbia now has ten forestry camps, seven Community Correctional Centers, and twelve community-based residential centers. The forestry centers house thirty to sixty residents while the community residential centers house small groups consisting of about twelve persons each.

In 1978 British Columbia expanded its Community Service Program; at last count, there were Community Service officers in twenty-eight locations in the province. This step, in addition to the increase in the number of smaller community-based residential centers, a large community volunteer program in which members of the general public are involved in working with offenders, and the increased involvement of businessmen and industrial representatives in British Columbia lends support to the alternatives concept. Legislative action and implementation of several important alternative programs indicate Canada's support of these programs. These efforts are not the total solution but are good indicators of a more sophisticated approach to corrections in Canada.

Saskatchewan

In Saskatchewan two programs will be described because they provide additional information concerning the procedures in the operation of alternative programs. One program is handled by the Corrections Branch of the Saskatchewan Department of Social Services and is known as the Fine Option Program, similar in nature to work or service order programs.[25] The other program is sponsored by the John Howard Society of Saskatchewan and made functional by the courts and is entitled the Mediation Diversion Program.

The Fine Option Program provides the alternative of community service work to persons who have been fined and are unwilling or unable to pay their fines. Prior to the development of this program, persons who defaulted on fines faced incarceration. In 1970-1971 over two thousand admissions to the province's correctional facilities were for fine default and accounted for almost thirty thousand days of custody care, a very costly program for taxpayers. The Fine Option Program was started in 1975 and in 1978 was available throughout the province. It operates under the Correction Branch of the Department of Social Services, but almost all policy decisions involve liaison with the Attorney General's Department, which has jurisdiction over the courts and the police. The program has a complement of two field officers who are responsible for developing and monitoring the program, one secretary, and the director. The ongoing administration of the program is contracted to various nonprofit and local government agencies on a fee-for-service basis. These local agencies are responsible for receiving an offender into the program, for interviewing the offender, and for arranging suitable placement with a nonprofit organization. The agency who provides the work placement also supervises and records the hours of work performed by the offender. This agency receives no reimbursement for this service but is beneficiary of the offender's work.

There is no exchange of money in the Fine Option Program. The courts accept vouchers from Fine Option agencies showing hours of community service work performed. The number of hours required to settle a fine is determined by dividing the amount of the fine by the provincial minimum wage rate, $3 per hour in 1978. Fines may be settled by a combination of community service work and cash payment. All fines that can result in incarceration for default are eligible for settlement by community service work in the Fine Option Program. Offenses defined by the federal criminal code, province acts, and municipal laws, may all be handled through the Fine Option Program.[26]

The community service work provided under Saskatchewan's Fine Option Program must benefit the general community rather than private industry or business. It cannot displace persons already employed nor replace jobs normally filled. In city areas it may include park redevelopment, work for the Humane Society (animal care), the John Howard Society, senior citizens' homes, recreation centers, and similar organizations. Most of the work in rural areas is done for local governments and may include refuse removal, park improvements, and maintenance of recreational facilities.[27]

Saskatchewan has sixty-seven Indian reservations, and the chief and his council operate the Fine Option Program on these reservations. This work may include house construction and farming, as well as other work such as recreational facility development.

Another alternative is the Mediation Diversion Program.[28] The Mediation Diversion Program was first proposed by the John Howard Society of Saskatchewan in September 1976. The program was motivated by the beliefs that the justice system was too isolated from the community and the victim and that the justice system had failed to limit its intake to criminal situations in which it could be effective. Urbanization, professionalization, the mystification of law, and radical social and technological change have all contributed to this isolation of the public from social institutions. The fundamental objective of this program is the implementation and maintenance of a noncriminal procedure based upon victim-offender mediation of the conflict, with support and assistance from other members of society and especially the courts, which could act as a friend to both the complainant and the respondent. The procedure emphasizes interaction of the people involved, shared values, reconciliation, acceptance of personal responsibility, and cooperative action.

The Mediation Diversion program is especially aimed at husband-wife and landlord-tenant disputes, assault, vandalism, and minor fraud and theft where there is no major question of or challenge to the offender's guilt. Thus the program is designed for resolving a conflict between two parties. The following are examples of the situations at which this specific program is aimed:

1. Family disputes.
2. Neighborhood disputes and other disputes wherein the complainant and respondent share some form of preexisting relationship.
3. Shoplifting and theft under $200.
4. Willful damage involving damages amounting to less than $200.
5. False pretenses and fraud.
6. Joy-riding and car theft.

The Mediation Diversion program is not applicable if any of the following circumstances exist:

1. The complainant or the respondent requests formal criminal justice processing.
2. The incident causing the complaint involves the use of, or threatened use of, firearms or other restricted weapons.
3. The incident involved violent behavior resulting in physical harm to a victim where there was no preexisting relationship between the complainant and the respondent.

4. The incident occasioning the criminal complaint is clearly a single feature of a present and persistent pattern of criminal behavior.
5. The respondent is not normally a resident of the community in which the act occurred.[29]

The John Howard Society recommended that the procedure in resolving the conflict include the use of legal assistance, the courts, local police representatives, and others but that the complainant and the respondent should know whether others are involved, that is, whether formal civil or criminal charges are involved.

The procedure followed in the Mediation Diversion Program includes these steps:

1. A *screening* step to determine which cases could be included in this program.
2. *Referral* of a case to this program is made verbally or in writing from police or prosecutors, as appropriate.
3. An *intake* step includes interviews of the complainant and the respondent in order to identify their agreement to or rejection of mediation. If either party rejects mediation, the case would be returned to the source of referral. Parties would be assured access to legal counsel.
4. A *mediation meeting* then takes place at a time arranged during intake. Both the respondent and complainant meet with a volunteer mediator whose responsibility is to aid the parties in coming to an agreement rather than to judge or to impose settlement. Failure to obtain agreement at this step results in a return of the case to the source of referral.
5. An *agreement* is recorded in writing and signed by both parties; both parties are asked to sign again when the agreement is fulfilled.
6. Finally, agencies that are involved in the program and volunteers provide or arrange for required or requested services.[30]

Normally it is expected that mediation meetings are held within ten days of referral and that any agreement made should not extend beyond ninety days. Program records are maintained in local offices, and a central registry is maintained in provincial offices. These records are open to recognized criminal justice officials when necessary for their work. At the end of the mediation diversion agreement period, the referral agency is notified, in writing, of the status at time of termination and the general results. The Mediation Diversion Program appears to be a workable alternative to incarceration and lengthy court procedures. It provides for conflict resolution procedures that can be easily adapted to special situations. It allows cultural and racial minorities to incorporate their own value systems into the process. The procedure provides the victim of a crime real and immediate opportunity to experience justice done and recognition of his experience. The program makes no distinction, beyond the demands of justice and the protection of rights, between juvenile and adult. It offers a vehicle for an improved interface of criminal justice agencies and other social institutions at the level of day-to-day struggles as well as at senior levels of administration and planning. The results of this and similar projects where victim and accused may confront each other before formal court procedures are undertaken will probably begin to be evaluated in early 1980s. The idea is not new and it has worked in other times. The question seems to be, Can a modern technological world accept such a down-to-earth approach to social deviation?

Conclusion

The general approach to discovering and implementing alternative programs in Canada exemplifies the concept of alternatives. Canada and specific provinces have developed ideas and initiated pilot projects. Based on an intelligent and thorough evaluation of the present and predicted future success of the programs, these concepts have been translated into workable programs and have been implemented as permanent parts of the justice system through legislative action. This encouraging trend is, perhaps, best illustrated in the Community Services or Work Programs in Canada today. For this reason I have included the Procedures Manual of the Fine Option Program of Saskatchewan as an exemplary model of this trend (see appendix 4a).

Notes

1. Canadian Ministry of Correctional Services, *Report of the Minister,* pamphlet (Ottawa: Government Printer, 1975).

2. Secretariat, Royal Mounted Police, *Annual Reports,* 1975, 1976 and 1977, pamphlets (Ottawa: Canadian Penitentiary Board, National Parole Board).

3. Public Affairs Officer, *General Statistics,* pamphlets (Ottawa: Canadian Penitentiary Services, March 1977, March 1978).

4. Canadian Prison Services, *Probation and Parole,* pamphlet (Ottawa: Canadian Prison Services, 1977).

5. Canadian Prison Services, *Returning to Society, Community Correctional Centers,* pamphlet (Ottawa: Canadian Prison Services, 1977).

6. Province Ministry of Correctional Services, *The Community Work Order,* pamphlet (Toronto: Correctional Services, December, 1977).

7. Law Reform Commission, *To Jail or not to Jail,* pamphlet (Montreal: Law Reform Commission of Canada, 1977).

8. Canadian Prison Services, *A Better Way, Returing to Society,* pamphlet (Ottawa: Canadian Prison Service, 1977).

9. Ministry of Correctional Services, *Correctional Volunteers in Action,* pamphlet (Toronto: Correctional Services, August, 1977).

10. Victoria, Government Printer. *Annual Reports on Corrections,* pamphlets, 1976, 1977, 1978.

11. Canadian Church Council, *Alternatives*, a package of pamphlets addressed to citizen volunteers and potential volunteers with information designed to assist in working with sentenced persons, available from The Church Council on Justice and Corrections Alternatives, 404 Jarvis Street, Toronto, Canada, M4Y2G6, 1977.

12. Canadian Penitentiary Services, *A Key to Change, The Living Unit Concept,* pamphlet (Ottawa: Canadian Penitentiary Services, 1974).

13. Canadian Prison Services, *Meeting the Challenge, Temporary Absence,* pamphlet (Ottawa: Canadian Prison Services, 1977).

14. Ministry of Correctional Services, *Report,* 1975 (Ottawa: Government Printer). See also additional reports by the Ministry for the years 1977, 1978 and 1979.

15. Canadian Prison Services, *Returning to Society, Community Correctional Centers,* rev. pamphlet (Ottawa: Canadian Prison Services, 1979).

16. Ministry of Correctional Services, *Correctional Institutions and Programs for the Adult Male Inmate,* pamphlet (Toronto: Ministry of Correctional Services, June, 1977).

17. Ministry of Community and Social Services, *A Report, Newsletter,* October, 1977. See also the following: *Reorganization and Progress Report,* newsletter, Toronto: November, 1977; *Implementation, Establishment of the Childrens Service Division,* newsletter, Toronto: August, 1977; *Description of the Changes Planned, The Mandate Letter,* newsletter, Toronto, June, 1977.

18. Ministry of Correctional Services, *Community Resource Centers,* pamphlet (Toronto: Ministry of Correctional Services, October, 1977).

19. Province Ministry of Correctional Services, *The Community Work Order,* rev. pamphlet (Toronto: Correctional Services, 1977.

20. Province, Ministry of Correctional Services, *Ontario's Probation and Aftercare Service for Juveniles,* pamphlet, Toronto Province Ministry of Correctional Services, July, 1977.

21. Canadian Church Council, *Alternatives.* See especially pamphlet concerned with volunteers.

22. Ministry of Correctional Services, *Correctional Volunteers in Action,* rev. pamphlet (Toronto: Correctional Services, 1978).

23. Province Ministry of Correctional Services, *Annual Report for*

British Columbia (Victoria, B.C.: Government Printer, 1979).

24. Calvert R. Dodge, *A Nation without Prisons* (Lexington, Mass: D.C. Heath, 1975). See chapter on Outward Bound. Outward Bound is a wilderness training program structured to build self-confidence and trust in others. The program was initiated in England's naval units during World War II and was originally aimed at young people. It has become a worldwide organization for persons of various ages.

25. Department of Social Services, *The Fine Options Program,* pamphlet (Regina, Sask.: Department of Social Services, Province of Saskatchewan, 1977).

26. Department of Social Services, *The Fine Option Program, Procedure Manual*, pamphlet (Regina, Sask.: Department of Social Services, Province of Saskatchewan, 1977).

27. Saskatchewan Social Services, *Fact Sheet on the Fine Option Program,* pamphlet (Regina, Sask.: Department of Social Services, Province of Saskatchewan, 1977).

28. John Howard Association, *Mediation Diversion Project, A Project Proposal and Summary,* pamphlet (Regina, Sask.: John Howard Association, 1976), pp. 4-8. Reprinted by permission.

29. Ibid., pp. 7-8.

30. Ibid., pp. 9-10.

See also:

Solicitor General, *Report of the Commission of Inquiry into Certain Disturbances at Kingston Penitentiary,* pamphlet (Ottawa: Government Printer, April, 1972).

Canadian Prison Services, *Inmate Training,* pamphlet (Ottawa: Government Prison Services, 1977).

Ministry of Justice, *The Vanier Center for Women,* pamphlet (Ottawa: Government Prison Services, July, 1977).

Ministry of Justice, *Industrial Change in Canadian Prison Systems,* pamphlet (Canadian Prison Services, 1977).

Ontario Province Ministry of Corrections, *Careers in Corrections,* pamphlet (Toronto: Ontario Ministry of Corrections, August, 1977).

Education Division, *Correctional Education in Ontario,* pamphlet (Toronto: Ministry of Corrections, August, 1977).

Appendix 4A
Fine Option Program
Procedures Manual

Contents

Preface

The Fine Option Program is intended to offer an alternative to incarceration for non-payment of fines in Saskatchewan. The alternative is the opportunity to work off the fine by volunteer service in the community.

To accomplish this, the Fine Option Program staff will work with community groups to develop work options for the offender. As well, the Fine Option Program will enter into agreements with numerous community-based organizations to act as Fine Option Assigning Agencies who will administer the Fine Option Program at the local level.

The Fine Option Program Field Officers are located at Prince Albert and Regina. Enquiries and concerns should be directed to the appropriate offices as follows:

North
Fine Option Field Officer
Fine Option Program
Department of Social Services
101 15th Street East
Prince Albert, Saskatchewan
S6V 3P7

The Fine Option Program Procedures Manual is reprinted as an exemplary alternatives program by permission of the Department of Social Services, Province of Saskatchewan, Canada.

South
Fine Option Field Officer
Fine Option Program
Department of Social Services
2240 Albert Street
Regina, Saskatchewan
S4P 2Y3

or
Mrs. Margery Heath, Director
Fine Option Program
Department of Social Services
2240 Albert Street
Regina, Saskatchewan
S4P 2Y3

Eligibility

1. The Fine Option Program is available to anyone assessed a fine by a Court in Saskatchewan *where time to pay is allowed* by the Judge, Magistrate or Justice of the Peace.
2. All fines are eligible for settlement through the Fine Option Program (i.e.—Federal, Provincial or Municipal Statutes).
3. Fines assessed by issuance of Summary Offence Tickets require an appearance in Court to qualify for settlement through the Fine Option Program.
4. Fines may be settled by the Fine Option method regardless of the person's age or means to pay.
5. The individual assessed the fine must be responsible for settlement of his/her fine through the Fine Option Program. (e.g.—A wife cannot work out her husband's fine.)
6. Access to the Fine Option Program is by way of personal presentation of the Notice of Fine (issued by the Court) to a Fine Option Agency.

Determination of Volunteer Work Period

1. The amount of volunteer work required to settle a fine will be determined by the amount of the fine, divided by the minimum wage, as set from time to time by the Government of the Province of Saskatchewan. (i.e. $150 fine ÷ $3.00 = approximately 50 hours of work.)
2. Where an offender is presently employed, a week-end or evening work option will be offered if available in the community.
3. A fine may be settled by a combination of work and cash.

4. All work will be considered of equal value (minimum wage) regardless of tools or skills required to perform the work. No credit will be allowed for use of equipment.
5. Where an offender completes a portion of the work required to settle the fine and does not pay the balance of the fine by cash, his period of incarceration will be reduced accordingly. The reduction will be calculated by multiplying hours worked by the minimum wage to establish credit.

The Court

"The Court" includes all judicial and quasi-judicial jurisdictions which have the authority to levy fines (i.e.—Judges, Magistrates, Justices of the Peace, etc.)

1. The "Notice of Fine" form will constitute the referral to the Fine Option Program.
2. The "Notice of Fine" form shall be given to every offender who is assessed a fine and is given time to pay by a court of competent jurisdiction.
3. The "Notice of Fine" is printed in triplicate; a) Copy #1 is retained by the issuing court b) Copies #2 and #3 are given to the offender at time of sentence.
4. The Fine Option Agency will advise the Court that the offender has chosen to work out his/her fine by returning the third copy of the Notice of Fine *to the issuing home Court*. This advice will contain the expected completion date and must be postmarked prior to default date. Allow fourteen days from default date for receipt of advice before issuing warrant.
5. Upon the completion of the work option by the offender, the Court will receive Form D.S.S. 8,914 (green copy) stamped "Fine Paid by Volunteer Service". Court should allow fourteen days from completion date before issuing warrant.
6. Partial completions of work options will be stamped "Incompleted". Dollar value of work should be noted as payment on Warrant of Committal so that incarceration time will be reduced.
7. Procedures for processing—See Page 4, Nos. 1 and 2—Provincial Court Office Procedures.

The Fine Option Assigning Agency

The Fine Option Assigning Agency will provide administrative service to the Fine Option Program on a contractual basis. The Fine Option Assigning Agency will be responsible for interviewing and assisting the offender in choosing a work option. It will be responsible for notifying the court of the offender's progress in the Fine Option Program and for facilitating the smooth operation of the Fine Option Program at the community level including the development of work options as required.

The Fine Option Assigning Agency will:

1. Receive from the offender personally *both* copies of the Notice of Fine form *prior to default date.*
2. The second copy of the Notice of Fine must be completed and returned to the issuing home Court *immediately.* Postmark must be prior to default date.
   (a) Completion date should be determined by calculating the number of hours to complete the fine plus two weeks. Example—$150 fine ÷ $3.00 (minimum wage) = 50 hours of work or approximately 1½ weeks of work. Add two weeks and completion date would therefore be 3½ weeks from day offender is to start work.
   (b) *It will be the responsibility of the Fine Option Agent to request an extension of time from the Court when the offender has been unable (for good reason) to finish working out his fine by completion date.*
3. Interview the offender completing Form D.S.S. 8,912.
4. Complete placement Form No. 8,914. Arrange with employing agency and offender a suitable starting date. Mail all copies of Form 8,914 to the employing agency along with the offender's work record, Form 8,918. Give offender appointment slip.
5. Completed Work Options:
   (a) Upon receiving Form No. 8,914 from employing agency, stamp all copies "Fine Paid by Volunteer Service" over signature of supervisor.
   (b) Provide Offender with White Copy as Receipt.
   (c) Mail green copy to issuing home Court immediately.
6. Incomplete Work Options:
   Same procedure as in No. 5, but stamp "Incompleted".
7. When offender does not report for work, complete Form D.S.S. 8,914 showing nil hours worked. Remit green copy to Court as soon as possible, *but no later than expected date of completion shown on Notice of Fine.*
8. In the event of injury to the offender while participaing in the Fine Option Program, see Page 10.
9. Procedures for Reimbursement:
   (a) At the end of each month, the Fine Option Assigning Agency will remit to the Fine Option Program the following:
      (1) Monthly statement of list of offenders.
      (2) For each offender, attach the following forms:

      (i) One copy of interview form—No. 8,912 (blue).
      (ii) One copy placement form—No. 8,914 (blue)
      (iii) Notice of Fine form.
(b) Reimbursement will be at the rate of $10 per match-up.
(c) Be sure the name and address of the Fine Option Agency is shown on the Monthly Statement.

Employing Agency

The employing agency or organization refers to the group offering the work or service situation to the Fine Option Program.

1. The employing agency or organization is responsible for the supervision of the offender.
2. The Fine Option Assigning Agency will mail the placement forms No. 8,914 and work record No. 8,918 to the employing agency. These are to be completed by the employing agency and returned to the Fine Option Agency immediately upon completion of required hours of work, *but no later than completion date shown on form No. 8,914.*
3. If the offender does not report to work within three days of arranged date and has offered no reasonable excuse for not showing up return forms no. 8,914 to Fine Option Agency showing nil hours worked (see page 9, No. 4).
4. Injury to a Fine Option participant must be reported immediately to the Fine Option Agency.
5. An offender shall not be required to participate in treatment or counselling programs in conjunction with working out a fine.

**Guidelines for Maintenance of Satisfactory
Work Performance**

To ensure that all participants in the Fine Option Program perform an adequate quality and quantity of community service work in lieu of cash payment or incarceration, the work placements should meet the following conditions:

1. The Work Option shall:
    (a) benefit the community rather than a private individual;
    (b) be seen by the community as worthwhile work; and
    (c) be seen by the offender as a worthwhile endeavor.
2. The offender shall be supervised.

3. Hours of work shall be recorded and the work record signed by the supervisor.
4. Work performance under the Fine Option Program should be comparable to work-for-pay situations with regard to expectations of:
   (a) punctuality and
   (b) notification to employing agency of absenteeism for sickness, etc.
5. Problems arising between supervisor and offender regarding quality or quantity of work performed should be referred to the Fine Option Field Officer for assistance.
6. All Fine Option offenders must perform the work or task assigned and it is the responsibility of the supervisor to ensure this performance. A charge of fraud could result if hours of work are recorded when, in fact, work has not been done by an offender.

Workers' Compensation Benefits

All participants in the Fine Option Program are covered by Workers' Compensation. In the event of injury, the following procedures should be followed.

1. The Fine Option Agency must complete two copies of Form 5—Employer's Report of Accident and send original copy to:
   > The Director,
   > Fine Option Program,
   > Department of Social Services,
   > 2240 Albert Street,
   > Regina, Saskatchewan.
   > S4P 2Y3

   This must be sent in within three days after any accident requiring medical aid or loss of work time. Duplicate should be retained on file in Fine Option Agency.
2. The Fine Option participant should be provided with Form 4 to complete and send to:
   > The Director,
   > Fine Option Program,
   > Department of Social Services,
   > 2240 Albert Street,
   > Regina, Saskatchewan.
   > S4P 2Y3

   This must be sent in within three days of accident or injury.
3. The Fine Option participant must seek medical attention within three days of injury. A doctor's report will be required by the Workers'

Compensation Board.

4. Fine Option Participants are covered by Workers' Compensation only during the hours of work as determined to settle their fines.

Appendixes

FINE PAID
BY
VOLUNTEER SERVICE
FINE OPTION PROGRAM

Upon receiving, from the Employing Agency,
a Form 8,914 which shows that the required
number of hours were completed the above
stamp should be affixed over the signature
of the supervisor. The 8,914 is the only
form which requires this stamp.

INCOMPLETED
FINE OPTION PROGRAM

When a Form 8,914 is received and indicates
the required number of hours were not completely worked out the above stamp is affixed
over the signature of the supervisor.

**DEPARTMENT OF THE
ATTORNEY GENERAL**

NOTICE OF FINE

_____ HAS BEEN FINED **$** _____ TO BE PAID ON

OR BEFORE _____ . FAILURE TO PAY THE FINE WILL RESULT IN _____

DAYS/MONTHS IMPRISONMENT. INFRACTION(S): SECTION _____ ACT/CC _____

COURT LOCATION: _____ SASKATCHEWAN.

DATE: _____ FILE/INFORMATION # _____

HOME COURT ADDRESS: _____ JUDGE / J. P. _____

INSTRUCTIONS FOR PAYMENT

1. IF PAYMENT IS MADE BY MAIL, THE PAYMENT MUST BE EITHER BY A CERTIFIED CHEQUE OR MONEY ORDER TO THE HOME COURT ADDRESS.
2. IF PAYMENT IS DELIVERED TO THE MAGISTRATES' OFFICE, PAYMENT MUST BE MADE BY CERTIFIED CHEQUE, MONEY ORDER OR CASH.
3. MAKE ALL CHEQUES OR MONEY ORDERS PAYABLE TO THE **PROVINCIAL MAGISTRATES' ACCOUNT.**
4. ANY PAYMENTS MUST BE ACCOMPANIED BY THE **NOTICE OF FINE** FORM.
5. SETTLEMENT OF FINE BY FINE OPTION PROGRAM — SEE INSTRUCTIONS BELOW.

FINE OPTION PROGRAM

SHOULD YOU BE UNABLE TO PAY YOUR FINE AND DO NOT WANT TO BE IMPRISONED, YOU MAY WORK THE VALUE OF THE FINE OUT AT COMMUNITY SERVICE WORK. IF YOU CHOOSE THIS METHOD OF PAYMENT, YOU ARE REQUIRED TO REGISTER WITH YOUR LOCAL FINE OPTION PROGRAM AGENCY BEFORE THE DATE OF DEFAULT SHOWN ON THIS FORM. THESE FORMS MUST BE PRESENTED TO THE FINE OPTION AGENCY. INFORMATION ON LOCATION OF FINE OPTION AGENCIES IS AVAILABLE FROM THE COURT, POLICE, COURT WORKERS, LEGAL AID OR PHONE COLLECT TO THE FINE OPTION PROGRAM, DEPARTMENT OF SOCIAL SERVICES, 565-3333, REGINA.

NOTE: IF YOU HAVE NOT PAID YOUR FINE OR REPORTED TO THE FINE OPTION PROGRAM BY THE DATE OF DEFAULT A WARRANT OF COMMITTAL WILL BE ISSUED.

GRAPHIC BUSINESS FORMS LTD. REGINA, SASK.

COURT COPY

Province of  *Saskatchewan*
DEPARTMENT OF SOCIAL SERVICES

CORRECTIONS BRANCH

F I N E   O P T I O N   P R O G R A M

FROM: Fine Option Agency   DATE: _____

_____   TO: _____ Court

_____, Sask.   ATT: _____ Magistrate

                                             ADDRESS: _____

NAME OF OFFENDER: _____   INFRACTION(S): _____

ADDRESS: _____   COURT DATE: _____

BIRTHDATE: _____   FILE/INFORMATION # _____

                                             COMPLETION DATE: _____
NAME OF EMPLOYING AGENCY:

ADDRESS:

SUPERVISOR:

AMOUNT OF FINE: $ _____

NUMBER OF HOURS REQUIRED TO SETTLE FINE _____ (Amount of fine ÷ by minimum wage
                                                       = number of hours required)
TASK ASSIGNED (DESCRIBE)

_____

TO BE COMPLETED BY EMPLOYING AGENCY

Number of hours completed _____ @ _____ = $ _____
                                           (minimum wage)

Amount of fine: $_____

Less value of community work: $ _____

Balance owing on fine: $ _____

I hereby certify that the above-named worked the indicated number of hours.

Date: _____   Supervisor: _____

NOTE: FINE OPTION AGENCY — USE FINE OPTION STAMP ON THIS FORM ONLY WHEN FINE IS SETTLED
       IN FULL.

                                                          D.S.S. 8914

Province of **Saskatchewan**

DEPARTMENT OF SOCIAL SERVICES

CORRECTIONS BRANCH

F I N E   O P T I O N   P R O G R A M

REFER TO FILE

NAME: _____   DATE: _____ 19 ____

ADDRESS: _____   PHONE: _____

BIRTHDATE: _____   MALE ☐   FEMALE ☐

SOCIAL SECURITY NO. _____

MARITAL STATUS: Single ☐   Married ☐

ETHNIC ORIGIN: Native ☐   Other ☐

EMPLOYMENT: Employed ☐   Unemployed ☐   Student ☐

EDUCATION: Grade Completed _____

AMOUNT OF FINE $_____   DATE ASSESSED _____

CASE/FILE NO.   _____   TO BE PAID BY _____

COURT _____   JUDGE _____

_____
Fine Option Assigning Agency

_____
Address

D.S.S. 8912

F I N E   O P T I O N   P R O G R A M

OFFENDER'S WORK RECORD

DATE _____

REQUIRED HOURS OF WORK _____

OFFENDER'S NAME _____

DATE	IN OUT A.M.		IN OUT P.M.		NUMBER OF HOURS

TOTAL HOURS WORKED _____

_____
Signature of Supervisor

D.S.S. 8918

FINE OPTION PROGRAM

VOLUNTEER'S REFERRAL CARD

VOLUNTEER'S NAME _____

ABOVE NAMED TO REPORT ON _____
                                        Date/Time

TO _____
            Name of Agency

AT _____
            Address

FOR THE PURPOSE OF WORKING OUT A FINE

FINE OPTION PROGRAM

VOLUNTEER'S REFERRAL CARD

VOLUNTEER'S NAME _____

ABOVE NAMED TO REPORT ON _____
                                        Date/Time

TO _____
            Name of Agency

AT _____
            Address

FOR THE PURPOSE OF WORKING OUT A FINE

M O N T H L Y   S T A T E M E N T

Date: _____

To: Fine Option Program
      Department of Social Services
      Corrections Branch
      2240 Albert Street
      Regina, Saskatchewan
      S4P 2Y3

Statement for the month of _____ 19_____

The following people were matched to work options (list names)

_____
Name of Fine Option Agency

_____
Signature of Agent

Attach: Copy Form 8912   )
              Form 8914   ) for all match-ups listed above
              Notice of Fine Form)

THE WORKERS' COMPENSATION BOARD
SASKATCHEWAN
1840 Lorne Street, REGINA. S4P 2L8   Telephone 565-4370

WORKER'S REPORT OF ACCIDENT
OR
INDUSTRIAL DISEASE Form 4
(REV. 1/76)

TO BE SENT TO BOARD OFFICES IF DISABLED LONGER THAN THE DAY OF ACCIDENT

Please PRINT BELOW information
ch is not complete OR
incorrectly shown at right ⟶ ⟩ ⟩

WORKER'S NAME & ADDRESS

CLAIM NO.

LAST NAME
MR
MRS
MISS

FIRST NAME(s)

ADDRESS

| Postal Code | Telephone Number | DATE OF BIRTH | Day | Month | Year | Sex | Marital Status |

EMPLOYER'S NAME & ADDRESS

ACCIDENT DATE   FIRM NO.   RATE CODE

S.H.S. NO.   Social Insurance Number   Occupation

EMPLOYER   TYPE OF BUSINESS

AREA OF INJURY   S.H.S. NO.   BIRTH DATE

ADDRESS

| DATE OF ACCIDENT | Day | Month | Year | Time a.m. p.m. | Date and Hour You Reported Your Accident | Day | Month | Year | Time a.m. p.m. | State Name and Position of Person to Whom You Reported: |

Place of Accident   Province

Did it happen on Employer's Premises? YES NO   If 'NO': State where:

Are you related to your employer? YES NO   If 'YES' Specify:

Are you a Director or other Official of the Company? YES NO   If 'YES': Specify:

Was the work you were doing at the time for the purpose of your employer's business? YES NO   Was it part of your regular work? YES NO   State if anyone other than your employer or fellow workers were to blame for the accident:

Describe FULLY what you were doing at the time, mentioning the part of plant. works. equipment. machine. tools. article or other matter or conditions connected with the accident: (USE REVERSE SIDE OF FORM IF NECESSARY)

State ALL injuries you sustained. indicating right or left if applicable   Give names and addresses of persons who SAW the accident — two if possible

Had you any prior related condition? YES NO If 'YES'. Specify:

Have you had any previous accidents which were reported to the Board? YES NO

Who rendered First Aid?   Date: What Hospital were you treated at. if any?

FULL Name and Address of ATTENDING DOCTOR (PLEASE PRINT)

NORMAL WEEKLY WAGE (if paid by the week)
. . . . Hours at $ . . . . Per Hour $ . . . .
OR
NORMAL MONTHLY WAGE (if paid by the month) $ . . . .

Date and Hour You Last Worked   19   at   a.m. p.m.

Date and Hour You Returned To Work   19   at   a.m. p.m.

| Date started with present employer: | Day | Month | Year | Show your normal days of rest | SUN | MON | TUE | WED | THU | FRI | SAT |

If you have not yet returned to work. estimate how long you will be off:

What were your total earnings for the 12 months immediately preceding your accident or. if employed less than 12 months. show earnings for actual period:

If you worked after first lay-off. give dates:

$ . . . . From . . . . To . . . .

How much time did you lose during that period?

Normal working hours on day of lay-off: From   .m. To   .m.

. . . . Weeks   Sickness . . . . Weeks
Days . . . . Weeks   Lack of Work . . . . Weeks

Normal pay on day of lay-off: $ . . . .   Wages received on day of lay-off: $ . . . .

Has your employer (excepting day of accident) paid or allowed you anything during disability period? YES NO If 'YES'. Amount: $ . . . .

I declare all the above is true and correct, and I claim compensation for the above mentioned accident.

Date:_____   Signature _____

THE WORKERS' COMPENSATION BOARD
1840 LORNE STREET, REGINA
S4P 2L8
TELEPHONE 565-4370

FORM 5

EMPLOYER'S
REPORT OF ACCIDENT

CLAIM NO.

FIRM NO.

CODE

PART 1

TO BE SENT TO BOARD OFFICES WITHIN THREE DAYS AFTER ANY ACCIDENT REQUIRING MEDICAL AID

WORKER'S LAST NAME

FIRST NAME(S)

FULL ADDRESS

EMPLOYER'S NAME

MAILING ADDRESS

TYPE OF BUSINESS | TEL. NUMBER

DATE AND HOUR OF ACCIDENT ___ 19 ___ AT ___ M.

| SEX | MARITAL STATUS | DATE OF BIRTH | DAY | MONTH | YEAR |

DATE AND HOUR ACCIDENT REPORTED ___ 19 ___ AT ___ M.

SOCIAL INSURANCE NUMBER | S.H.S.P. NO.

TO WHOM REPORTED

NAME ___ TITLE

DATE ENTERED YOUR EMPLOY | OCCUPATION

NAME AND ADDRESS OF ATTENDING DOCTOR

HISTORY OF ACCIDENT - IMPORTANT - STATE NATURE OF INJURY. DESCRIBE FULLY what happened to cause the injury. Be sure to include the SIZE, WEIGHT and DESCRIPTION of any OBJECT which may have been involved. (Use reverse side of form if necessary)

Place of accident _____ Province: _____

On Employer's premises? NO YES If "NO", elaborate _____

Is injured worker related to employer or partner? NO YES   Director or other officer of the company? NO YES   If related, does he/she reside with you? NO YES

Do you have reason to believe the accident occurred other than described? NO YES

At the time of accident, was the work being performed other than for the purpose of the employer's business? NO YES

Was there any serious and wilful misconduct involved? NO YES

Was any person not in your employ to blame for or involved in the accident? NO YES

Was there a previous similar disability which prevented the worker from performing full duties? NO YES

"YES" ANSWER TO ANY QUESTION REQUIRES EXPLANATION ON REVERSE

Disabled longer than the day of accident? NO YES   **IF YES, COMPLETE PART 2**

PART 2

NORMAL WEEKLY WAGE (if paid by week)
.... Hours at $.............. Per Hour .... $...................
OR
NORMAL MONTHLY WAGE (If paid by month) $...................

TOTAL EARNINGS WITH YOU FOR THE 12 MONTHS IMME-DIATELY PRECEDING ACCIDENT OR, IF EMPLOYED LESS THAN 12 MONTHS, FOR ACTUAL PERIOD

$.............. FROM .... 19..... to .... 19......

TIME LOST DURING THAT PERIOD?
TOTAL .... WEEKS   SICKNESS .... WEEKS
HOLIDAYS .... WEEKS   LACK OF WORK ...... WEEKS

| SHOW NORMAL DAYS OF REST | SUN | MON | TUE | WED | THU | FRI | SAT |

DATE AND HOUR LAST WORKED ___ 19 ___ at ___ a.m. p.m.

DATE AND HOUR OF RETURN TO WORK ___ 19 ___ at ___ a.m. p.m.

NORMAL WORKING HOURS ON DAY OF LAY-OFF FROM ....M. TO ....M.

NORMAL PAY ON DAY OF LAY-OFF $............... | WAGES PAID ON DAY OF LAY-OFF $...............

IF WORKED AFTER FIRST LAY-OFF, GIVE DATES

ESTIMATE HOW LONG HE/SHE WILL BE OFF WORK

GIVE PARTICULARS OF ANY PAYMENT, ALLOWANCE OR BENEFIT MADE OR TO BE MADE FOR DISABILITY PERIOD

DATE ....
           Signature   Official Title

Rev (9/75) 2

**Fine Option Program Statistics for the Fiscal Year
April 1, 1976, to March 31, 1977**

Referrals from court	6,167
Entered fine option	3,399
Completed	2,920
Incomplete	479
Paid fines	54
Value of fines of Fine Option clients	$ 347,762.80
Value of fines worked out	$ 290,276.89
Days in lieu eliminated—60,700 3/4 days @ $20/day	$1,214,015.00

5 Denmark

During the past fifteen years the Danish penal institutions and the probation and community treatment or aftercare service have been characterized by extensive and rapid reforms. Denmark has long had a reputation of being unafraid to take a humanistic approach to the problem of assisting those labeled "criminal."

Denmark's 5 million people are served by 84 district courts, each of which has a court that functions as a court of first instance in most criminal cases. Criminal cases may be appealed in higher courts up to the Supreme Court. There are no juvenile courts in Denmark.

While the first Danish Criminal Code dates back to 1866, the present criminal code represents a modernization process which began on April 15, 1930. The code has been revised several times since, the last major revision occurring in 1974. These revisions in the criminal code changed the Danish penal system's attitudes and approaches to community treatment and aftercare programs. Some of these changes are as follows:

1. Capital punishment was abolished.
2. Corporal punishment was abolished.
3. Imprisonment with hard labor was abolished.
4. Youth prison was introduced in a form that had been greatly influenced by the English borstal system.
5. Special forms of detention of an indeterminate character were introduced for professional and habitual offenders. These forms included ordinary detention, security detention, equivalent to the U.S. maximum security prison, and correctional workhouses for nonviolent professional criminals.
6. Special measures were provided for mentally abnormal offenders and for alcoholics.

These changes required the establishment of a number of new penal institutions and the reorganization of the entire Danish penal system. One example of change was the opening of a former manor house as Denmark's first youth prison. It is now an open prison for young offenders with special emphasis on education. Inmates from other penal institutions may be transferred to the state prison at Sobysogard for the purpose of obtaining a special education at schools outside the prison, often assisted by teachers employed at the prison.

The changes mentioned occurred between 1930 and 1938. In 1938 the local prisons, which were formerly owned and administered by the local authorities, were taken over by the state. Since April 1, 1973, the state has also taken over the probation and aftercare service, including the institutions called hostels for probationers and parolees. Today there is one national central administration for corrections. Additional changes in 1973 included the following:

1. Youth prison was abolished.
2. Correctional workhouse was abolished.
3. Security detention was abolished.
4. Imprisonment for mentally abnormal offenders was abolished.
5. Harsh penal measures for alcoholics were abolished.

In addition, the application of detention was reduced for certain dangerous offenses. Today, in Denmark, apart from the small number of persons sentenced to detention, the only measures involving deprivation of liberty are ordinary imprisonment and lenient imprisonment, lenient imprisonment consists of a very short sentence, sometimes lasting only a few days.

While abolishing or changing these penal programs, Denmark did not eliminate certain programs of especially positive value, such as instruction and vocational training for young offenders and special programs for mentally abnormal offenders.

Punishment for Criminal Offenses

According to the Danish Criminal Code the minimum age of criminal responsibility is fifteen years. For persons under fifteen the authority is vested in the Child and Youth Welfare Authorities, which may impose measures according to the Children and Young Persons Act.

Action that is deemed necessary in emergencies or acts of justifiable self-defense are not punishable as specified in the criminal code.

The court must decide that the act was willfully committed or whether a negligent act is also punishable. Legally, all attempted crimes receive the same punishment as committed crimes. In practice, however, the punishment for attempted crimes is less severe.

In addition, the code stipulates that persons who, at the time the offense was committed, were irresponsible owing to insanity or similar conditions or to a pronounced mental deficiency are not subject to the punishment rules as legally sane criminals receive. The court may impose special measures such as special probationary measures, commitment to a mental hospital or to an aftercare program if it deems this action necessary in behalf of the public safety. The decision of changing such special measures, including a final release from these institutions, remains with the courts, but usually the institutional treatment will be followed by a supervisory period during which recommitment can be enforced by the supervising authority subject to the approval of the court.

Types of Sentences

Fines, lenient imprisonment, and ordinary imprisonment, as well as suspended sentences, are the sentences given offenders in the majority of cases. The fine is the most frequently applied punishment, and in 1977 fines made up about 25 percent of all criminal code sentences and the majority of noncriminal code offenses. Fines are imposed mainly for minor offenses, but fines may be used as an additional punishment attached to a sentence of imprisonment or suspension of imprisonment. If a fine is not paid voluntarily, the offender is committed to serve a term determined by the court, normally as lenient imprisonment. The alternative term is usually for not less than two days, nor more than sixty days.

Denmark's lenient imprisonment sentence may be applied for a term ranging from seven days to six months. Currently about 8 percent of all criminal code offenders receive this type of sentence. It may apply to offenses such as driving while intoxicated. Persons receiving this type of sentence are usually housed in open institutions offering inmates the facilities of work and social activities, purchasing food beyond the institutional diet, receiving special furniture for their room, and finding their own work. In a recent year, 275 of over 600 offenders serving lenient imprisonment were placed in open institutions where they are able to enjoy a fairly liberal social environment.

Imprisonment, which is currently applied in about 25 percent of all criminal code sentences, may be imposed for life or for a definite period, not less than thirty days nor more than sixteen years. Sentences of imprisonment are normally served in the so-called state prisons, which may be closed, cellular prisons or semiopen institutions. In Denmark the term *state prison* is still used to distinguish the ordinary prisons from the local prisons even though all penal institutions are operated by the state.

A sentence of imprisonment for life is indeterminate, but it is intended that offenders serving such sentences shall be pardoned and released after a period of ten to twelve years.

The suspended sentence may be compared with the British system of probation or a suspended sentence supervision order. In Denmark a suspended sentence means that the sentence is suspended for the probation period and will not take effect unless the probationer commits another punishable offense or violates other conditions determined by the court.

The object of the suspended sentence is the ultimate and rapid reestablishment of the offender in the community. It calls for the offender to establish a relationship with his probation officer that will help the offender contribute to the well-being of his family and community in the process of his own resocialization. The courts may impose the suspended sentence with a determined penalty, without a determined penalty, or with a combined unconditional and suspended sentence. The unconditional sentence requires that the offender must spend some part of the sentence in an institution.

Approaches to Treatment within the System

Like most other nations, Denmark has been confronted with the problem of an increasing number of crimes committed by an increasingly younger age group. There is a tendency also of younger people to commit more serious crimes.

The minimum age of criminal responsibility was set at fifteen years by law. The possibility of waiving prosecution against young offenders between fifteen and twenty, was liberalized. These two practices were designed to help youths avoid the stigma of a criminal record and the possibility of a life of serious crime. These aids, it was hoped, would be provided by the Child and Youth Welfare Authorities and would be provided up to age twenty-one and, in some cases, to age twenty-three. A large number of young offenders, however, end up in Denmark's penal institutions, either because the facilities of treatment of the Child and Youth Welfare Authorities are no longer found adequate or because of the seriousness of the crime.

The social assistance arrangements and other alternatives provided either by the welfare authorities or by private agencies should be voluntary. Compulsory programming of any part of this system has the effect of infecting it with all of the stigma associated with the involuntary penal system, with consequent negative responses by the committed offenders.

It would be preferable to build a system in which families in trouble with the law could trustfully apply for assistance for family guidance as soon as their children showed signs of aberrant behavior. But this system could hardly be realized if the Child and Youth Welfare Authorities became known as an organ empowered to commit children and young persons to institutions without the consent of the parents.

Denmark's original prison system was modeled after American systems, commonly known as the Auburn system and the Philadelphian system.

Denmark has had problems like those of the United States in changing these systems into what we may call a community-based treatment program. Denmark, nevertheless, began changing its system of corrections despite the drawbacks caused by penal institutions constructed on these now outmoded models.

In the early prison system the committed offender had, for all practical purposes, absolutely no privileges. Today, in Denmark, the aim of rehabilitation is not to subject the prisoner to any deprivation of privileges except as required for the safety of the community or, in some cases, the safety of the prisoner himself. Full access to outside telephones, full mail use, the spending of earned money, leaves of absence, and educational and work opportunities outside the institution are permitted. Thus offenders may spend much of their institutional commitment in the free community. While these leaves are particularly applicable to inmates committed to corrective workhouses and youth prisons (borstals), they are also applicable to other institutions in a wide number of cases. In open institutions leaves are normally granted as a matter of routine, while in closed prisons the provisions are used in a more limited manner. The excellent record of offenders on leave has allowed the leave concept in Denmark to grow and become applicable to a broader number of cases. In 1973, for example, only 8 percent of the total number of leaves were abused, and criminal offenses during leaves amounted to only 1.2 percent of all leaves granted. A few years ago the Prison and Probation Administration started to expand the inmate's opportunities for contact with the outside world. An essential feature in this movement with respect to opening the prisons to the surrounding society is that the prisons have tried to use organs in ordinary society instead of constructing special systems within the prisons. This applies to education, where the community educational system is increasingly taking on the responsibility of education of the inmates. This also applies to psychiatric assistance, not only by a temporary transfer to a hospital, but also by completely entrusting the welfare of the inmate and future decisions concerning him to the psychiatric hospital. The trend in making incarceration less total can also be seen in the possibility of obtaining permission to work for a private employer. Thus ordinary society is more directly involved in the treatment work. This must be seen as part of the general process of normalization, which has been one of the major aims of the reform efforts. The effort is to increase inmate participation in activities outside the institution, and it is increasingly important that the inmate, while serving of his sentence, gets a chance to leave the institution. Another effort is represented by programs that bring citizens into the institution from the outside community in order to demythologize the public conception of offenders and penal institutions or in order to participate in the activities of the prisons for treatment purposes. There have been successful experiments to create study groups with participation by citizens from the surrounding community or to allow participation in sports, games, the establishment of youth clubs, and the like.

These efforts have a dual purpose. Not only is the aim to integrate the prison into the surrounding community, but it is considered equally important to engage the inmates in shaping the daily life of the institution, thereby increasing their own sense of responsibility for what happens there.

The prison system has deliberately been opened to the press, the radio, and television; press meetings have been arranged by the Department of Prison and Probation—tours of the penal institutions are now often conducted by the inmates as guides. The open prisons have also arranged open house days, where everyone living in the neighborhood is invited to visit the prison and its inmates.

For many years experiments with representative arrangements have been made in order to give the inmates a chance to express their views. In 1971 regulations were issued that established formal channels for securing inmate participation in the decision-making process in the penal institutions. If the director does not agree with the elected representatives of the inmates, he must submit the matter to be decided by the Department of Prison and Probation.

A few years ago an organization of ex-prisoners was started, called KRIM. Persons interested in the problems of offenders may join the organization even if they have never been incarcerated. The organization has been very active and has been critical of the Prison and Probation Administration, but a certain cooperation also exists between them. The organization has representatives in some committees set up by the central prison administration.

Formerly the inmates had no possibilities of voting in general elections or referenda. The General Election Act of June 1970, however, provides for electors committed to any penal institution to be able to cast their vote at the institution. As a result, election meetings are held in most penal institutions with participation of representatives of the different political parties. The inmates are entitled, through badges or the like, to signify their political affiliation.

In most of the open prisons the inmates are not locked up in the cells for the night. The inmates are provided with a key to their own cell, and they have a small cupboard which they can lock. The inmates also have access to a pay telephone without any control from the institution. Conjugal visits are also allowed in some of the open prisons where it has been found to be practical. At some open institutions the visitors may not stay at the inmate's cell, but the institutions have special visiting rooms with very little control during the visit; after visits the inmates may be searched in order to prevent illegal effects to be smuggled into the institution such as narcotics and similar drugs.

Probation and Aftercare

Since the middle of the nineteenth century, private organizations have worked in assisting prisoners after their release from prison, and since 1905 they have worked with probationers. In 1951 all the existing discharged prisoners' aid societies were amalgamated into one national organization, the Danish Welfare Society. The society was a private organization aided by grants from the state in proportion to the number of current supervisions and social inquiry reports, covering all costs of administration such as wages, rent, travel expenses, and office equipment. The welfare society had a close cooperation with the prison administration.

It was, however, considered more convenient to have one national correctional administration to cover all penal institutions, probation, and aftercare, and from April 1973 operation of the probation and aftercare administration was transferred officially from the Danish Welfare Society to the Ministry of Justice, Department of Prison, which was renamed the Department of Prison and Probation. The change was primarily administrative in nature, and the existing institutions and offices were taken over unchanged, and staff became public employees. The Danish Welfare Society still exists as a private organization with economic means to support offenders, where the ordinary social system and the probation and aftercare service have found no possibility of assisting offenders.

A typical local probation and aftercare office covering a county has a case load of three hundred to four hundred, and it will make about two hundred social inquiry reports per year. The staff consists of a principal probation officer, four social workers, and two to three full-time clerks. A psychiatrist is attached as a consultant, and there are a few student employees (studying social guidance), law students, and conscientious objectors. The ratio of three hundred to four hundred cases per worker sounds high, but it must be kept in mind that many volunteers may be active as assistants to the paid worker and that contacts may be much closer to a one-to-one basis.

Apart from the professional social workers, about fifteen hundred persons in Denmark undertake the supervision of about 70 percent of the total case load of the approximately six thousand persons and make a large number of the social inquiry reports. The remaining 30 percent of the case load—usually the most complicated cases—are supervised by the professional probation officers from the local offices. The private supervisors are assisted and supervised by the local offices, and they get a monthly payment for their work. About seven hundred of the private supervisors (a number of them also making social inquiry reports) are persons employed in other social institutions, including the penal institutions, or in the police forces.

The probation officer's tasks include the use of job search, education, welfare, and private citizens in a joint effort to successfully resocialize the former offender.

Over the last several years welfare work in the local prisons has been increased. It is considered vitally important to establish a contact with an offender as early as possible in order to remedy the social consequences of imprisonment.

Trends

In recent years Denmark has made deliberate attempts to reduce the application of penalties involving deprivation of liberty. Recent research, according to Danish officials, suggests that any treatment via the process of incarceration is negligible in Denmark. Bringing together persons with pronounced difficulties in social adjustment may not be the best way to achieve good treatment results. Often the negative influences of *incarceration* are far greater than any therapeutic benefits achieved among members of inmate treatment groups. The social environment of the prison is often so strong that it is extremely difficult to compensate for it even through the efforts of the staff. An offender released from a Danish prison after having served his sentence has a greater risk of relapsing into crime than he had before serving the sentence. This finding, by the Danes, is similar to research findings in the United States and in other countries.

The most characteristic feature of Danish criminal policy has been a shifting from sanctions involving deprivation of liberty to treatment in the community with suspended sentences or other alternatives to incarceration.

The increasing application of suspended sentences in connection with the transfer of the probation and aftercare administration from the Danish Welfare Society to the Ministry of Justice caused problems in insuring that the economic resources of the probation and aftercare work were increased so that such services may be available to the offenders through their contacts during the probation period or to the ex-offenders through their aftercare period.

The criminal code revisions of 1973 decriminalized many former offenses, and at the same time most indeterminate sentences and other special penal measures of relatively long duration were abolished. The drug offenses and tax evasion cases, however, are among several items that may be revised or be inserted in the new criminal law. The target, with regard to drug offenses, is the professional drug offender or seller rather than the addict.

Community Living

It is the general policy that probationers and parolees should be received by the community as equals with other citizens and not be segregated in special institutions. Unfortunately there are still shortages of housing in Denmark, and when no flat or room is to be found, the clients without permanent residence are usually placed in shelters and lodging houses run by the local community, in youth hostels, in institutions for alcoholics, in homes for the elderly, or in institutions of the Salvation Army and the like.

Where it is considered appropriate, and if the client wishes to do so, the probation officer establishes a contact with the institutions of the probation and aftercare service with the aim of making permanent arrangements for the client.

There is always a group of clients in need of close supervision in separate institutions where the staff is prepared to pay special attention to their behavioral problems. Therefore the Prison and Probation Administration runs a number of institutions intended for probationers and parolees, who come there for shorter periods on a voluntary basis or according to an order from the probation officer. At present there are four rather small hostels, a home mainly for older habitual offenders, a school for vocational training courses (also used for persons serving sentences of imprisonment), and three institutions for drug addicts.

The offices and institutions of the probation and aftercare service are directly responsible to the Director General of the Prison and Probation Administration.

Rather than taking up residence at one of the institutions of the probation and aftercare service, a parolee in trouble may, on a voluntary basis, return for a short period to the prison. In practice this is not done very often, and the duration of such a stay is, of course, decided by the parolee himself.

Current legislative moves toward law revision in Denmark deal with the decriminalization of minor offenses against property. This suggests changing the provisions for determination of the sentence of all offenses against property, which covers about 85 percent of all offenses of the criminal code in Denmark. As a result of these changes the ordinary maximum penalty was reduced from two to one and a half years of imprisonment, and the higher maximum for recidivists committing subsequent offenses was reduced from three to two and a half years. As part of the reform the government proclaimed to Parliament with detailed instructions to the public prosecutors that it would insure the reduction of applications of incarceration.

Finally the minimum penalty was changed for a number of offenses, so that now fines can also be applied where, formerly, imprisonment was obligatory, and by determining the penalty, the court should not emphasize the offender's previous criminal record.

Experiments with Alternatives

Housing for Law Offenders, The Skejby Experiment

Research concerned with priority needs of law offenders often ranks housing in first or second place. The offender released from prison may have no living accommodations or, for other reasons, he may prefer not to return to the housing he once shared with his parents or other relatives. The Youth Hostel in Skejby provides alternative housing. The Skejby experiment, begun in 1973, mixes offenders with non-offenders on the theory that people who have difficulties in adjusting socially are easily influenced by their companions. Thus in the Skejby experiment there is a mixture of peer group members including court clients and nonclients as well as a small staff. The experiment also involves families who have volunteered to cooperate by serving as volunteer foster parents (not in a legal capacity) for clients. Clients may come to Skejby and be assigned to a family outside the hostel, to another hostel, or to a commune or other lodging. If necessary, the supervisory program at Skejby may be continued for several years after clients have left the program. More recently the hostel has begun to assist collectives or communal houses consisting of members of the client and nonclient groups who settle into an extended living situation together.

Most of the client and nonclient members of the program are working or receiving some type of training. When a client is unemployed, the hostel staff provides the client with repair work or other activity at the hostel. The hostel has been successful in obtaining work or training for almost all its clients, most of the time because of its many contacts with businessmen who have shown a genuine tolerance toward clients in the work situation.

The Skejby Youth Hostel is located at Skejby, a suburb of Arhus, a town with about 250,000 inhabitants. The building itself provides twenty-two single rooms, each with a washing basin, a cupboard, bed and some additional furniture. Recreation rooms are available. There are washing machines, baths, televisions, a billiard table, table tennis, a discotheque, and hobby rooms. In addition, there are two apartments for the director and deputy director of the hostel. About half of the rooms are occupied by clients and about half are occupied by nonclients. Both female and males occupy the hostel. The age group of Skejby residents is between eighteen and thirty years, although it may occasionally accept older or younger clients. The average age is about twenty-two.

Normally clients are referred to Skejby by the prison and probation system of Denmark. Applications for clients are prepared by a member of the probation branch staff or by the prison welfare officer. About one-third of the clients are persons who are released on parole and one-third are probationers. The remaining one-third of the clients are offenders who have not been sentenced to incarceration. Nearly all the clients are under some form of correction department supervision, and compared with an average prison population in Denmark, these clients have a higher number of negative social background factors such as broken homes and alcoholic parents. Of those clients sent to Skejby 25 percent have regularly used drugs and about 25 percent are alcohol abusers. All clients are admitted on a voluntary basis. The only requirements are that they be in need of residence and that they have not used drugs for at least one month before moving in.

The nonclient group at Skejby is admitted by applying directly to the youth hostel, and they are admitted on the condition that they have not been involved in criminal activity or had any serious mental problem or social problem during recent years. They must also demonstrate a willingness to cooperate in the program, that is, that they will spend several evenings at the hostel working with clients, attending meetings, making efforts to assist clients, and mixing with them. About one-third of the nonclients are interested in careers in social work and another third are interested in lodging per se, lodging and developing their own social life. Females outnumber males in the nonclient group.

The hostel has five staff members including the director and assistant director, a social worker and two teachers. There are usually two or three conscientious objectors and two or three people from social work schools doing their practicums at Skejby.

Rent is charged both clients and nonclients, but it is minimal. Occassionally members of the client group may be excused from paying rent for a variety of reasons.

The Skejby program involves two regular meetings each week, a meeting of all residents and a small group meeting of six or seven members and a permanent staff member. These meetings are therapeutic in nature and deal with many personal problems.

Extensive research has been made of a group of forty-four clients who stayed at Skejby between September 1973 and May 1975. By December 1976 twenty-eight of these clients had permanently moved from Skejby. One of the findings was that clients leave or are expelled from Skejby within about three months after arrival, or they remain at the hostel for an average stay of about eight months. A person, therefore, is either expelled rather early in the program and is returned to prison or some other corrective system, or he settles down at Skejby and adapts to its program. Clients who were carefully selected from the many candidates tended to remain for the longer period. Criteria for the success of the program include the client's imprisonment or expulsion from the hostel, a record of his work absences, unplanned breaks in work or education efforts, financial support, social destructiveness, and negative social incidents. In measuring negative social incidents, for example, residents who were clients decreased their number of negative social incidents from 4.0 to 1.6 from the time of their arrival at Skejby to the time of their departure (length of stay averaged about nine months to one year). The percentage of recidivism appears to decrease with the increase in the length of time at the hostel. This rate is well below rates of recidivism of other systems of corrections for similar periods of incarceration or treatment in Denmark. The nonclient group has not been adversely affected by the client group at Skejby. After an observation period of eighteen months only one nonclient received a court sentence, for drunken driving, and one person was charged in a drug offense. The strength of the moral system of nonclients appears to have withstood any negative influences of the client group, and according to the research data the nonclient group appears to have positively affected the client group.

While it is too early in the experiment to give any final evaluation, there is a clear indication that the mixing of clients and nonclients in a combined living situation where they may help each other, has a positive effect and tends to reduce criminal tendencies and negative social actions. The Danish Department of Prison and Probation recognizes the merits of the experiment. Here is an alternative to prison that may promote the resocialization of law offenders and, at the same time, introduce nonclients to a greater awareness of the criminal's problems and how they may be solved.

Involvement of the Community as Volunteers

In October 1975 another experiment, with headquarters in the youth hostel at Ringgarden in Copenhagen, was begun. The main goal was to develop a continuous pattern of aid to law offenders from the various welfare and social service agencies. The program of aid for the law offender begins as soon as the police have interrogated him. The social worker is assigned to interview the client and offer him assistance. A cooperative effort was developed with the remand prison so that early intervention could be maintained. Social workers were given access to prisons so they could begin to relate with the client and start the helping service. If sentence to an institution is involved, the social worker and the offender plan a program together so that the time spent in prison may be properly used to improve the client's education or prepare him for work. The period in remand prison is also used to develop contacts with welfare and social agencies that may be of assistance to the client during his time in the correction system network.

This helping service is continued until the client is released or paroled from prison or until a conditional sentence is given. It is always the same social worker who works with the client throughout the period of involvement in the correction system. This method of assigning a single social worker to each client helps provide the continuity often missing in other forms of social services for law offenders.

The youth hostel is small, accommodating only about eight poeople, but rooms that were once used to house clients are now used to house offices of social workers who, in turn, attempt to locate housing for clients. Rooms are also available for nonclients, but they are not often used. Nonclients are welcome to use the recreation facilities of the hostel or to attend meetings and participate in other activities. Police also often bring persons stranded in Copenhagen to the hostel for overnight lodging rather than arrest them as vagrants. Thus the people who make use of the hostel may include clients, nonclients, girl friends, fiancees, sisters, brothers, fellow workers, and ex-clients and to some extent, friends of the staff members.

Final evaluation of the program was not available at this writing, but staff members, clients, and correction system officials appear to feel that the program is successful and warrants continued support. The volunteer workers appear to be a key factor in the program's success.

In December 1976 Denmark was expanding its use of volunteers in the treatment of offenders. Earlier, in November 1975, a planning committee set up by the Danish Ministry of Justice submitted a comprehensive report on the planning, organization, and carrying out of a program to involve the community members as volunteers in the treatment of nonincarcerated law offenders. The committee reported that Danish prison and probation systems did not effectively use local community agencies in resocialization efforts but that an abundance of these resources was available, perhaps more than similar services in neighboring countries in Europe. The report also suggested that staff supervisors for offenders be well-trained professionals but that volunteer supervisors from the community could help considerably in the resocialization of offenders. The report further suggested that contact persons, as they are known (that is, lay volunteers), should be welcomed into the program. The lay supervisor should live near the offender's home and should not have more than two persons to supervise. The report also suggested that contact persons should not be relegated to menial duties by prison or probation administrators. The aim of the report was to emphasize that contact persons can offer an intimate relationship, a personal contact that can be called on much more often than professional staff members. In the committee's recommendation it is this availability of a friend that is significant. These close contacts are extremely useful when help is needed in simple things such as establishing arrangements for transportation to work or for a job or therapeutic interview. A person in need of alcoholic rehabilitative services is helped by a contact person to meet with members of Alcoholics Anonymous Association, a help in the resocialization process, especially because it is immediate rather than delayed assistance.

Denmark is beginning to develop its alternative programs through the use of volunteers. It seems to be emerging from the old style of custodial treatment to a new style of community care modeled after the Swedish system and is incorporating some of the concepts of the United States and from other countries in Europe. From this standpoint it will be interesting to see how this country develops its approach to resocializing its law offenders in the future.

References

Brydensholt, Hans Henrik. and Ingstrup, Ole. *Involvement of the Community as Volunteers.* Pamphlet pub. by State Prison at Kragskovhede, Denmark, December 1976.

Brydensholt, Hans Henrik. "Kriminalforsorgen", in *Prison and Probation Report, 1977,* Pamphlet pub. by Ministry of Justice, Department of Prison and Probation, Copenhagen, 1978.

Lonberg, Arne. *The Penal System of Denmark,* Pamphlet pub. by Ministry of Justice, Department of Prison and Probation, Copenhagen, February 1975.

Nielsen, Hakon. *Involvement of the Community as Volunteers,* Mimeographed. The Ringgard Project, Neighborhood Services for Offenders in Denmark, 1976.

Philip, Bodil. *Involvement of the Community in Housing: The Youth Hostel at Skejby* mimeographed, December 1976.

Danish Parliament, *The Danish Criminal Code. Part VI: Penalties, Rules for Custodial Treatment,* Copenhagen, Government Printers, 1974.

6 England and Wales

England has had noncustodial programs for criminal offenders since the beginning of the probation system in Great Britain in the late nineteenth century. Since World War II interest in the development and support of noncustodial sentences for criminals has increased rapidly even with the increased rates of crime in the country. In 1974 England ranked ninth among twenty modern nations in the number of incarcerated prisoners per 100,000 population. At that time England and Wales had 81 prisoners per 100,000, compared with West Germany's 84 and Denmark's 70 incarcerated persons per 100,000 population. East Germany had 222, the United States had 250, prisoners per 100,000 population, Norway had 37 and the Netherlands had 22 imprisoned persons per 100,000 population at that time.[1] There is growing doubt concerning the effectiveness of custodial treatment either as a reforming device or as a deterrent in Britain. The English appear to have greater faith in the noncustodial system. In general they support the theory that prison inevitably has a damaging effect on the prisoner and his family and that the increasingly high cost of providing for an adequate custodial penal system is wasteful. This support for alternatives has not only been voiced by various groups but has become incorporated in the laws of the land. A number of recommendations made by the Advisory Council on the Penal System were published in 1970 and embodied in the Criminal Justice Act of 1972. These and other changes have been consolidated in the Criminal Courts Act of 1973.[2] Changes in the laws have also affected younger criminals. The juvenile system is now considered nonpenal and committal of juveniles under seventeen is made to the local social service authority. There are also special provisions for mentally disordered offenders, whom the courts have power to commit directly to mental health hospitals. In some cases the Crown Court can issue an order restricting certain mentally ill criminals to the hospital. The Crown Court is the upper tier of criminal courts in England and Wales, and it is staffed by full-time professional judges who work with lay magistrates. Contested cases are heard by jury. The great majority of criminal cases are handled by the magistrate court, which is staffed mainly by lay justices with professional support from clerks of the court. There are alternatives to prison in England and Wales for adult criminal offenders above the age of seventeen.

Absolute and Conditional Discharge

When an individual has been found guilty of an offense, but the court also believes that a prison sentence would be detrimental to the case, an absolute discharge is mandated or a conditional discharge is given. In effect the court states that it would be inexpedient to inflict punishment and that a probation order is not appropriate. The conditional discharge stipulates that if the offender is convicted of a further offense within a specified period of time not to exceed three years, the offender may be liable for sentencing for the initial or original offense.

Binding Over

In binding over the criminal offender must deposit a specified amount of money with the Crown Court. The sentence also requires that the offender be on good behavior during a period of time set by the court. This binding-over process, in short, holds the offender at the mercy of the court until final judgment is made. If the offender fails to comply with the court's directives or commits a further offense, his recognizance deposit is forfeited, and he may then be given a sentence for his original offense. In some cases magistrate courts also have the power to require offenders to pledge money and to conduct themselves as good citizens. Failure in this case, however, is punishable only with forfeiture of the sum of money pledged.

Fines

As in many European countries, the fine is the most widely used of all penal sanctions. It is not restricted to traffic and regulatory offenses but is used widely for offenses against property and the person. The Crown Court has been given unlimited power to fix the amount of the fine. Magistrate courts are limited to a maximum of approximately $800. In England the humanitarian aspect of this alternative is that the court has been given a mandate by British law to consider the offender's income, his family, his expenditures, and his general financial situation. The fine, in other words, is considered payable by the Crown Court in terms of the offender's total means. The enforcement of this method of penal sanction is made by representatives of the magistrate courts, including in many cases staff specialists and the police. The methods for enforcing this alternative to imprisonment include placing the offender under supervision as in probationary systems, direct deduction of portions of the fine from earnings paid by employers of the offender, seizure of some but not all property, and, as a last resort, actual incarceration for a specified but usually short period of time. Before this final step is taken, the offender must appear again in court, and his means are again investigated as well as his reason for not paying the fine. Even in this final stage of the court's review of the case, a second chance may be given, and the warrant for imprisonment may be suspended to give the offender additional time for payment. Even if the offender is committed to prison, if he is able to arrange for payment of the fine through other people, he may purchase his release by paying the amount due. The English court continues to have power given to it by Parliament that allows it to remit fines for compassionate reasons.

Probation

Originally probation was a device used to protect women and young offenders from long tems in harsh prison environments. Probation in contemporary England is increasingly seen as a way of placing a wide range of criminal offenders under professional social workers, mental and emotional health care specialists, and other particularly well qualified therapists or helping agents. A probation order cannot be made without the offender's consent. In fact the probation order is more a contract between the offender and the court. The period of probation may range for not less than one year nor for more than three years. The stipulations of the probation contract include continual communication with a representative of the court, usually a probation officer. This communication may involve interviews, regular visits, and telephone calls made by the offender to the probation officer. It may also include visits to the offender's home, phone calls, and other contacts made by the probation officer. English probation orders are similar in many respects to the typical probation order in most American courts. The order includes a general requirement that the offender maintain good conduct. It may also require the offender to undergo mental or other medical treatment such as drug detoxification. The order may also include an assignment to an approved probation hostel. These hostels, operated by voluntary groups as well as by the British probation service itself, are publicly financed and provide residence, group experiences including therapy, and other measures of social support for offenders in groups of about eighteen or twenty. While these hostels do not provide daytime occupation for the offender, they often provide assistance in helping the offender find and keep a job.

Recently a new type of facility has been developed in England, called the Day Training Center. Probationers may be assigned to one of these centers for a period usually not exceeding twelve weeks. These centers concentrate on training the probationers in job application methods, work habit formation, reading and writing skills, and other basic but extremely important social and job skills. Each of these day training centers can accommodate about fifteen offenders.

Technically the court issues a probation order instead of actually sentencing the offender. While the probation order provides the offender with a wide range of services, it also allows the court to issue a more severe sanction should the offender commit an additional offense or otherwise fail to live up to the probation contract. The supervision of criminal offenders is one of the responsibilities of the probation and aftercare service in England and Wales. In England and Wales there are fifty-six separate areas of local probation services and aftercare services. These areas or districts are responsible for preparing investigative reports for the courts on individual offenders, for the administration of rehabilitative programs, for the welfare of offenders in prison, and for the operation of probation hostels and homes or day training centers.

Suspended Sentences

The British courts have the authority to suspend a sentence that included imprisonment for a specified period of not less than one year nor more than two years. Again this type of sentence stipulates that if the offender is convicted of any further offense punishable by imprisonment, the court may order that the original sentence be carried out. Normally the court is expected to make this order a fact by incarcerating the offender. If an offender is given a lengthy suspended sentence (more than a year), the sentence may order the offender to be placed under the supervision of a probation officer to attend some type of therapeutic program.

Ancillary Measures

The British courts have had increasingly wider powers, but no directives, to impose alternatives to imprisonment in the last decade. The courts have powers to order a convicted felon to pay compensation to his victim for personal injury. If there was loss or damage caused by the offense, the offender may pay compensation for this by order of the court. If he has property or money in his possession at the time of the arrest, this may be used for restitution or reparation. In some cases where a major loss was incurred by the victim of a crime, the court can make a criminal bankruptcy order,[3] to facilitate the repayment of assets for the benefit of the offender's creditors. The courts may also impose an order of forteiture of property in an offender's possession or control at the time of his arrest where it had been employed for the purpose of, or with the intention of, conducting criminal conduct or facilitating the commission of an offense. In cases where an automobile or some other motor vehicle was used in the commission of a crime, offenders may have their driving privileges suspended by the Crown Court.

There is an additional alternative to imprisonment, called Community Service or Community Service Orders. It should be noted, however, that British courts have wide discretion in passing sentences and are increasingly more likely to use the alternatives. The penalty for murder in England is life imprisonment and is fixed by law, but any other indictable offense, and many lesser offenses, can now be dealt with by any of the alternative measures described. In England in 1975 the courts were able to dispense with 56 percent of all indictable offenses with fines. Conditional discharges of sentences were granted to about 10 percent of the total indictable offenses, while suspended sentences accounted for almost 9 percent. Immediate sentences still accounted for over 10 percent of the total indictable offenses. Probation accounted for an additional 8 percent. The British courts used the detention center and borstals mainly for young offenders in 4.3 percent of its indictable offenses in 1975.[4] The ages of those in this group ranged from seventeen to twenty-one. The Community Service Orders were issued to about 1 percent of the total indictable offenders while absolute (unconditional) discharges accounted for 0.7 percent of the indictable offender population. While the Community Service Order commitments are relatively lower than most of the other sentences, this method of sentencing looks promising for the English criminal offender.[5]

The Community Service Order

Before 1973 England experimented with the concept that offenders may be assigned to work in the community as an alternative to prison. A few of the fifty-six probation and aftercare districts conducted the actual experiment, and by August 1976 Community Service Order programs existed in fifty-three of the fifty-six probation and aftercare districts. The court may issue a Community Service Order in cases where an offender is convicted of an offense punishable by imprisonment. The order requires the offender to perform work for the community for a period of between 40 and 240 work hours.[6] The selection of the tasks is developed and organized by the probation service but may also be suggested by voluntary organizations working in the community. One of the objectives in selecting a task is to choose work that the offender may view as helpful to the community and that makes the offender feel that he is paying for his misdeed. While no money is paid to the offender, his sentence or debt to society is repaid as he is credited for work hours performed. Offenders may work individually or in small groups, and in many cases offenders and nonoffenders work together. This often provides a training environment and helps develop better work habits, punctuality, cooperation, and problem solving. Perhaps the principal worth of the Community Service Order is that it affords the offender an opportunity to experience achievement instead of simply paying a fine or completing a term of probation or parole. The Community Service Order enables the offender to demonstrate to himself and to others, often for the first time in his life, that he can be of value to his fellow citizens and that he can shed the labels of deviant, inadequate, or dangerous. Often Community Service Orders direct the offender to work in a mental health center, an old age home, a public park, or a community hospital or a health center. The experiences of helping the disadvantaged have often been the key to changes in the attitudes and behavior of offenders, for they begin to develop concern and responsibility for others in this work environment. The more practical benefits appear to identify skills and work interests that they have often overlooked. The work itself often helps the offender to get a grasp on his own future career interests before committing himself to lenghty training or employment. In addition, the Community Service Program offers offenders a chance to escape isolation, to make better use of leisure time, and to establish contacts from which he may rebuild an acceptable and positive social world for himself.

Offenders who are issued Community Service Orders must report to a Community Service supervisor who is involved directly in the program. The supervisor may also assist the offender in dealing with other authorities while he becomes accustomed to the new work experience. More successful community service programs have usually involved small groups of offenders, usually four to six, and a supervisor. This size allows for a maximum of interaction for group and individual problem solving, for integration of more acceptable behavior, and for a feeling of togetherness. Within these groups there is often a development of a microcosmic concept of the community and concern for others, the shedding of guilt complexes, and the building of new role behaviors that are positively reinforced. The Community Service Order Program has its limitations, as all such alternatives do, in that certain offenders may be restricted from participating. These may include sex offenders, offenders who have committed serious violent attacks or offences against children, and serious drug offenders. But the program is not entirely closed to these people, for the courts have the power to make the final decision. Offenders most likely to be incorporated into the program because of its rehabilitative nature are vandals, car thieves, minor assaultists, weapons carriers, shoplifters, and house burglars. They have demonstrated certain skills in a negative manner. The Community Service

Order Program may help these offenders redirect their skill and ability in positive directions. The Community Service Order Program appears to be unsuitable for addicts of any kind including alcoholics or for persons with serious personality disorders.

The average offender assigned to community service work in Nottinghamshire may serve as a fairly representative example. He is likely to be between the ages of seventeen and twenty-one years of age, to have an average of six previous convictions, and to have experienced both a custodial sentence and a period of supervision such as probation. He is likely to be a resident of the area in which he is convicted. His past record includes a mixture of offenses "rather than a clear tendency to one particular type of offense." However, many of the offenders show a number of motor vehicle thefts.

The conviction that resulted in a Community Service Order would probably have normally resulted in a prison sentence. Several of the probation and aftercare areas in England, including the Nottinghamshire Community Service Team are undertaking additional research into offender suitability for the program. One of the instruments for selection has included the Eysenck Personality Questionnaire which offenders may complete voluntarily. This test purports to distinguish tendencies toward neuroticism and extraversion. It is believed that the Community Service Program may prove more advantageous to the offender showing a greater tendency toward extraversion than to neuroticism.[7]

The average offender assigned to the Community Service Order program cannot cope with the maximum of 240 hours within the twelve-month limit placed by the court for completion. The British Home Office Research team has suggested that 200 hours seems to be a more reasonable sentence for a one-year time limit and that shorter periods of time may be given to certain types of offenders so that eventually Community Service Orders might consist of a short term of 75 hours, a medium sentence of 125 hours, or a maximum of 175 hours, plus or minus 25 hours in each sentence category.[8]

Research into all types of alternatives is very important. In England, as in other countries, alternatives to prison are often given more verbal than financial and legal support. A more relevant use of all the alternatives based on research concerning the circumstances of both the offense and the offender would result in a more rational and reasoned approach to assignment, by the courts, of offenders to beneficial programs. An example of this reasoning suggested by critics of Britain's alternatives is the drunken driver. For his first offense he is fined, but for the second offense he is committed to prison. Research results, if similar to data found in the U.S., would give substantial evidence to the courts to support commitment of the offender to a detoxification center or other more therapeutic experiences rather than to incarceration. Just as there is a hierarchy of fines and other penal sanctions for various crimes in England, there could also be written into law, according to British reformists, a hierarchy of alternatives. Additional research now being conducted may help justify this idea. These alternatives would be tailored to the severity of the offense, the circumstances of the offender, and the number of times the offender has been arrested or has appeared in court for the same or similar offenses At present many groups in England are recommending a more sophisticated approach to penal sanctioning. In summary, however, these proposals

1. Recommend that legislation be passed to prohibit the use of imprisonment for certain offenses, including default in alimony (maintenance) payments, simple drunkenness, soliciting for sex, possession of less than one ounce of marijuana, and all the various vagrancy offenses.[9]
2. Suggest that it be mandatory for courts to state why each prison sentence is necessary for the protection of the public when an offender is committed to prison. These reasons can then be used as grounds for an appeal or for a decision in favor of an alternative.
3. Recommend that the use of prison for offenders who have failed to fulfill the conditions of noncustodial orders (mainly fines) should cease.
4. Recommend that all penalties attached to criminal offenses be reviewed and a scale of noncustodial penalties placed into law according to severity of offense, number of previous court appearances, and so on.[10]

During 1975 over 64,300 people were sentenced to imprisonment in England and Wales. In addition, about 68,000 persons were in custody pending trial or sentencing. Another 5,500 people spent some time in prison for default of alimony or maintenance payment. Of the 64,300 imprisoned persons almost 43,000 were involved in offenses of property such as theft and fraud or in victimless crimes such as drunkenness, vagrancy, and sexual offenses by consenting adults. Only about 30 percent of these offenses are considered serious threats to society by the reformists, and for these 22,000 persons incarceration may be considered beneficial. The major effort by various groups including the Law Commission, the Home Office Working Parties, the Advisory Committee on the Penal System, the Criminal Law Revision Committee, and others is to press for a more mature approach to the sentencing of offenders and for the legalization of appropriate alternatives for certain crimes. In many cases alternatives such as Community Service Orders are not being used for offenders who would ordinarily have received a sentence to imprisonment. In 1975, for example, only about 45 percent of all Community Service Orders were a direct alternative to prison. The prison population in England in 1976 was a daily level of about 42,000, which was considered intolerably high with overcrowding everywhere.[11] Yet many courts were issuing Community Service Orders to offenders who would ordinarily have been given probation in the first place. In 1978 critics of the judicial system in England were emphasizing the need for a greater degree of discretion in sentencing. Penalties for different crimes were so broad that the use of alternatives was becoming less clear in terms of resocialization of offenders. The range of penalties for rape is one example. A person found guilty of rape can receive a sentence ranging from a fine or suspended sentence to a period of imprisonment up to and including life. Without directives such as the First Offenders Act of 1958, prohibiting the use of prison for certain nonviolent types of offenses and suggesting the alternatives, for other offenders, it remains certain, according to critics of the system, that sentencing to prison and the inappropriate use of alternatives will continue. The use of alternatives, according to those critics, must not become the total answer

Private Efforts Supporting Alternatives

In England and Wales alternatives to imprisonment were suggested as far back as 1872, when the Select Committee on Drunkenness recommended legislation to enable alcoholics to voluntarily submit themselves to control. Even before this time, private groups were actively involved in the alternatives-to-prison campaign. A description of one of the organizations, the National Association for the Care and Resettlement of Offenders (NACRO), should serve to demonstrate the possibilities of organized efforts for alternatives made by citizen groups.

The National Association of Discharged Prisoner's Aid Societies, which later became the National Association for the Care and Resettlement of Offenders (NACRO), was developed in March 1966 at a time when the British Probation Service assumed authority for the prison and aftercare work. The organization developed as a result of the recommendation of the report of the Advisory Council on the Treatment of Offenders, *The Organization of After Care, 1963.*[12] NACRO was established with grant-in-aid from the Home Office to fulfill aims such as centralizing many services necessary to enable the independent voluntary groups to develop more systematic and meaningful efforts on behalf of offenders. Almost from its inception NACRO began broadening its parameters of work to include alternatives to prison. It supported a major shift from custodial efforts to treatment in the community. It also began efforts to provide programs for persons who had a high risk of getting into trouble, and it tried to change environments and neighborhoods of less fortunate persons. In 1972 NACRO broadened its efforts through NACRO Community Enterprises, to include the development and management of pilot or experimental programs for offenders and potential offenders. NACRO has now become a major nongovernment agency working for the improvement of the system and facilities for offenders and ex-offenders in England. The organization's chief concern now centers on improving and increasing the range of noncustodial facilities and programs for offenders. NACRO works through existing agencies such as probation and aftercare services, voluntary organizations, and relevant local authorities including the government, police, prison services, and judicial departments. Services of the organization range from development of information and research to training and consulting work and special pilot projects. Some of these projects are described.

Lance: Housing the Homeless

In Manchester, as in other urban communities, a central problem is the concern for the homeless. Many homeless people drift about in society with no real power to determine their own future. Often their housing is so inadequate that it contributes to a delinquent attitude. Most of these homeless people are caught in a vicious circle with no base from which to find a job and no money to find housing. The Lance project aims to provide a wide and flexible range of help for single, homeless people in Manchester and Stockport, England. The project was begun in 1973 to provide support hostels with full board and lodging, hostels that have some resident staff but in which residents cook for themselves in communal kitchens, supported rooms where rent is paid but no staff is available or is available only on call, assistance in finding a room or other lodging, a supported landlady's service, and a walk-in referral center. Single, homeless persons are referred to Lance by a wide variety of public and voluntary agencies. In a three-month period the program affected the lives of some 317 homeless persons.The project now has over ten houses with over eighty-two beds, but it also makes referrals to other housing for its clients. Most of the houses accept people of all ages and of either sex. Part of the task of the Lance workers is to help the client find other agencies which can refer job agencies and other service agencies to him.

Onward Workshops

Loss of or lack of work habits such as desire, punctuality, respect for work, and so on, and the inability to find a job in the first place are two major problems of offenders. While the Onward Workshop Project cannot be construed as an alternative to prison, it may be considered a preventive measure or a preventive alternative to recidivism. The project consists of of two parts. The first part consists of a workshop that takes offenders and ex-offenders and other high-risk groups of people and trains them in job search, application, and interview skills, work habits, and other skills. The workshop can handle fifteen members at a time and has a staff of a manager, assistant manager, and two instructors. The second part of this project is a supported workshop that provides actual work and pay for twelve main-grade workers and three supervisors as well as a workshop manager. This type of workshop aims to be self-supporting after about twelve months. Often workers graduate from this work to other types of work in industry. Most referrals to the project come from the probation and aftercare services while others are referred from social service and employment agencies as well as from the Lance project for single, homeless persons. The courts are now considering the workshop as an alternative to prison sentences. Workers are expected to participate in a normal working day. In the first part of the program workers receive a small bonus for attending class, and the bonus does not affect the offender's or participant's supplemental or sickness pay. The bonus is obtained from the sale of products manufactured in the workshop. After a satisfactory period of involvement in this program, workers are encouraged to move to a job, part two of the workshop program, or to government retraining facilities. Activities of the workshop involve furniture restoration, upholstery, antique rejuvenation, and similar production products.

Talbot Road House

The difficulties that confront homeless, single women are often even more acute than those faced by homeless men. There are very few hostels in England that are prepared to accept women. When a woman offender locates a hostel room she may lack the money to rent it. In some cases these homeless women include teenage offenders who also have babies to care for. Talbot Road House in Manchester was developed as an experimental project in December 1974 and was aimed at women who were placed on probation or who had just left prison. It also made some provisions for prisoners' wives and battered women. The project is managed by NACRO in connection with the Greater Manchester Probation and After Care Service and is financed in part by the Home Office and in part by voluntary sources. The Talbot Road House usually consists of six- or eight-bed units, with a living room. Single women share bedrooms while women with babies are given private rooms. All residents either have their own cooking facilities or share cooking equipment with one or two others. Rules are minimal, and each resident has her own front door key and room key. The house provides short-term accommodation up to three months and employs a residential worker and a detached worker to provide practical and social help and other agency referral for residents. During the first year of the project sixty-two women were accommodated, over half of whom were between sixteen and twenty years of age.[13] A house committee, which consists of staff, a liaison probation representative, and a NACRO representative, meet weekly to select referrals, to assist in helping residents, and to work in other ways to help residents find jobs, learn social and job skills, and generally adapt to a new life.

Lifeline Project

The Lifeline Project Day Center is situated in the center of Manchester and provides a concerned and caring environment. Its staff offer advice, day-to-day support, and practical help to people involved in drug abuse. It is managed by NACRO and financed by local agencies and in part by the Home Office. The project also provides advice and information to friends and relatives of drug users, as well as to professional workers such as probation officers, lawyers, social workers, and teachers. This often takes the form of meetings with various groups, including school and college students, to disseminate information and to channel outside volunteer help for the participants. The center aims to help the drug user break the chain of events that led to drug abuse. The center provides a midday meal, help for users to sort out mental and emotional problems, money, housing, employment, and family problems. Legal aid is also given. While the program is not an alternative to prison, modified versions of it have been used as alternatives by courts in the United States and other nations.

NACRO Education Project

Developed in its experimental stage in May 1974, the project aims to help offenders and ex-offenders to overcome educational difficulties and to continue education that may have been started in prison. The project is funded for its experimental stage by the Home Office and charitable organizations. The project involves the assistance of the National Education Advisory Service of England to assess a potential student's needs; it also provides educational information and works out educational plans or contracts for each person and develops educational applications for school and for monetary grants-in-aid. By 1976 the program had assisted over 450 offenders. Placements have included enrollment in high schools, colleges, residential educational institutions, art schools, technical schools, and others.

Another segment of the program now involves a student group in Cambridge which is based in a residential unit that can accommodate ten students. Some fifty to sixty persons lived in the unit during the years 1975 through 1978. Any offender who either has been released from prison or is serving a noncustodial sentence may enter the program if he is seventeen years of age or older. No examinations have to be passed to enter, but educational ability must be assessed before one is accepted into the program. Advice and counseling, as well as other assistance, is provided early in the program to help the participant find and keep meaningful goals that can be accomplished in his educational pursuit.

Multi-Facility Project

This program incorporates many of the projects already described but includes additional residential units such as probation hostels in Bury, Altrincham, and Eccles, all of which include bail offices, a probation-bail hostel in Withington which opened in 1978, the Minshull Street Day Center (to treat alcoholics, gamblers, and illiterates), and other hostels. The aim of the Multi-Facility Project is to channel the offender into the program, residential unit, or counseling service that may best answer his needs. Several of the residential units are coed. The program is operated on a cooperative basis with the help of NACRO and the Greater Manchester Probation and After Care Service but involves other voluntary and service agencies.

Whitechapel Day Center: The Sharp Project and
Stopover

Liverpool's congested urban industrial area is beset with even greater problems of homeless offenders and ex-offenders as well as other high-criminal-risk persons, both male and female, than is the Manchester area. The Whitechapel, Sharp, and Stopover Projects provide all the services described in the Lance, Talbot Road House, and other programs. The Whitechapel House is a day care program, for example, and includes everything from a hobby and craft shop to television rooms, a small library of daily papers, magazines, and periodicals, a workshop, a small clothing store, and low-cost food. District probation officers may issue meal tickets that may be cashed in at the center. Cooperating churches also cash these vouchers for food. The money for these cashed vouchers is recoverable from the Probation Service. Medical attention, including surgery, is also available along with other types of aid, such as job skill training, employment referral, and counseling. Since it began in mid 1975 it was discovered that some 10 percent of over two thousand clients are illiterate, and educational services have been developed. In 1977 staffs were expanded to serve the growing number of clients.

Other projects include the Wiltshire Scheme, which offers housing in a rural environment and educational and employment help and works with the courts for clients. The 134 Project in London is similar to the housing programs for the homeless. It has made use of properties which have been renovated and converted into rooms with communal kitchens, bathrooms, and living rooms. Residents may stay for two months while they find permanent employment and residential accommodations. Up to twenty persons can be accommodated in the project's main house in Brixton, while three other smaller homes serve smaller numbers of persons. The Hammersmith Teenage Project helps teenagers twelve through sixteen years of age and is situated in a building in the center of Hammersmith. The staff includes a director, social worker, teacher, youth worker, five persons known as linkers (staff members who have backgrounds similar to those of their clients), a secretary, and a research worker. Teenagers are referred to the project by various agencies, including the court. The project may serve as an alternative to incarceration, since judges may defer sentencing on the understanding that the offender will work with the project during the period of time. The minimum penalty rather than the maximum penalty for the teenager's crime may be imposed. When the youth is assigned to the project, he is introduced to his linker. The linker spends a substantial amount of time with him, his family, his friends, and his school. The youth is encouraged to examine his relationships with his peer group, teachers, neighborhood, and family and to learn practical skills. Videotapes of family problem situations, and so on, drama, discussion, group sessions and other methods are tools used to help the youth cope with and overcome problems in his own environment. The program also incorporates a full-time educational program for those who refuse to go to school or who have been expelled. Youths who are still in school work in the project after school and on weekends. The project makes maximum use of volunteers and neighborhood community agencies. NACRO continues to develop new projects and to expand older experimental projects that have been successful. One of its central aims is to develop and expand those projects that provide housing, employment, and education, as well as counseling for the offender and ex-offender with emphasis on providing alternatives to prison. It is also involved at present in changing the overall environment of high-risk people by helping to create and to expand housing developments and housing associations to improve entire neighborhoods and districts of cities.

NACRO has also called to the attention of Parliament the importance of reform in the laws regarding offenders. Its Second Memorandum to the House of Commons Expenditure Committee in February 1978 exemplifies this effort. In summary, the memorandum called for four ways to reduce the rising prison population in England.

1. It recommended that prison sentences with a maximum of five years be reduced except for penalties for murder, kidnapping, rape, and deliberate infliction of personal injury. It also suggested that the law direct the court to explain that the sentence is essential for the protection of the public and to give reasons in support of this view.[14]

2. NACRO suggested that certain offenses should no longer carry a sentence of incarceration. These should include
   a. Fine defaulting: Imprisonment for nonpayment of fines should be abolished and an alternative substituted.
   b. Maintenance (alimony) defaulting: An alternative to imprisonment is more logical.
   c. Drunkenness: Assignment to a detoxification center outside the criminal justice process would be the best solution to alcoholism.
   d. Using cannabis (marijuana): Imprisonment for marijuana users (with small amounts of cannabis in possession) should be abolished.
   e. Vagrancy and begging: English vagrancy laws should be repealed; instead, various public resources should be considered to offer a positive environmental change.
   f. Soliciting and importuning: Imprisonment for these offenses should also be abolished according to the NACRO memorandum.

3. Prison sentences should be reduced for the following types of offenders:
   a. Mentally ill offenders: Alternatives should include a greatly expanded use of mental health agencies and halfway homes for the mentally retarded.
   b. Prisoners on remand: NACRO suggests that when bail is refused (because of, for example, lack of money) the offender should be given legal aid to appeal to the Crown Court. Rooming houses should be used as temporary housing agencies instead of remand prisons for homeless offenders awaiting trial while on bail.
   c. Juveniles on remand: NACRO recommended that juveniles should be placed in the custody of responsible adults while awaiting court appearance instead of being placed in custody.
   d. Prisoners awaiting deportation: NACRO has recommended that the criteria for the imprisonment of persons awaiting deportation or removal should be strictly and more narrowly defined by law or directive so that persons innocent of any crime (in terms of all other English law except illegal entry) are not held in prison while they await deportation.

4. A much greater use of alternatives to prison is proposed by NACRO.

These alternatives should include:

a. A much wider development of accommodations for offenders including hostels, supported basic units, rooming houses, and independent accommodations.

b. Employment and educational opportunities including placement and work-habit training services.

c. Court presentation of alternatives in living accommodations: This interesting recommendation by NACRO suggests that the judge be shown specific possibilities for the offender's new accommodation as well as for employment and educational facilities, that these possibilities be specific to each offender's case, and that they be presented in some systematic manner.

d. Alternatives to custody for juveniles: NACRO suggests that the best chance for providing appropriate noninstitutional alternatives for juveniles is in the development of a comprehensive "range of intermediate treatment facilities which should include alternative education programs."[15] NACRO also suggests that there should be facilities offering work experiences, work skill training, community service programs, and other services. Local authorities and programs to recruit foster or community parents should be used for young offenders who would otherwise be incarcerated.

In this memorandum to the government and others like it, NACRO has suggested that new programs of experimentation with alternatives to prison should receive government support to a much greater extent. One idea includes a greater expansion of the Community Service Order in terms of length of the applicable program and supervision by people outside the justice system.[16]

In summary England and Wales have developed an exemplary approach to resolving important issues with regard to imprisonment. The alternatives discussed indicate that England and Wales have a good chance of finding a workable solution. Increases in crime rates and demands for more prison space by other groups, tend to impede the progress of the alternatives movement. The early 1980s may help us predict the progress of alternatives to imprisonment in England.

Notes

1. Hans V. Hofer, *Dutch Prison Population*, mimeographed, University of Stockholm, Institute of Criminology, Department of Sociology, Stockholm, 1975, p. 4.

2. Home Office, *Non-Custodial Treatment of Offenders in Britain*, mimeographed, Whitehall, September 1976, p. 1.

3. Ibid., pp. 4, 5.

4. Ibid., p. 5.

5. Ibid., p. 5.

6. Ibid., p. 8.

7. Home Office, *Report on the Nottinghamshire Experimental Scheme,* mimeographed, London, undated, pp. 10, 11.

8. Home Office, *Guidelines for Suitability for Community Service,* mimeographed, London, undated, p. 2.

9. NACRO, *The Use of Prison and Its Alternatives*, pamphlet, London, 1977, p. 11.

10. Ibid., p. 11.

11. Ibid., pp. 2, 7.

12. NACRO, *NACRO's Beginning* (London, 1977), p. 5.

13. NACRO, *Talbot House: Housing the Homeless* (London: L&T Press, 1976), p. 2.

14. NACRO, *Memorandum to the House of Commons Expenditure Committee* (Education, Arts and Home Office Sub-Committee), Enquiry into the Administration of the Prison Service, November 1977, p. 5.

15. Ibid., p. 6.

16. Ibid., p. 8.

A large selection of two-page to four-page pamphlets describing the various programs are published by NACRO. Copies may be secured from NACRO, 125 Kennington Park Road, London SE 11. Additional information may be secured from Her Majesty's Stationery Office, London:

Community Service Orders, Pease, et al., eds., H.O. Research Study, No. 29, 1975.

Community Service Assessed in 1976, Pease et al., eds., Study No. 39, 1977.

A Review of Criminal Justice Policy, 1976.

A list of other relevant papers on alternatives in England may also be secured from Home Office, Research; Research Unit, Romney House, Marsham St., London SW1P 3DY.

7 The Netherlands

Visitors to The Netherlands often see a neat, industrious, and orderly country. It also appears to be a colorful country with congenial, composed, and intelligent citizens. These impressions are not superficial. Respect for man and concern for his welfare are interwoven in the Dutch cultural fabric. Investigations of The Netherlands' criminal justice system indicate that this humanistic outlook is not limited to Holland's free citizens but includes its accused and committed residents as well. The Dutch are efficient in handling criminal cases. Their police and court staffs are knowledgable and well-trained. Social concern even permeates the penal sanction system. It is important, therefore, to examine alternatives to prison in The Netherlands within the context of its entire justice system. A sketch of this system may help in understanding this nation's total approach to its social deviants. The Netherlands has many of the elements of other industrialized nations and could be examined for comparison's sake. Unlike other industrialized nations, The Netherlands does not have many of the elements of other nations' incarceration philosophies, of punitive treatment. Recent statistics indicate that prison populations in Holland amount to between 20 and 21 per 100,000 population, compared with the United States, which has between 225 and 250 of its citizens under lock and key per 100,000 population.[1]

The Legal System

The development of the Dutch criminal justice system with its humanistic approach dates back to 1823 when its probation services were originated. It was in the Penal Code of 1886, however, that criminal procedures were simplified and the door was opened to changes that continue today. The Legal Organization Act of 1827 and the Criminal Procedure Code of 1926 were other instruments that served to lay the foundations for today's approaches in Holland. The law was simplified by the division of crime into serious offenses and minor offenses. Sentences were divided into only three main categories: Imprisonment for serious offenses, detention for offenses involving negligence and most minor offenses, and a system of fines for both serious and minor offenses. There are no minimum penalties for separate offenses, but there is a minimum penalty of one day of incarceration or a small fine for certain offenses. As a result of these stipulations the law does not recognize any mitigating circumstances, as do most other Western legal systems. This allows a Dutch judge considerable freedom to examine each case on its own merits. Like many other countries, the Dutch have many separate laws for serious and minor crimes, including drug use and sale of drugs, traffic violation, and economic offenses concerned with fraud. These laws are interpreted and administered by highly professional people. By law judges are highly qualified and professionally trained. Nonprofessional people cannot administer judicial procedure. Trial by jury was abolished about 1813 when the Napoleonic Code was being used in The Netherlands for the last time. Private citizens may not initiate criminal proceedings although they may register complaints. The Dutch government begins all prosecution through its public prosecutors.

Another important provision of Dutch criminal law is the principle of legality. This means that an act can only be penalized by reason of written provisions of laws in existence prior to the commitment of the act. Dutch legislators wrote precise descriptions of the criminal behavior in each of the various acts. Because of this specificity, judges cannot declare guilty verdicts on the grounds of "contravention of the unwritten laws."[2] A forbidden behavior is legally described in Dutch laws, and a maximum penalty is attached to this description. The principle of legality gives the judge boundaries by definitions of offenses, and it eliminates judgment of cases by analogy. This means that behavior not included in the definition cannot be penalized simply because it is similar to the specific behavior described in the law.

The Dutch criminal law is similar to other nation's laws in its recognition of certain general defenses against criminal liability. Persons in the following categories can make such a defense:

1. Extreme youth: Children under the age of twelve years cannot be penalized for their offense. A special criminal law is applicable to youths between twelve and eighteen.
2. Mentally disturbed persons: Defense may be made on the grounds of mental retardation or derangement.
3. Excusable error: If a person believes he is acting according to the law, having received incorrect directions from a legal authority (a policeman, for example), he may plead excusable error. If it is proved that he broke the law while acting in good faith, he is excused from all penalties.[3]

The Netherlands penal system includes three main punishments for adults: imprisonment, custody, and fines. Penalties for juveniles breaking the law include training school assignment, custody, fines, and reprimand. Mentally disturbed persons may be institutionalized, but this is not a specific penal sanction. The laws applicable to mentally disturbed persons include stipulations for the care and treatment of mentally disturbed juveniles as well as adults.

The Police System

Two types of police departments make up the bulk of The Netherlands police: the government or state police, under the authority of the minister of justice, and the municipal police. State police usually operate in communities with populations under 25,000 and municipal police operate in communities with more than 25,000 inhabitants. Municipal police are answerable to the government minister of home affairs. Both police departments are responsible to the local buromaster (mayor) while maintaining law and order in his jurisdiction. When an investigation of a criminal case is being conducted, both police departments must answer to the prosecutor and ultimately to the minister of justice. All police investigations and powers are administered under The Netherlands Code of Criminal Procedure. This code mandates that police follow instructions of the public prosecutor, a position similar to the district attorney in the United States. Holland also has military, railway, economic, and other special police units.

The Court System

The Netherlands judiciary system includes a hierarchy of courts as follows:

1. The High Court.
2. The Court of Appeals.
3. The district courts.
4. The cantonal courts.

Qualified judges for these courts receive their lifetime appointments from the queen, and they cannot be removed from office. The High Court, like the U.S. Supreme Court, has the task of ensuring that justice is administered correctly through all courts. It also serves as the court for adjudication in cases of malpractice of ministers and certain high officials. The High Court has never had to act in the capacity of reprimander for unorthodox conduct of high officials. If a verdict of a lower court is anulled by the High Court, the case is referred back to the same lower court or to another for a new trial. The lower court judge receiving the case is bound by the decision of the High Court with regard to the right of the defendant to appeal. Other than these rights, there are no binding orders. The actual adjudication of offenses is handled by the other three lower courts. A single judge who handles minor offenses presides over a cantonal court. Three judges who try serious offenses and who may judge verdicts of cantonal courts on appeal preside over district courts. A police magistrate tries less serious cases and is limited in sentencing powers to sentences of six months or less. A juvenile judge tries both serious and minor offenses, which may include drunkenness and disorderly conduct of juveniles. The Court of Appeal judge hears appeals presented by district courts.

The Public Prosecutor

The public prosecutor in The Netherlands is responsible for the prosecution of offenses, the supervision of criminal investigations, and the upholding of the law by the public. On a hierarchical ladder these three tasks are managed by (1) the attorney general at the high court, (2) the attorneys general at the Courts of Appeal, and (3) the public prosecutors at the district courts and cantonal courts.

The attorney general of the High Court has the special task of maintaining a system of justice administration by all courts. His job is somewhat similar to the U.S. Attorney General's Office. Particular tasks include recommendations to be made to the High Court on each case being judged and prosecution of ministers and other high officials. To date, his office has never had to carry out prosecution of ministers or high officials. The attorneys general of the Courts of Appeal prosecute cases that have been appealed and are responsible for seeing to it that sentences pronounced in the courts are carried out. The public prosecutors prosecute cases in the district and cantonal courts and are responsible for carrying out lower court sentences.

The Chain of Actions by Dutch Police and the Public Prosecutor

The Dutch police may take certain compulsory measures when someone is suspected of criminal behavior. These measures include arrest, detention for interrogation for a maximum of six hours, search of body and clothes, and a house search with a warrant from the minister of justice. If enough evidence is at hand and, in addition, certain other conditions are present, (chance of immediate escape, violent behavior), a suspect may be held for two additional twenty-four hour periods by order of the public prosecutor's assistant or a higher police officer or for a period up to eighty-six hours by order of the public prosecutor. An examining magistrate may be called into the case if needed, for example, if the police investigation was unsuccessful. The examining magistrate has greater powers, including the power to force witnesses to appear and to detain them. He may also authorize more extensive house searches and authorize a warrant to hold the suspect in custody for trial for a period not to exceed two six-day periods. Only the district court may extend this remand period and then only for a period up to ninety days. This custody is for serious offenses only. If a trial date has been set beyond the ninety-day period, further extension of custody may be granted if there is a possibility of escape and of obstructing the investigation or if there is a danger that further criminal behavior will occur.

The public prosecutor is the only authority for prosecuting cases in The Netherlands. Most cases, however, are not prosecuted. Often in cases where an indictment is clearly supported in both economic and property offenses, the defendant may be offered the option of settling the case out of court. The public prosecutor is not obliged to initiate prosecution proceedings. Often settlement is made through a cash payment or cash payment agreement. In many minor offenses the defendant and the victim may be able to make a settlement on the spot, and payment of any fine levied by the policeman may also be made at this time. The offenses in this category may include minor traffic offenses, breaking local by-laws, and small property damage. In traffic offenses the accused is directed by note (ticket) on his windshield to go to the nearest police station and make settlement. If this is done, no criminal offense report is made.

If settlement is not suggested by the police, or if suggested settlement is refused, a written report is made by the police and presented to the public prosecutor. This procedure is also standard where the police are not authorized to suggest a settlement or do not desire to settle the case at that point. The public prosecutor analyzes the report from the police and may choose one of several alternatives. He may decide not to prosecute, to make a settlement suggestion, to table any decision until he hears more about the case or accused, or to order a further investigation. More than 50 percent of Dutch criminal cases are handled through the expediency principle. This means that a public prosecutor may waive prosecution if the suspect agrees to attend a drug clinic, alcoholic rehabilitation program, or similar treatment program.[4] In recent years about 85 percent of all economic cases and about 45 percent of all fiscal offenses were also settled without prosecution. These figures emphasize that the members of the Dutch criminal justice system strive to minimize needless incarceration and time-consuming but often unnecessary legal proceedings. The public prosecutors use their alternatives often, and this use of alternatives is much more a role of Dutch public prosecutors than it is of public prosecutors in other Western nations where the efforts made by public prosecutors are concentrated on getting a conviction. In The Netherlands the job of the public prosecutor is to expedite judicial proceedings but with a concern for the citizen as well as for the state. The Dutch public prosecutor, for example, may use his legally allowed time limit for handling a case by tabling a decision. This means that he may decide to take no further criminal action if the accused does not become involved in any reportable misconduct during a certain time period. He may also suggest that during this time period the accused must arrange to pay compensation to the victim, to follow a set of probationary type rules, or to follow some other out-of-court action.

The public prosecutor is held accountable for his decisions, and he must report each decision to prosecute to the Prosecution Council at the High Court level, even in cases in which some type of adjudication is fairly well assured. The point of this procedure is to expedite the judicial process by respecting the needs of the state as well as the needs of the accused. More cases are now dismissed than prosecuted, and public knowledge of this is causing concern in the justice system. Justice officials are presently attempting to solve this dilemma since public knowledge of leniency may cause some persons to take advantage of this system.

The Netherlands judicial system includes about 400 judges. There are about 150 public prosecutors. The probation departments of Holland include about 550 full-time probation counselors. A major portion of all resocialization work, however, is actually conducted by members of private agencies although much of the work is government funded.

Preliminary Investigation and Trial Procedures

A summons in The Netherlands must specify the rights of the suspect or defendant, the name of the court and time of appearance, and normally the names of the witnesses the public prosecutor plans to bring to court in support of his allegations. In cases where the accused feels that there is reasonable expectation of a conviction, he may petition the court to examine the charges without public hearing. The court will then hear the case in chambers.

The police and public prosecutors do not have the power to compel witnesses to give evidence or to send a suspect to a clinic for psychiatric examination. A preliminary investigation in The Netherlands is not mandatory, but a public prosecutor may refer a case to the judge, and the judge may then authorize an investigation including the production of evidence from witnesses and clinical examination of the suspect. A suspect may receive the services of a Dutch attorney at his own expense, or, if he is unable to pay, such services will be paid for by the government. Lawyers paid for by the government have rights similar to privately paid lawyers. These rights include serving as defense, appearance in courts, attendance at interrogations of the accused, inspection of the accused's state file, and access to copies of all police reports. He may also, of course, bring witnesses to court for the defense.

The court hearing takes place before one of three judges and is moderately accusatorial, more so than the preliminary investigation. The suspect is entitled to inspect all papers and other documents in the case, call in witnesses, and make a plea with or without counsel. His position at this point is the same as that of the public prosecutor. While the court hearing is accusatorial, it is much less so than similar proceedings in England, the United States, Canada, and other countries. The judge is actively engaged in an examination of the evidence. An important fact is that the accused may not plead guilty in the Dutch law of criminal procedures. A confession of the accused may be an important part of the evidence but is not sufficient enough in itself for conclusions to be made. Interrogation of the accused under oath, at this stage, may not be made.

The trial itself is regulated down to the last detail including procedure for questioning witnesses, the questioning of the suspect by the judge, the presentation of police reports, reproduction of statements made by witnesses, and the presentation of recommendations by the public prosecutor. In serious cases witnesses may be heard by the court. This is especially true when the suspect denies the offense. The judge is not bound by any demands for certain penalties made by the public prosecutor. The suspect and his counsel are given the last word in court. The entire procedure calls for enough supplementary evidence, enough witnesses to ensure a proper decision; the suspect's own statements, even in a confession, are not sufficient proof, nor are the judge's own observations. If the decision is not acquittal, the suspect may appeal to a higher court unless the offense was a minor one or the sentence was very light. The public prosecutor may also appeal cases to higher courts except minor offenses. Appeals may be made to the higher court within fourteen days of the lower court's decision, and a further appeal may be made to the High Court. The High Court may refer the case back to the lower court that made the decision or to another court for reexamination of the case, or it may make the final decision itself. After all possibilities of appeal have been exhausted, the accused may still appeal for "mercy" within eight days after final sentencing. The mercy plea is a plea that the sentence be suspended.

The Dutch system, in which every attempt is made to settle infractions without sentencing, may be one reason that armed resistance to arrest is rare in Holland. It may also be the reason that over 80 percent of the defendants confess to the charges either during the preliminary investigation period or in the hearing. This attitude and procedure appear to foster the expeditious handling of cases in Dutch courts. Often the questions are concerned with what to do with the defendant rather than with gathering additional evidence in order to obtain a conviction. Often the public prosecutor is more concerned with the total situation of the accused and the victim rather than accusatorial procedures. The family, the circumstances of the criminal act, the community—all are important aspects to be considered by the public prosecutor in this humanistic approach. This process of adjudication contains serveral notable points that may be summarized as follows:

1. Prosecution by private citizens is not permitted, although complaints by private citizens may be registered.
2. Many cases are settled at the police department level. Similarly, many cases are settled at the prosecutor level.
3. The right to prosecute is limited by time periods specified by law. These time periods, however, allow the public prosecutor to settle the cases with several alternatives. One procedure, a "conditional nonprosecution," is written into Dutch law.
4. Pretrial custody is a very serious matter, and the accused person's rights are guarded. Dutch law now stipulates that time spent in remand custody is deducted from any sentence. One criticism of the Dutch judicial system is that remand custody periods continue to be lengthy, thus shortening the period of time spent in prisons after sentencing. Prior to 1974 almost half of the prison population in The Netherlands consisted of persons in pretrial custody.[5] Since that time the trend has been to avoid lengthy commitments of accused persons to remand custody to await trial.

The Probation System

We must also view the Dutch probation system differently from almost all similar systems of alternatives to prison and corrections. The Dutch began their probation system in 1823, inspired by the Englishman John Howard. The system developed along the same lines as the American and English probation systems except for its philosophy, the major difference. While probation officers are, in fact, a part of the official Dutch sanctioning system, they are professionally trained social workers. The English and American probation officer, on the other hand, is corrections oriented. In some cases probation officers in the U.S. as well as U.S. parole officers have been authorized to carry guns. Most probation officers today remain attached to the local court, police department, or similar justice agency. The Dutch probation officer directs his efforts, not as a policeman watching over a culprit, but rather as a helping agent nurturing his ward. One example of this orientation is the preparation of the presentence report. In England, the United States, and other countries, this report is provided to the judge by the probation officer, as a background to help the judge decide on a proper sentence. In The Netherlands it is not called a presentence report but a rehabilitation report. Many probation officers see it as an instrument for helping a human being returning to society as a law-abiding and functioning citizen. Dutch probation officers try to report, as accurately as possible, the offender's personality, social background, and infractions to help the judge establish a meaningful and helping relationship between the social worker and the client. The philosophy of the probation officer when using this report is that his role is a helping rather than a sanctioning one. In this role he might suggest that if the court desires an objective report of facts related to the court's fulfillment of its job as a sanctioning agency, then it should call on the police or other office of the state rather than the probation officer for its presentence report.

While on probation a Dutch citizen may find himself in contact with many agencies. The essence of the entire rehabilitation or probation period is contact with the community. A network of voluntary workers in Holland carries out tasks in a highly efficient manner. The volunteers enlist the assistance of trade unions, various industry groups, the Dutch equivalents of America's junior and senior Chambers of Commerce, and the churches. These contacts are continually maintained and nurtured so that the public has become a part of the rehabilitation network. Many persons in each neighborhood are available and willing to take risks in helping others. While part of this risk taking may have stemmed from underground work during the Nazi invasions, the concept was generated in the Dutch culture long before that time. The theme of the social workers in support of the probation program is that "the greater the choice the better we can match the probationer to his supervisor,"[6] who is usually a volunteer. Since the probation officer is also a professionally trained social worker, the volunteers can turn to the probation officer for advice. The voluntary organizations have been in competition with one another to do better with their probationers. Merger of these old established agencies was attempted in 1912 and failed, but there is again a trend toward merger. Four such agencies began merger procedures in 1973 but have contended that these agencies must be kept separate from the Ministry of Justice. This merger will represent an end to 155 years of voluntary forms of charity for probationers and the beginning of an organization of professionally trained helpers. Results of volunteers' working side by side with probation officers have generally been good; no judicial action was taken against probationers in more than 70 percent of the cases over the past several years. As probation helping services become more professionalized through merger and development of standards and goals, recidivism itself will not be the only measurement, and additional in-depth measurements must be developed.

Penalties for Crimes

Having briefly examined the Dutch judicial system, we may now view its system of sanctions other than the probation alternative. The major stipulations concerning sanctions were developed in the Dutch Penal Code of 1886, the Criminal Procedure Code of 1926, and the Legal Organization

Act of 1827. Part of the probation provision dealing with conditional release was enacted in 1915. Provisions for caring for mentally disturbed prisoners came into law in 1928. Solitary confinement was provisionally abolished in the 1930s and completely abolished in 1953. Laws regarding fines were introduced in 1925 and have since been revised. Over 90 percent of all sanctions in The Netherlands are in the form of fines, and only about 5 percent of all sanctions are in the form of incarceration. Even conditional sanctions that include liberty deprivation are rare, amounting to only about 1 percent of all sanctions.

Liberty Deprivation

While liberty deprivation sanctions in The Netherlands differ little from those of other modern Western nations, their actual use differs considerably. The Dutch rarely use liberty deprivation as a sanction, and such sanction is most often used for the protection of the public rather than for punishment or for a deterring effect. The sanctions include (1) imprisonment, (2) detention, (3) substitute detention, (4) assignment to a state workhouse, (5) commitment to the care of the government, and (6) commitment to a mental health facility. A convicted person in Holland may be imprisoned for a period of from one day to life. A one-day sentence could be imposed even for such severe crimes as murder. The laws of The Netherlands do not specify any minimum sentence.

Originally detention, the second form of sanctioning, was applied to persons whose crimes were not severe enough to warrant imprisonment with its degrading forms of forced labor. Detention, therefore, was a popular alternative. Today most short prison sentences in Holland are served in a modern version of the detention house. Short term in this case means a sentence of fourteen days or less. A person may receive a sentence to a house of detention for a maximum of one year, but this sentence is not often used. Extensions of this sentence by law may go to sixteen months, but, again, such sentences are rare.

A seldom-used sanction in recent times is incarceration in a state workhouse. Originally this type of punishment was aimed at nonindictable offenses. These included vagrancy, pimping or use of money secured from prostitution for a living, begging, drunkenness, and similar misdemeanors. A minimum period of three months and a sentence of up to three years may be imposed on persons found guilty of these crimes. The broad discretionary powers of local law enforcement personnel have all but eliminated this type of incarceration in favor of much simpler sanctions or none at all.

In cases where the offender is considered mentally handicapped and cannot be held responsible for his acts, the Dutch laws provide that, upon conviction of a crime, mental health treatment shall be provided. The Dutch words *Ter Beschikking Regering* (T.B.R.) ("at government disposal")[7] apply to mentally deficient persons. T.B.R. originated in the Dutch Penal Code of 1886 and stipulates that "offenders who cannot be held responsible for a criminal act on account of a defect or disease of the mind are not punishable for that act".[8] But persons to whom this stipulation applies are to be held for special treatment in special facilities. T.B.R. reached a peak in the late 1950s with about eight hundred persons called patients placed at government disposal. The trend has been away from T.B.R. in recent years. There are about ten T.B.R. facilities in Holland. Other persons may be committed to T.B.R. who have been found incapable of abiding by the law. This allows for treatment of habitual criminals such as pyromaniacs or kleptomaniacs.

In The Netherlands courts also have the power to provide for conditional sentences.[9] A conditional sentence may be a fine, detention, T.B.R.,[10] or imprisonment not to exceed a year if the conditions are not upheld. This conditional sentence allows the court to suggest a set of conditions to which the offender must adhere during the time of the sentence. The conditions may be psychiatric assistance, some form of work, or involvement in a rehabilitation program. In recent years about 93 percent of all Dutch sentences consisted of fines with no conditions attached. Only about 5 percent of the nearly three hundred thousand annual convictions include prison sentences and about 1 percent receive sentences to detention, a form of incarceration which allows a greater latitude of treatment measures, work releases, etc. Thus the conditional sentence was minimized to a great extent. This total sanctioning system is unique in its minimal use of liberty-depriving sanctions. This minimal use of prisons and incarceration other than prison does not appear to increase crime rates, as one might expect.

The Dutch approach to juveniles who commit crimes is also unique. One example of this is the custodial arrest of juveniles. Custodial arrest is used for liberty deprivation for as little as four hours or as much as fourteen days. This detention device appears to have a significant shock effect on juvenile deliquents, especially first timers. Some of the effects of this sharp and sudden imprisonment depend on the events that occur during these hours or days of detention. If the family becomes deeply involved and shows an attitude of love and care as well as a new feeling of involvement in teaching responsibility, the results of such detention are positive. If counselors are available to assist the youth through this crisis and to dealing with his personal problems, the results of incarceration for this shock period are usually much more significant in terms of reducing recidivism. This punishment may be served in installments at any time within a sixty-day period to help avoid interruption of school or work, but the sooner it is imposed the more likely that the shock effect will take seed. Another provision of this short custody period is that, unlike most sentences involving deprivation of liberty, it may be served in a private institution where specialized therapeutic services may be available.[11]

If a juvenile is convicted of a crime, rather than a misdemeanor, he may be sentenced to spend one to six months in a Dutch equivalent of the American reformatory or training school. For juveniles in need of long periods of reeducation and especially juveniles who are uneducated or socially retarded, a long-term commitment to the care of the government is possible where these schooling and socialization services are available. This indefinite commitment is reviewed every two years and, in any case, expires on the day the youth reaches his majority. A commitment to an institution for special treatment is developed especially for youths who are found to be partly or totally irresponsible for their offenses. Such a commitment is not regarded as punishment but as a service in the interest of the youths.

The Dutch have made considerable efforts to protect children, and no child under twelve years of age may be charged with a criminal offense. When a child has been involved in such an offense, social services are called on. The juvenile court system is aimed primarily at youths between twelve and seventeen years of age although it can be applied, in certain cases, to older youth. These older youth, up to age twenty-five in some cases of mental deficiency, may also be heard under special provisions of the General Penal Law. During the three years ending in December 1977, between twenty thousand and twenty-three thousand Dutch youths were found guilty of juvenile offenses. About 89 percent were fined, and only 8 to 10 percent were incarcerated conditionally or unconditionally. Unconditional sentences accounted for only about 4 percent of the liberty-depriving sentences given to youths during these years.

The Dutch concluded around 1900 that prisons do not resocialize, deter, or prevent crime or serve other rehabilatative needs. The decline in prison sentences appears to have gathered momentum in recent years. During the period from 1957 to 1972 the Dutch decreased the daily average number of prisoners a significant 40 percent, from thirty-five prisoners per 100,000 population to twenty-two persons per 100,000 population. These decreases could indicate that the Dutch are holding only their hard-core criminals in prison and for longer periods. This is not the case. In the fifteen-year period ending in 1972 the average time spent in prison has decreased from three months and a few days to about one and a half months. This is a drop of about 50 percent. The courts in The Netherlands continue this evolutionary system of prison abolishment by the simple mechanics of sentencing fewer people and sentencing them to shorter terms. Critics of the Dutch system have suggested that part of this phenomenon may be explained by the fact that more Dutch people who are accused of criminal acts spend longer periods of time in remand prisons awaiting trial. There is some credence to this criticism according to some researchers.[12] The Dutch passed rules in

1973 that require courts to deduct all time spent in remand custody from any sentence imposed by the court.[13] The average time spent in remand is about two months for persons accused of felonies. This may be compared with the average of three months spent in remand by accused persons in Sweden. Imprisonment in The Netherlands in terms of numbers of prisoners and time spent in prisons remains considerably lower, in any case, than other Western nations even when we consider the time in remand.

Alternatives

The alternatives to incarceration are neither profound nor exemplary compared with alternatives in England and the United States. The Dutch rely, to a considerable extent, on the expediency principle in relation to prosecution. This gives a considerable amount of discretionary power to the Public Prosecutor's Department. This discretionary power affords many possibilities in dealing with criminal cases. For the last twenty to thirty years, primarily from the end of World War II to the present, the rule has been to ask, Why prosecute? rather than, Why not prosecute? In most other countries the question would be, Why not prosecute? or How strong can we make the case in order to assure a high penalty? Even in Holland the question Why prosecute? must still be asked within some boundaries, which include the upholding of Dutch parliamentary law with regard to criminal behavior. That is, the discretionary power given the public prosecutor is limited. If, for example, a recommended conditional sentence consists of suspension of incarceration, then the public prosecutor also has the responsibility of recommending some adequately organized group or system outside the Dutch Criminal Corrections system, which can effectively deal with the convicted criminal. The court, of course, has the final word in any such action. The history of the Dutch criminal justice system demonstrates a significant correlation between the sentences recommended and the sentences imposed, attesting to the realistic use of the public prosecutor's discretionary powers in line with the thinking of Dutch judges. In some cases the public prosecutor may wish to exercise his power by recommending the services of a therapeutic agency instead of incarceration; however, if such an agency does not exist or if it has no room for the client, the alternative may not be used. This happened in 1970 when adequate socio-psychiatric treatment was frequently not available to drug users.[14]

In cases of relatively minor offenses the harmfulness of the sanction may far outweigh its usefulness. When this happens, avoidance of criminal sanctions is suggested. This action suggests that some other alternative be used—psychiatric observation, counseling, or special programs related to this type of treatment. Most alternatives to deprivation of liberty in The Netherlands apply in cases of minor criminal acts.

Examples of alternatives, thus far, have included probation and therapeutic services. Additional alternatives include the following:

1. *Settlements*: Unless prison is the only penalty for the crime, an accused person may "buy off" the offense without the intermediary of the court.[15] The sum is paid to the Public Prosecutors Department.

2. *Fines:* In The Netherlands the fine is the most important alternative to imprisonment. Fines may be imposed for many offenses and may be substituted for imprisonment. They may also be imposed along with imprisonment. Fines may not be imposed as alternatives to prison for offenses that are punishable by imprisonment for periods exceeding six years. In the last ten years fines have been the alternative in about three-fourths of the simple property crimes. Fines have also been the alternative for about 50 to 60 percent of the morality offenses (including abortion) and offenses committed under the Road Traffic Act.[16] Between 92 percent and 95 percent of all fines are collected within seven months from the date of sentencing. Imprisonment for nonpayment, appears to encourage payment of fines.

3. *Restoration of the legitimate situation*: In this case the alternative consists of performing some duty or service that has not been performed or undoing that which was unlawfully done and to make good the damage or loss caused, all at the expense of the convicted person.

4. *Loss of benefits that have accumulated as a result of unlawful acts or omissions*: If the offender has benefited financially, by or through the offense committed, these benefits must go to the state.

5. *Payment of surety*: This measure is part of the socioeconomic legislation, and payment may be liquidated if the offender complies with whatever conditions are imposed. If the conditions are met, the offender's money is returned to him.

6. *Confiscation and withdrawal from free circulation*: In this case certain property of the offender may be confiscated. This penalty may be imposed in addition to other penalties but may also replace the major penalty.

7. *Legal pardon and a small or symbolic sanction*: Legal pardon is a conviction without the enforcement of a penalty. It is only applicable in the lower courts (cantonal) and juvenile courts. It is used when the offense is minor or when the personality of the offender, home conditions, and other criteria are considered decisive elements related to the sanction.

8. *Reprimand*: Usually the reprimand is a form of punishment for children and is rarely administered. Of 5,799 penalties and measures administered during 1969, for example, only 124 reprimands were administered.

9. *Conditional sentence*: The conditional sentence is similar to the probationary sentence in the United States and, in Holland, is given to a

maximum of three years. These conditional sentences give the Dutch courts many alternatives to imprisonment. These may include one or more of the following:

a.   Assignment to a rehabilitation program.
b.   Psychiatric treatment.
c.   Assignment to a clinic or mental health center.
d.   Assignment to a foster home or other substitute home.
e.   Making good the damage done.
f.   Placing a ban on visiting certain establishments (bars or cafes, for example).
g.   Placing a ban on fraternization with certain other people.
h.   Placing a ban on driving a motor vehicle on certain days and similar types of alternatives.
i.   Assignment to certain work for the community.[17]

A Dutch citizen convicted of a crime may also be deprived of certain rights including the right to hold specific offices, to serve in the armed forces, to take part in elections for public office, to act as counsel, or to engage in certain types of work.

These alternatives to prison are similar to those of many other Western societies. These alternatives along with the general attitude of the Dutch society become important parts of the complex set of reasons for the low number of persons confined to Dutch prisons today. In 1973 the European Committee on Crime Problems, Sub-Committee No. XXVII, issued a paper that discussed alternative penal measures to imprisonment. In its discussions of the Dutch penal system the committee concluded that it should always be possible for offenses to be dealt with out of court and for offenders to be referred to social agencies instead of court. Another recommendation by this committee was that out-of-court settlements should be possible and that they should be negotiated by the prosecuting attorneys. The committee recommended that custodial sentences not be the only type of sanction for a crime and that other alternatives should be available. A further recommendation was that alternatives should include space for conviction without penalty, compensation for the injured party, and enforcement of alternatives, as much as possible, in the convicted person's own environment. Finally the committee recommended that if an offense was committed during leisure time, its enforcement can be made during leisure time so that the connection between offense and sanction is immediate and clear.[18] For example, a person convicted of drunken driving after regular work hours would be banned from driving after work hours. The committee also recognized that such procedures would require the training of court staffs in the fields of psychology, psychiatry, and sociology, and that a greater number of experts would be required to adequately inform the court of services and possible results of sanctions. Perhaps one of the most important recommendations made by the committee was that sanctions should be "accompanied by participation on the part of the convicted person"[19] as often as possible.

These descriptions of the seemingly permissive attitude of the Dutch judicial system would suggest that Holland may become a center of international crime. Although The Netherlands is strategically located, the logistics of criminal activity make such a possibility doubtful. The Netherlands serves international criminal activity only to the degree that such activity is economically or logistically better suited to Holland than, for example, Chicago, Hong Kong, or Istanbul. The leniency or humanism of its judicial system is only one of many factors that attracts a particular type of criminal activity.

The Netherlands' judicial system must be judged on its usefulness to its people and its government. It may also be compared sociologically with its neighbors. The Netherlands manages its judicial system differently from other countries. It has, by far, the lowest rate of incarceration, and this, as far as this particular discussion is concerned, is the important point. The Dutch prison population continues to fall, and the Dutch have far fewer incarcerated individuals than their neighbors. The United Kingdom has three times the number of prisoners per 100,000 population, and the United States has ten times as many persons under lock and key per 100,000 population.

The result of Holland's changing laws and its policies of imprisoning only the most dangerous criminals has reduced the number of prisons, and the number of inmates in existing prisons, and increased the turnover of prisoners as a result of shortened prison sentences.[20]

These changes are significant in several respects and from different viewpoints. To the prison abolitionist they are very positive. To the reformer or to the person concerned solely with supporting alternatives to imprisonment, they offer great hope. To others such change may be less heartening. Staffs of prisons in The Netherlands were banned from carrying firearms in 1973, and in emergencies the prison warden must call on the local police or special "airborne" police squads. The chances for disruption in prisons are raised, of course, because only the more dangerous person is likely to be confined. This person is all the more likely to to be desperate and to attempt to escape. The reputation of a prison relates, at least in part, to its rehabilitative or resocialization reputation. Even if this prison rehabilitative record reputation is generally poor, the rehabilitation concept remains a viable reason for the prison to exist. This factor may almost be eliminated in any country, including Holland, as the quality of the inmates declines. Since there are fewer prisons in The Netherlands than there were some years ago, selective differentiation is less possible and contacts with local family, friends, legal counsel, case workers, and other helpers for the prisoner are made more difficult.

While these negative aspects of such change must also be dealt with eventually, the positive factors, for the majority of defendants and for the Dutch population in general, must far outweigh these disadvantages.

The Judicial System's Operation and Crime

What does a decrease in prisons or a liberal attitude in favor of the accused have to do with crime in The Netherlands? At first inspection one might conclude that the result would be a widespread rise in criminal activity. This, however, is not the case.

In 1963 there were 148,418 crimes known to the police. Of this total 54 percent were solved. In 1972 there were 348,171 crimes known to the police and only 36 percent of these were solved. During the intervening years these rates were similar and the figures for 1977 and 1978 did not differ to any great extent.[21] While these figures indicate that the elimination of harsh sentences, long prison sentences, and the attitude of judges have given rise to rampant crime in Holland, another examination of additional factors indicates that this is not quite the case. The Dutch consider crimes against the person and morality crimes particularly troublesome, as do the people of most other nations. These particular crimes have not risen significantly between 1968 and 1978. When crimes of violence and morality are on the upswing, as appears to be happening in most countries, public outrage is usually manifested in stiffer laws and sanctionings. Nations often move from liberal views on criminals and penalization to harsh views. The Dutch have been spared this pendulum approach. Other crimes in The Netherlands, especially theft, have increased. Research of social, economic, and other factors would be required to understand this rise in nonviolent crimes. We cannot, however, make any direct links between fewer prisons, different rehabilitative methods of liberal judicial systems for convicted persons in The Netherlands, and certain crime rates. Analysis of trends of crime in The Netherlands suggests that in the next few years murder will probably remain at about the same level. Holland does not have much violent crime. Each year there are about five convictions for murder per million inhabitants. There will probably be little change in assault and battery offenses. Sexual offenses have declined. Holland has a rather open view with regard to sexual acts between consenting persons, and the display of pornographic literature to adults is common. Property crimes, larceny, and related offenses, and simple cases of theft will continue to rise. These simple cases of theft are related to a large increase in the theft of bicycles. About three-quarters of all crimes committed in The Netherlands are nonviolent offenses.

In 1974 these rises in crime were not adequate to cause the legislature to change its attitude concerning imprisonment. The Dutch Parliament held debates on the Ministry of Justice budget. A clear majority contended that the Dutch prison system was a social problem itself, and the government was requested to develop a concrete plan for solving this problem.

From these figures we may conclude that crime has increased in Holland, as it has in many other countries. Crimes of property theft and vandalism have increased, while violent and morality crimes have not. The Dutch have remained steadfast in their belief that criminals are the result, in general, of the larger social environment, and it is to this environment that they address their efforts. The criminal is resocialized by means other than incarceration as often as possible. This is the philosophy of the Dutch judicial system. Let us examine decreases in the prison population from this point of view.

Incarceration Rates

An important requirement of any judicial system is that penal sanctions should impose the smallest burden on the community and the least interference with the criminal's ability to fulfill his responsibilities to his family. A broader view of this concept is taken by the Dutch, who feel that punishment should teach the person not to behave in antisocial ways but, at the same time, interfere as little as possible with his freedom. In addition, the Dutch appear to demand that the severity of a penal sanction be in proportion to the seriousness of the crime committed. If either freedom or disproportionate penal sanctions are given to the criminal, then the sentence is unjust to both the community and the offender. Severe punishment arouses resentment and rebellion and often stigmatizes the offender, lessening his chances of reintegration into the community. Thus a continued pattern of crime is often the result of the judicial process. Often the severity of punishment is less important that its certainty of being given and the degree to which potential offenders are aware that it will be given for the proposed crime. The Dutch have also learned that financial sanctions and retributory sanctions are at least as effective as custodial sanctions.[22] Victims of crime are satisfied by a program of restitution. The Dutch have incorporated this concept into their criminal justice system to a large extent.

How is this philosophy reflected in the numbers of people incarcerated in The Netherlands? Number of prisoners per 100,000 population is 21 and there has been a significant drop, about 50 percent, in the amount of time spent in prison by each individual criminal during the fifteen-year period ending in 1972. Average time spent in prison has decreased from 3.2 months to under 1.1 months.[23] The courts in The Netherlands continue this evolutionary system of prison abolition simply by sentencing less people to shorter terms. Critics have suggested that part of this phenomenon may be explained by the length of time spent in remand prisons by the accused awaiting trial. There is validity to this agreement according to some researchers.[24] The Dutch passed obligatory rules in 1973 which require courts to deduct all time spent in remand prison, from any incarceration time imposed by the court. The average amount of time spent in remand is about two months for persons accused of felonies. In Sweden, accused persons spend only about one and one-third months awaiting trial. If we add the time that a Dutch citizen spends in remand custody to the time spent in prison, the total incarceration time remains considerably less than in many other Western nations. Of 14,474 Dutch prison sentences imposed in 1975, 75 percent were imposed for less than three months and another 20 percent ranged from three months to one year. Only 4 percent received terms longer than one year. It appears that the brevity of sentences is the single most important factor in creating Holland's relatively small prison population. This trend is promoted beyond the court's philosophy of shorter sentences with regard to incarceration. Prison employees may contribute to this effect, since Dutch prison guards belong to trade unions and these unions have "succeeded in holding down the population to insure good working conditions". Costs may be another factor, since it costs about $500 a day to keep a prisoner locked up.[25] This low prison population has been maintained by a rather large bureaucracy with little citizen involvement in the criminal justice system itself. The system is composed of a large number of professionals. Citizen enters the picture after the defendant is convicted. Neither citizens nor prisoners control the court system. But the element of trust in leadership and in civil servants appears to be high in The Netherlands, and this may account for the feeling that the system is doing the right thing. Unconditional imprisonment has become almost a thing of the past in The Netherlands. While fines occupy a secondary position in the Dutch system of penalties, they form a major part of the system of penalties. Several groups who have investigated the Dutch criminal justice system have suggested that imprisonment should be made the exception rather than the rule and that other alternatives including fines should be considered first.

The Culture's Contribution to Low Prison Populations and Alternatives

The Netherlands is involved in dynamic growth and movement that equals or surpasses that of most other European nations. It also has a high rate of population growth. Of its 13 million population, with a density of one thousand persons per square mile, over 18 percent consists of youths between the ages of fifteen and twenty-five years of age. In many other countries and

especially in the United States this age group accounts for a dispropor-
tionately large number of crimes. This is not the case in Holland. There is
also considerable urbanization, and the old and traditional types of jobs are
rapidly changing. Ideological values of other nations, industrialization, and
modern media messages are influencing the people of The Netherlands.
Foreign workers in large numbers and immigrants from former Dutch colonies have crowded into The Netherlands in recent years, adding to the
population that came from Indonesia after World War II. The Netherlands
is also a world travel traffic island for tourists. Many of these tourists include youths who have become dissatisfied with their own homelands.
Many have settled in The Netherlands as members of the Dutch culture.

From this picture of The Netherlands one might expect an increase in
violence on the streets. The Netherlands has many of the characteristics that
other modern countries have which contributed to a rise in crime in Germany, England, and the United States. The Dutch have not had a correspondingly rapid rise in predatory crimes such as burglary crimes of
violence. A combination of interwoven factors contributes to this encouraging picture. The Dutch, for example, have one of the most comprehensive
programs for maintenance of incomes. One facet of this program is the effort made by the Dutch government to assist people who are not satisfied
with their jobs. If the work appears to be boring or difficult to adjust to,
steps are taken to make changes. Factors such as salary, working conditions, and location of work in relation to the employee's home may all be
considered. In addition, work-motivating factors such as job responsibility,
promotion, and recognition are also examined, and steps may be taken to
involve the employer, the employee, and the government in improving the
situation.

The Netherlands maintains a high regard for the individual. For the
youth culture this high regard is evident and relevant to their behavior.
There is an extensive system of youth centers and programs for youth.
These programs are not government directed but instead are developed by
the youths themselves with little influence from recreation center directors
and other officials.

Public funding of these youth centers is substantial, but the centers are
not operated by the government. Communication between social workers,
police, and the youth at these centers is kept open. The rebellious attitude of
youth found in some countries is not as evident in Holland.

The Dutch attitude toward drug addiction, alcoholism, and other forms
of inappropriate social behavior is more sophisticated than that of many
other countries. Such behavior is managed without police and law enforcement involvement. As a result of this nurturing attitude, Holland attracts
many foreign youths to its drug centers and cities. This benevolent attitude
permeates the Dutch population and has influenced the crime picture to a
great extent.

In The Netherlands there are over eight thousand professional social workers employed in hundreds of agencies to provide client-centered approaches to problems confronting people. These agencies work toward developing better environmental living conditions, better social relationships in families and among neighbors, and they work in other ways to improve family living situations. When trouble appears in some area, a maximum effort is made to decrease tensions, maintain channels of communication, and correct the problem. Members of these social agencies along with probation, parole, and rehabilitation services actively participate together in advocating changes in the laws and the social welfare systems of the country. The Dutch media devote considerable time to public service programs, especially where rehabilitation is the message. The Netherlands' League for Penal Reform helps supply the media with subject material and data for its programs. Seminars, conferences, organized groups, and consultive bodies all have included wide public representation to help influence legislative changes.

Many of the present judges who serve life terms on the bench in The Netherlands were prisoners of war during the Nazi occupation in World War II. Their personal experience with prisons and incarceration may account for the views of many of these judges. Dutch authorities are convinced that prison is counterproductive but that short periods in prison may help focus on resocialization and community and family assistance for the convicted citizen. Emphasis is not placed on "the deterrent effect of prison or penal sanction."[26] This is a singularly profound view, since most of the world's legal and sanctioning systems are constructed around the theme that incarceration deters crime.

The Dutch have come to believe that punishment does not alter those situations or factors that lead to criminal behavior. Incarceration may simply be another device to stigmatize a person. This stigma is most often applied to street criminals from lower-class minority groups who do not have the money or means to avoid legal conviction and consequent penal sanctions.

The United States appropriates large sums of money to fight crime in the streets; the Dutch take a different approach. Most members of Parliament see a rise in crime rates from a different viewpoint from that of Americans. The Dutch leaders view a rise in crime as an indicator of social ills. Appropriations are directed toward examining and alleviating these social ills rather than to the symptoms of social ills such as crime.[27]

The Dutch culture is tolerant of divergent positions and respectful of individual liberties. They are also independent and strong believers in individualism. The influence of the Spanish, French, and Nazi invasions have only served to solidify this individualism and at the same time have increased the Netherlanders' sense of community responsibility. Social problems are viewed collectively, and while individualism is essential as a characteristic of the Dutch citizen, it does not mean isolation from his fellow citizen. This is in contrast to much of American thought. The Dutch have a feeling of mutual responsibility, and this may be one of the keys to their attitudes about incarceration and criminal resocialization.

Conclusion

I have presented a brief sketch of the police and judicial systems of The Netherlands and of the Dutch attitudes toward penal sanctions and incarceration, and I have made several suggestions as to why the system seems to be working well. It appears that shorter sentences, fines, and other alternatives have not caused a sharp increase in criminal activity in Holland. The root of the system appears to be the Dutch philosophy that contends that man is basically good and that his wrongdoing is to a great extent a problem of society. While I have not singled out an exemplary alternative program for criminals, the Parliament, the public prosecutor's discretionary powers, upheld by judges, and the people of Holland through their government and through community action have been greatly responsible for low incarceration rates. Finally, other nations are interested in improving their judicial systems, reducing the economic and social expenses of incarceration, and increasing judicial effectiveness. If this statement applies, then these nations should examine the Dutch system in much greater detail.

Notes

1. Hans V. Hofer, *Dutch Prison Population*, mimeographed, Scandinavian Research Council for Criminology (University of Stockholm, 1975), p. 4, reprinted with permission. See also Polly D. Smith et al., *How Holland Supports Its Low Incarceration Rate: The Lessons for Us*, mimeographed summary of The Netherlands Criminal Justice Investigative Seminar, (Philadelphia: American Foundation, 1978), p. 1, reprinted with permission; and Erik J. Besier, Statistical Yearbook of The Netherlands 1976 (The Hague: Central Bureau of Statistics). Reprinted with permission.

2. Jan Fiselier, Jan Fokkens, Lodewijk G. Moon, "Criminal Law, Criminality, and the Correctional System in the Netherlands." Paper presented at the First Monchengladbach Seminar on Comparative Criminal Justice in The Netherlands, 1977, used with permission from Jan W. Fokkens.

3. Ibid., p. 2.

4. Ibid., p. 13.

5. Ibid., p. 14.

6. Alfred Heijder, "The Recent Trend toward Reducing the Prison Population in The Netherlands," *International Journal of Offender Therapy and Comparative Criminology* 18 (1974):237, 238. Reprinted with permission.

7. L.H.C. Hulsman, "Criminal Justice in The Netherlands," *Delta, A Review of Arts, Life, and Thought in The Netherlands* 1 (1974):14.

8. Alfred Heijder, "Some Aspects of the Dutch Probation System: A Search for Identity," *International Journal of Offender Therapy and Comparative Ciminology* 17 (1973):107. Reprinted with permission.

9. Fiselier et al., "Criminal Law, Criminality, and the Correctional System," pp. 6, 7.

10. "Detention at the Government's Pleasure, T.B.R.," mimeographed Central Recruitment and Training Institute of the Prison Service and the Care of Criminal Psychopaths Service, Pomstation weg 34, The Hague, Netherlands, p. 1. (T.B.R. are initials for Dutch words meaning "Detention at the Government's Pleasure.")

11. Robert Tollemache, "Crisis Agencies and the Treatment of Offenders in The Netherlands," *Howard Journal of Penology and Crime Prevention*, 8 (1973):307.

12. Hofer, "Dutch Prison Population," p. 13.

13. Hulsman, "Criminal Justice in The Netherlands," p. 14.

14. W. Breukelaar et al., "Alternatives to Penal Measures of Imprisonment other than Suspended Sentences, Probation and Similar Measures; Notes on Legislation and Practice in The Netherlands," in *Report of the European Committee on Crime Problems, Subcommittee report No. XXVII* (Strasbourg, France, May 10, 1973,) p. 23. Reprinted with permission from W. Breukelaar, European Committee on Crime Problems and the Ministry of Justice, The Hague, Netherlands.

15. Ibid., p. 6.

16. Ibid., p. 7.

17. Fiselier et al., "Criminal Law, Criminality, and the Correctional System," pp. 32, 7.

18. Breukelaar, "Alternatives," pp. 24-26.

19. Fiselier et al., "Criminal Law, Criminality, and the Correctional System," p. 28.

20. Ibid., p. 29.

21. Ibid., p. 29.

22. Hofer, "Dutch Prison Population," p. 4.

23. Heijder, "The Recent Trend toward Reducing the Prison Population," p. 234.

24. Hulsman, "Criminal Justice in The Netherlands," p. 10.

25. Breukelaar, "Alternatives," pp. 27-28.

26. Holsman, "Criminal Justice in The Netherlands," pp. 11-12.

27. Ibid., p. 11.

References

Robert Tollmanche (see note 11) discusses several recently developed agencies and voluntary group programs as well as older, established programs for offenders in The Netherlands. Among these are the following:

Young Peoples Advice Centers.

Release, an organization which includes counseling programs and programs to promote changing social programs in The Netherlands.

Judicial Consultation Bureau (for the accused).

S.I.K.H. (initials of Dutch words designating a voluntary program to find and provide housing for persons in need, including paroled prisoners).

Plein 36, a help center to resolve immediate crisis which also may provide room and board for ten days or more.

Rehabilitation and social work agencies of The Netherlands, mainly the six major voluntary organizations.

De Corridor, a short-stay institutional camp which provides a short but sharp shock to the offender in a programmed communal activity mainly through guided group interaction activities. For a detailed discussion of the therapy program known as "Guided Group Interaction" see Lamar T. Empey and Maynard L. Erickson, *The Provo Experiment*," (Lexington, Mass.: Lexington Books, D.C. Heath and Co., 1972).

Psychiatric Observation Clinic, a clinic that takes a maximum of sixteen offenders for a period of eight weeks during their pretrial or remand period. It accepts only those charged with murder and more serious violent and sexual crimes.

T.B.R. (see note 10).

See also:

Detention at the Government's Pleasure: Treatment of Criminal Psychopaths in The Netherlands, mimeographed, The Hague: The Ministry of Justice, 1976, pp. 4-9, 11.

Prison Regulations and Extracts, Dutch Prison Services, Regulations Governing the Prison System Applicable to Prisoners in Houses of Detention, The Hague: Engels, 1975.

Smith, Polly D. "Mildness Breeds Mildness: A Look at the Dutch Penal System and Alternates," mimeographed (Philadelphia: American Foundation, May 6, 1977), pp. 2, 3, 4. Reprinted with permission.

The Netherlands Statistical Yearbooks, 1976, 1977, 1978, 1979, Section W: "Justice and Prisons." Pamphlets, Central Recruitment and Training Institute of the Dutch Prison Service. The Hague: Netherlands Prison System, 1977.

Punch, M. "Frontline Amsterdam: Police Work in the Inner City," *British Journal of Law and Society* 3 (1976):2.

Bianchi, Herman. "Social Control and Deviance in the Netherlands." In *Deviance and Control in Europe*, I. Bianchi, M. Simondi, I. Taylor, eds., New York: John Wiley and Sons, 1975.

Holsman, Louk. "The Penal System as a Social Problem [itself]." Paper presented at the Wingspread Conference on Rural Criminal Justice; *Issues and Answers* (May, 1974).

8 The Federal Republic of Germany

Hansjorg J. Albrecht

Alternatives to Prison in West-German Penal Law: Innovative and Alternative Sanctioning Strategies

If the terms *innovative* or *alternative* are used in connection with sanctioning measures, it is necessary to imply a traditional method of sanctioning as a background against which alternatives and innovations can be identified and tested.

In the criminal law systems of modern industrial states this traditional method is represented by the prison system and the penalty of prison sentence that, in the process of penal law reform, replaced the corporal punishment of the Middle Ages and, in the course of the eighteenth, nineteenth, and twentieth centuries, formed the main element in the penal system. Accordingly, I would like to evaluate these sanctioning measures that are not based on deprivation of liberty. Innovations or alternatives within the range of penal law sanctions can be defined according to two characteristics.

1. Alternatives can relate to a reduction of the punitive character, that is, less infliction of harm and a more humane treatment of offenders.
2. Alternatives can relate to the victim of the offense or to the society who, through the introduction of new sanctioning strategies, receives better protection in the sense of crime prevention, better treatment in the sense of reparation of incurred damage, and lower costs in funding the criminal justice and police system.

Traditional penal law ideology still connects the best possible social protection from delinquent behavior with the penalty of deprivation of liberty.

Hansjorg J. Albrecht is associated with the Max Planck Institut Für Ausländisches Und Internationales Strafrecht (Max Planck Institute for Foreign and International Criminal Law). Dr. Albrecht is located at the institute's headquarters in Freiburg im Breisgau, Federal Republic of Germany.

Therefore, alternative sanctions will be developed by way of reform and will be enforceable. The political and justice system and the public provide limits that do not necessarily correspond to scientifically expected or possible limits but are defined through mechanisms of conversions of diverse interests and politics and, therefore, also the law.

Political Limits and Possibilities of Alternative Sanctioning Measures

I shall attempt to outline the range, with regard to German penal law, in which alternative sanctioning measures can be developed. If we suppose that penal law sanctions by way of general or specific preventive effects supply protection, a model of the norm system becomes feasible which—if we consider a given range of punishable behavior—is built up in levels at which alternative sanctions, as they are understood here, occupy the middle area.

The first stage of punishable behavior could be totally withdrawn from penal law without affecting the envisioned protection of social and individual interests. This decriminalization strategy is not based on empirically won prognoses but rather on a consensus of the various social subsystems such as politics, science, and the mass media. In the Federal Republic of Germany such measures of decriminalization have been experienced, for example, in traffic and sexual penal law.[1]

At the opposite end, behavior considered to be serious or in need of deterrence (robbery, rape, murder) is assigned to traditional and severe sanctions.

In the middle range are offenses that are more suited to the development of alternative sanctioning measures. This is mainly behavior that is very widespread on the one hand, (mass offenses) and for which the judicial and the political systems, as well as the public, regard imprisonment and detention as unnecessary.

The view that severe punishment should be dispensed with arises from the specific status of the offender (juvenile offenders or delinquent children), and from the evaluation of the criminal behavior itself. This behavior can result in a drop in the need for punishment when it appears in the form of widespread acts such as shoplifting[2] or abortion, crimes where the victims are anonymous or nonexistent or where minimal damage occurs.

This decrease in the need for punishment, that is, the decline in political support for criminalization strategies, can also arise when the relevant penal norms are not seen by the public as being morally justifiable or when the administration of punishment becomes excessively inefficient. Since there is a limit to the integrative function of a penal norm, it can only exercise control over a minority of the population. The expansion of the list of criminal law offenses or the control of widespread acts through penal law measures raises questions about the effectiveness of penal law as an integration mechanism. If breaking a norm is no longer exceptional, then it is no longer apparent that a norm was broken. Instead it merely shows that lots of people behave in the same way. The resulting loss function can have an effect on penal norms as a whole but can also have a very obvious effect on individual sanctions. The function of imprisonment as an integrating factor can be diminished if it is used for acts committed on a massive scale or listed in the judicial register.[3]

In addition, the exercise of power, especially in the form of criminal law sanctions, is bound inevitably to the requirements of legitimacy.[4] Legitimacy today is represented by belief in statutes and rules that are formally correct and that have come into being in ways recognized as being legitimate.

Belief in the principle of legality and the ensuing legitimacy, however, presupposes a conception of the law and its enactment that includes equal treatment of all persons before the law.

If a certain widespread behavior can be punished only in a very small number of cases, as in traffic offenses, drunken driving, or petty theft, then the issue of equality of injustice[5] arises, since it becomes public knowledge that only very few such lawbreakers actually receive punishment.

When penal statutes thus lose their proper function and legitimacy, several remedial actions are possible: decriminalization and depenalization, downgrading sanctions by substitution of others that are considered lighter, or restrictions of imprisonment and detention to only a small portion of serious offenses.

The Legal System of Alternative Sanctions

In the area of mass delinquency, such as traffic and petty property offenses, the fine has been established as an alternative to imprisonment. A very important step in this direction was the enactment of the First Criminal Law Reform Statute (Erstes Strafrechtsreformgesetz) of 1969 in the Federal Republic of Germany. Thereby, the following provision (§ 14 StGB a.F., § 47 StGB n.F.) was introduced into the criminal code.

> A prison sentence of less than six months shall be imposed by the court only when special circumstances, arising from the act committed, or from the personality of the offender, show imprisonment to be essential in influencing the offender or in the protection of law and order.[6]

With this regulation the short prison term was declared *ultima ratio*, normally to be subsidiary to the fine. This limitation to discretion differentiates the West Germany penal law system from the normative systems of other countries. In Anglo-American systems the penalty of a fine usually is not limited to misdemeanors but can also be applied in felony cases.[7] In these legal systems, however, the penal judges are not obligated to work with a legally ordered priority of fines instead of short prison terms, as in the case in the West German penal system.

The introduction of this provision led to a reduction in the percentage of convicted persons sentenced to prison from 36.2 percent in 1968 to 16 percent in 1970 (see table 8-1). In this reduced portion fines were imposed and have since continued to play the leading role (four-fifths of all sentences) in penal law sanctions. Fines as an alternative could have an effect, however, only within a certain range that corresponds to prison terms of up to one year. When prison sentences of not less than one year are laid down by law, then fines can no longer be imposed. This means that in the case of felonies the concept of fines presently only may be used as an argument in any proposal to substitute or amend prison sentences of up to one year.

It was not only with the 1960s and with the reform of criminal statutes that fines became the most frequently applied criminal sanction. In 1931 Exner had already pointed out that fines had become the dominant sanction in German criminal law. He calculated that fines were applied at a rate of 25 percent in 1882 and that this rate rose to 70 percent by 1928.[8]

It is highly questionable whether the fine as an alternative to imprisonment can be developed and applied in the case of very serious felonies. In the period between 1965 and 1974 the proportion of punishments involving more than nine months of imprisonment (3 percent of all sanctions) stayed the same. This proportion of long prison terms proves to be an established structure that has not even changed since 1880, if the criminal statistics since that date are compared.[9] It would thus seem society's demand for punishment and protection allow no changes in sanctioning measures to penetrate the area of serious crime. From the fact that this proportion of prison sentences remains constant it can, however, be deduced that demands for punishment and protection through longer prison sentences are satisfied by quite a small proportion of total convictions. This means that a large area remains in which alternative and innovative penal measures can be developed.

Historically all changes in criminal sanctioning policy, which may include the use of a variety of alternatives, occurred within the old established criminal sanctioning structure especially with regards to dangerous criminals.

Table 8-1
Sentenced Persons by the Age of Twenty-one Years and Over, 1965-1974 (Federal Republic of Germany)
(in percentages)

	Fines	Imprisonment without Probation	Imprisonment with Probation	Up to 1 Month	1-6 Months	6-9 Months	9-12 Months	1-2 Months	2-5 Months	5-15 Months	Life	Total Offenses
1965	64.6 301,881	22.7 106,268	11.6 54,166	15.7	16.1		1.0	1.1	0.4	0.01	0.01	467,385
1966	61.7 307,143	25.1 125,206	12.3 61,425	18.2	16.7		1.0	1.1	0.4	0.01	0.01	497,866
1967	60.6 312,149	25.7 132,266	12.9 66,312	18.5	15.6	1.8	1.0	1.2	0.4	0.004	0.01	514,779
1968	63.0 361,074	23.1 132,609	13.1 75,036	17.0	15.0	1.8	0.9	1.1	0.4	0.01	0.01	572,629
1969	70.0 371,918	15.5 82,175	13.9 73,566	11.2	13.7	1.9	1.0	1.1	0.4	0.006	0.01	530,947
1970	83.9 464,818	7.5 41,276	8.5 46,972	1.4	8.7	2.6	1.6	1.1	0.5	0.07	0.01	553,692
1971	83.4 476,785	7.5 42,750	9.0 51,385	0.9	8.7	3.3	1.7	1.1	0.5	0.08	0.01	571,423
1972	83.5 494,399	7.0 41,503	9.3 55,148	0.7	8.8	3.4	1.7	1.1	0.5	0.09	0.01	591,719
1973	83.8 504,335	6.4 38,747	9.6 57,842	0.6	8.6	3.4	1.7	1.1	0.5	0.09	0.008	601,419
1974	82.4 494,266	6.8 40,863	10.6 63,863	0.6	9.3	3.8	2.0	1.1	0.5	0.1	0.01	599,368

Sources: Statistisches Bundesamt, *Bevölkerung und Kultur (Population and culture)*. Reihe 9. Rechtspflege (Wiesbaden, 1965-1974).

However, the opinions of judges and public prosecutors also indicate that the innovative potential of fines has become exhausted. This was shown in the empirical study about the attitudes of judges and public prosecutors toward fines and prison sentences.[10] Few of the judges and public prosecutors questioned wanted to see a further extension of the range covered by fines and two reasons for this opinion were mentioned most: (1) It was feared that the further expansion of fines would mean a weakening of general and specific deterrent effects; and (2) the assumption that fines extended to more serious branches would mean that they would be too high for people to pay. It can, therefore, be presumed that the judicial system does not see the possibility of extending the field covered by fines. The majority of judges is satisfied with the present range of the application of fines.[11]

In 1975 the total amount fine system changed to the day fine system by which a more just determination of the amount of the fine was expected. In the day fine system the amount of a fine is established in several steps. In the first step the guilt, or injustice of the act, is evaluated and defined in terms of justified days of imprisonment. In the second step the fine per day is calculated, taking into account the accused's income and financial situation. The monthly income minus eventual obligations is divided by the number of days in a month. In the third step the figures ascertained in steps 1 and 2 are multiplied, giving the total fine to be paid. The amount of the fine is related to the financial situation of the accused.

Other than fines and imprisonment with or without probation there were no further sanctioning possibilities for adults according to the penal code until the year 1975. In 1975 a fourth variation in sanctioning was introduced, the so-called caution with suspended fine (§ 59 StGB):

> If the court convicts a person of an offense incurring up to 180 daily fine-rations it can also issue a caution, fix the penalty and suspend enforcement of the said penalty, so long as
> 1. it can be expected that the offender, even without the effect of the penalty, will not commit further offenses,
> 2. there are special circumstances surrounding the act or the personality of the offender which indicate he should be spared from enforcement of sentence, and
> 3. the safe-guarding of law and order does not demand that he be sentenced.

While this sanction can be imposed by the court, a further alternative to conventional sanctioning methods was transferred to the public prosecutions office. It provided for the dismissal of a case with the imposition of forfeits and was introduced at the same time as the caution with suspended fine (§ 153 a StPO):

With the consent of the court concerned with instituting main trial proceedings, and with the consent of the accused person, the public prosecutions office may temporarily refrain from continuing with public prosecution procedure and, at the same time, impose upon the accused

1. reparation of the damages inflicted by the criminal act,
2. monetary contribution to a public institution or to the treasury,
3. public service of some kind, or
4. payment of a fixed amount of maintenance or alimony, providing that these forfeits and tasks are sufficient to assuage public interest in the prosecution of a minor offense.

I shall outline the development of these reactions by penal law and procedure to the divergences in the system of fining, caution with suspended fine, and the dismissal of the case with imposition of forfeits. In addition, I shall deal with the efficiency of fines and with the question of the willingness of the judicial system to use the other two sanctions.

Empirical studies so far have not been included within the range of evaluation and efficiency research. A somewhat disturbing picture that reflects an international research interest concentrated on deprivation of liberty and probation, even though in many countries the fine represents the quantitatively most significant penal control. Next to all criminological or penally thematicized ranges such as prison therapy, therapy out of prison, and diversion to name a few, there still lies a criminologically and sociologically unexplored area—the fine as a penal sanction.

Many advantages are ascribed to fines over imprisonment without probation, and of these I should like to mention only the most important:

1. The convicted person is not torn away from his family and social life.
2. The convicted person retains his profession and his place of work.
3. Because of the anonymous nature of fining, it is not so likely that one becomes stigmatized as a criminal.
4. In terms of cost analysis the fining is less expensive than institutional correction.

But these are only plausible-sounding ideas that lack empirical proof.

The Fine in Comparison with Imprisonment

First, I shall define objectives that enter into comparison between fine and imprisonment. I shall, however, confine myself to functional aspects and leave out humanitarian objectives. In connection with the decision whether a penal sanction is applicable or not, the humanitarian aspect is, however, indispensable in preventing the excesses of a purely functional approach.[12] In a study of the efficiency of fines the following objectives can be included:

Objective 1. Replacement of prison sentences by fines with consideration given to the specifically preventive effect of fines in terms of recidivism.

Objective 2. Reduction in the number of inmates in prisons.

Objective 3. No complicated enforcement of fines that would mean a mere shift in the work of the penal administration.

Objective 4. Individualized and thus fair methods of determining the amount of the fines, especially with the day-fine system.

In the area of traffic offenses, and particularly drunken driving, the question of the deterrent effects of fines initiated a discussion that was carried on for some time after enactment of the First Penal Reform Act.[13] Nevertheless, in the Federal Republic there are scarcely any empirical studies about the influence of penal law on behavior. The following presentation is therefore limited to the other areas mentioned before.

In one project records of criminal proceedings from 1972 ($N = 1,832$) and from 1975 ($N = 451$) concerning enforceable fines and prison sentences with or without probation were evaluated. After a five-year term the 1972 convictions were tested on their legal behavior. As a final step criminal judges, public prosecutors, and judicial officers in Baden-Württemberg were questioned about problems with the determination of the amount of fines and with the enforcement of fines.[14]

Facts Determining Punishment and Assessment of the Penalty

The essential principles for the assessment of a penalty are fixed in §§ 46, 47 StGB. They contain a list of social, biographic, and personality-related circumstances that may be used in the determination of punishment (within the limits stated in the legal code). One can, however, easily imagine that a penalty is not only determined according to normative but also according to pragmatic principles.[15] Information about the different admissable facts used to determine punishment is necessary for a systematic differentiation of the penalties that complex penal systems may create. This is especially true with the fine, because in the daily-rate system the public prosecutor and the judge must know the income and the pecuniary circumstances of the accused in order to determine the amount of the applicable fine. Today it is still believed that the fine discriminates against the poor and favors the rich. The introduction of the daily-rate system was intended to compensate for this structural weakness of the fine.[16]

The information gathered from the 1972 and 1975 convictions, however, is not very encouraging. In more than half of the cases the economic situation of the offender was not known, and thus the determination of the amount fined became an equation with an unknown quantity. As to the investigation of other facts, such as indebtedness, obligations of maintenance, assets, and similars, the record did not tell anything. To examine the question whether the current income of the offender, as far as it is known, really influences the amount of the fine or not, we compared the available data with the amounts fined. There was a close connection between both variables so that it can be considered empirically proved that a person's known income corresponds with a daily-rate fine according to the legal regulation. Nevertheless, this result should be interpreted with regard to the fragmentary information about the economic situation of the accused.

The various degrees of misdemeanors[17] or minor offenses may be distinguished clearly, but the structure of penalty determination in the field of minor and partly also of more serious offenses shows, that from the sanctional point there is probably an approximation to the fine proportioning prevailing in misdemeanor procedures. Nevertheless, the sanction is still not rated in terms of taxes. But it seems that the complicated structure of the day-fine calculation model does not meet the pragmatic requirements of a social control for highly frequent offenses.[18] A day-fine is a monetary fine as an alternate to imprisonment and is computed on the basis of the point that each day represents so many dollar equivalents based on the offender's income or previous income.

The Decision for the Fine or Imprisonment

With all offenses included in our study, the decision whether to impose a fine or to sentense a person to prison depended clearly on whether there had been a previous conviction. When a person had been convicted previously he was more likely to be sentenced to imprisonment. There was no difference in the particular type of offense as to the degree of damage done by the offender in any previous crime for which a conviction was acquired for offenses against property (theft and fraud) the amount of the damage plays a great part in the selection of the sanction, whereas with traffic offenses other determining factors in relation to sanctions could not be identified.

Problems of Enforcement

Before and also after the 1969 reform it was feared that pretrial detention and substitute imprisonment without probation[19] might leave a loophole for the continuance of a certain number of executed short-term prison sentences. However, an analysis of the payment of fines showed that just about 4 percent of persons fined actually served a substitute imprisonment. This rate does not increase when the few cases in which the fine is compensated through pretrial detention ($N = 4$) are added. This number could be alarming, especially with regard to the better cost-benefit relation attributed to the fine in comparison with imprisonment. The relation would change with a substantial increase of executed substitute prison sentences. Yet two-thirds of all fines are paid punctually, while in a further 20 percent of cases a reminder was sufficient inducement to pay.[20] It is surprising, however, to note that every tenth fine was paid only after the order of substitute imprisonment and the order to serve the substitute imprisonment was received. (Table 8-1 shows the enforcement procedure of fines.)

Persons required to serve a substitute imprisonment were shown to have a serious previous record compared with other offenders. In most of these cases the execution authorities had to establish the person's whereabouts. Interpretation of the results leads to the conclusion that the social and economic situation of the persons does not permit them to pay the fine and prevents them from developing defense strategies in order to avoid execution of punishment. For this group, one year after the sentence had become legally enforceable the major part of substitute prison sentences had already been carried out. In contrast, the enforcement procedures in the group of offenders who paid the fine after having received the order to serve the substitute imprisonment took much longer. This group has developed techniques such as requests for respite and applications for payment by installments that postpone the final decision. Persons serving a substitute prison sentence generally did not make applications for payment by installments or other methods and never got in touch with the competent authorities on their own accord. Their relationship with the judicial system may be defined by the term *deficient competence of action*.[21]

Preventive Effect of the Fine

The specifically preventive efficiency of the fine was judged by the criterion of legal behavior. That social integration or disintegration of the offender can be caused by punishment is not taken into consideration. Only the fact of reconviction is registered. The reconviction variable is an indicator of organizational behavior as well as an indicator of the behavior of the offender himself.

The group of offenders fined or sentenced to imprisonment with or without probation differed most significantly in terms of their previous conviction. This variable determines the use of the different sanctions applicable (and therefore the occurrence of the different types of sanction whose efficiency is to be compared). The sentencing proved to be very consistent, and only a small group of first offenders were sentenced to prison. (They were accused of very serious offenses, for example, great damage in case of theft or homicide caused by negligence.) A comparison of offenders with the same previous record who were fined or sentenced to prison with or without probation showed a much greater justification of the fine method, as only 16 percent of those fined were reconvicted whereas there was about 50 percent reconviction of persons sentenced to prison (with or without probation).

From the standpoint of the type of offense involved, traffic offenders without previous conviction were, as one could expect, much less often reconvicted than property offenders without previous conviction. Also in the group of offenders with previous conviction, traffic offenders showed less evidence of reconviction than property offenders in a comparable group, regardless of whether a fine or a prison sentence was imposed. No connection could be established between the amount of the fine and reconviction or seriousness of reconviction, regardless of the type of offense and the record of previous convictions.

A global view of the results shows that offenders with a long criminal career are most likely to be reconvicted. This refers to a vicious circle; the seriousness of previous conviction influences the severity of the sanction imposed, and the severity of the sanction influences the probability and the seriousness of reconviction. Another result justifies this argument: offenders with a serious previous record who receive only a fine for a petty offense, regardless of the type of offense, have the same rate of reconviction as offenders (comparable in several important aspects) who are sentenced to prison because of a more serious offense. This also means that punishment is determined according to the principle of proportionate sanctions, a principle that should never be neglected in the sentencing process.

From this we may safely conclude that fines are certainly not less effective than prison sentences with or without probation, though it seems impossible to prove the greater efficiency of the fine, judged by the criterion of legal behavior, by way of bivariate analysis.[22]

Caution with Suspension of Fine

The so-called caution with suspended fine was introduced into the German Penal Code on January 1, 1975. This form of sanction was intended to be used in extreme cases as an alternative to imposing a fine. With this sanction a caution is issued, and the fine sentence is suspended and held in reserve. This is less harsh treatment of the offender than fining, for no renouncement of economic advantages is necessary.

A study of the statistical frequency of implementation of this sanction during the first year after its introduction showed that it was rarely used. This may be due to the very constrictive framework of the ruling or to the attitude of the judges who, according to our interview results, could not get used to this form of sanctioning.

Reasons given by judges and prosecutors for not recommending the caution with suspended fine are

1. No other alternative is needed between the dismissal of a case with imposition of forfeits (§ 153 a StPO) and the fine, since these two institutions overlap and leave no room for a caution. Potential caution cases would thus be covered by § 153 a StPO.
2. The caution cannot easily be put into practice since it requires too much administrative effort; the dossier stays at court and must be kept there until the period of probation (from one to three years) is over. This imposes a greater burden on penal justice administration than imposing a fine.
3. Even if a penal judge wanted to use this ruling, he might not be able to because its legal framework is too limiting.
4. Such a ruling, whereby payments of a sum of money or other such forfeits are not imposed, is suitable for juvenile panel law, but not for adult penal law.

Judges and public prosecutors seem to consider criminal behavior on the part of adults to be more deserving of punishment than criminal behavior on the part of juveniles for whom they find it easier to waive sanctions.

The variable of judicial efficiency, if one can call it that, does not seem to play an important role here. In the evaluation or application of sanctions, the judiciary personnel seem, at least in part, to proceed not according to the criminal political goals that could be attained but rather according to how a measure can best be dealt with from the point of view of judicial or court efficiency. In other words the fastest method to clear the dossier is sought.

This is a consequence of the need to integrate the normative system into the requirements of functional penal procedure in order to avoid overload problems.

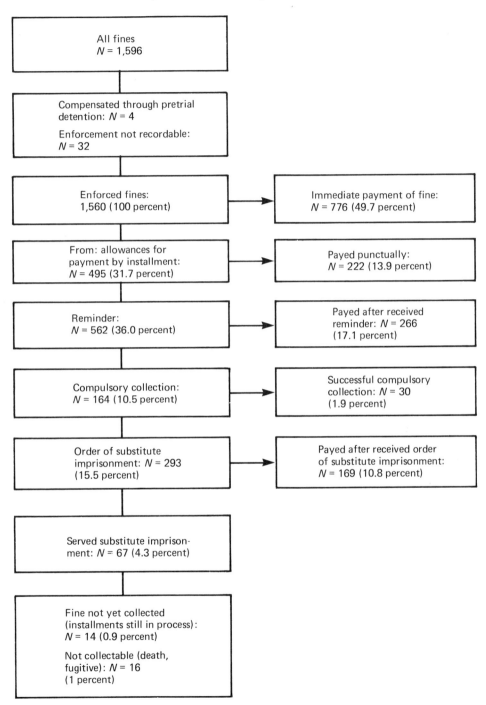

Figure 8-1 System of Fines, Federal Republic of Germany

Dismissal of a Case with Imposition of Forfeits

The variables *work effort involved* and *business procedure* were of some significance in the application of § 153 a StPO by the public prosecutor's office, at least shortly after its introduction. Implementation procedure is very time- and energy-consuming, since

1. a writ has to be sent to the court requesting consent to the dismissal of the case;
2. the consent of the accused has to be obtained;
3. the court then has to be informed of this consent;
4. the payment of money or other forfeits imposed has to be checked on; and
5. the case is finally dismissed only after payments and forfeits have been made.

As a contrast to this, it is easier for the public prosecutor to deal with the case if he moves for a fine by way of written penal order. This necessitates completing a form rather than the three writs required in the case of § 153 a StPO.

For the offender, application of § 153 a StPO means that he will not be registered as a convicted person and that the dismissal cannot be used against him in subsequent criminal law proceedings.

Several forfeits are envisaged by the ruling of § 153 a StPO, but of these the most important is a money forfeit, that is, the payment of a certain amount to the state or some public institution. From the material side, dismissal of a case with money forfeit is like a fine. Regarded politically, § 153 a StPO can be seen rather as a diversion strategy to avoid having to put the accused through the whole criminal judicial process because of one minor misdemeanor, while at the same time not having to do without material atonement by the accused.

The range in which § 153 a StPO can be applied is limited mainly to minor property offenses (up to a limit of 100 DM damage) and traffic offenses involving, for the most part, bodily harm through negligence in the case of minor injuries to the victim.

At the present time, no statistical surveys of the frequency of application of § 153 a StPO exist, so that for evaluation one has to rely on judiciary perceptions. At the beginning application of § 153 a StPO seemed to be limited because of the administrative burdens. The public prosecutors rarely made any use of this institution. A statement made by the Ministry of Justice of Baden-Württemberg and sent to individual public prosecution offices commented as follows:

The changes introduced on January 1, 1975, into the penal code and with regard to penal procedure are intended to achieve decriminalization in the petty crimes area and thus relieve the judicial system and speed up penal procedures. Proceedings according to § 153 a StPO are especially designed to meet these ends but this is still not applied often enough, mainly because of its complicated legal form. We do not fail to appreciate that case dismissals according to § 153 a StPO very often mean no lightening of the workload for the public prosecutors themselves. This cannot, however, be the main decisive factor.[23]

And further:

Since cases of minor guilt are relatively frequent, the procedure of § 153 a StPO can not be employed only in exceptional circumstances, as was the practice up to now in several public prosecution offices.

Therefore, the Ministry of Justice's guidelines on the use of § 153 a StPO state that it should be applied in all cases of petty property offenses (with damage less than 50 DM). This was followed by increased use of the ruling. In contrast to the caution with suspended fine, where the judge decides whether or not to implement it, such a central order or recommendation is possible in the case of § 153 a StPO since the public prosecution offices are organized according to a hierarchical system in which orders given by executives as to petition practice regarding certain measures that must be followed. The judges, on the other hand, can only be requested by the legislator to make more frequent use of certain sanctions.

Conclusion

Looking at the three alternatives to prison sentences that have been developed in the German penal law system within the last years or decades—fines, caution with suspended fine, and the dismissal of the case with imposition of forfeits—one can observe that although fines have become fully established (the penal judiciary system applies this sanction whenever practical and allowed by the legal range or limits), the caution with the suspended fine is rarely used. Penal judges have many reservations about the suspended fine which severely constrict the innovative potential that suspended-fine-with-caution-to-the-offender possesses in the penal sanctions area.

Section 153 a StPO, which can be called a diversion strategy, has asserted itself as an alternative to conventional criminal sanctions which also includes fines in these cases. Under the motto of destigmatization it offers the possibility of avoiding an official criminal record, thus preventing the harmful effects of traditional sanctioning measures. This seems to be one of the most important reforms, since a criminal record plays a very significant part in the selection of a certain penal sanction to be imposed upon a criminal who commits another criminal act and is found guilty. The decision not to put the case on record (that is, the first criminal act of which the offender has been found guilty) sets the course to be followed and can determine whether a criminal career has begun. The suspended fine is a useful tool in the network of innovative alternatives only when some other action that replaces the fine as a punitive sanction is utilized in some sort of resocialization effort. This is especially important when this alternative, whatever it is, proves to be more useful than the fine itself in preventing a return to criminal activity by the offender. Research must indicate to penal judges that keeping an offender's case relatively clean by the use of such mild sanctions as fines instead of incarceration or cautions instead of fines does, in fact, serve to reduce repeat offenses. Nevertheless, with or without conclusive research findings, the pattern of penal sanctioning in the Federal Republic of Germany is beginning to acquire a new design. The following points may help to summarize it:

1. Considerable room is left to develop alternative sanctioning strategies in West Germany, especially considering the historic development of fines in relation to prison sentences.
2. Fines, nevertheless, have become an established alternative to incarceration in the Federal Republic of Germany.
3. The decision on which to base penal sanctions within the range of minor delinquency has not been researched enough and there is little information on which a judge may base sanctioning policy. More information is needed to assist the penal judiciary to develop an appropriate approach in this area. This area of sanctioning takes a central position between complex penal procedures in the cases of serious offenses and the tax model of petty misdemeanors.
4. A regular cost-efficiency analysis of the fine in comparison with imprisonment could not be feasibly performed. We do know, however, from our experiences with infrequent enforcement of sutstitute imprisonment, that the fine measured with the criterion of the practicality of enforced collection relieved the penal sanction enforcement system of penal sanctions, that is, incarceration.
5. Therefore the concern that short-term imprisonment should be reinstated by way of enforced substitute imprisonment is not justified.
6. The analysis of legal behavior distinctly showed that sanctions within a certain behavioral or offense range (minor and intermediate delinquency) are interchangeable with regard to their effect on recidivism. That

is, within certain ranges of criminal behavior, one penal sanction or alternative sanction was as useful as another to reduce recidivism.

7. Considerable areas of use are indicated for certain penal sanctioning laws such as § 153 a StPO when one considers that the offenses for which it can be applied (such as minor property offenses with less than 100 DM—about $50.00—damage amount to almost 50 percent of all convictions for theft, and that theft represents the major portion of so-called classic criminaltiy. Within this range § 153 a StPO has established itself as an alternative to the fine.

8. Caution with a suspended fine, introduced as an alternative to the fine in certain exceptional cases, could not assert itself, since judicial practice could envisage no need for any alternative sanction in the area between the sanctions outlined in § 153 a StPO and sentence to a fine.

This discussion of a system of fines and caution sanctions used in West Germany suggests that the fine system can be a feasible substitute or alternative for harsher sanctions including incarceration. As Germany enters into the 1980s with this system of sanctions on its law books, the possibility exists of developing a wider range of treatment modalities for offenders that may serve as alternatives to prison. Presently, however, there appears to be a concern by the general public as well as specific groups in West Germany that leniency of penal sanctions is of no use in either deterring crime or treating criminals. Terrorism, drug abuse, and violent criminal acts brought to the public's attention have dampened the cause for alternatives to prison and created an increased demand for harsher penalties. There remains, nevertheless, a significant number of people and a number of significant persons supportive of the concept of alternatives and of prisons exemplified by this comment. ". . .prisons must be preserved as a treatment alternative of the last resort."[24]

Thus there is a high probability that West Germany will broaden its concept of prison alternatives modeled after other European, particularly northern European nations. This demand for reformation of antiquated approaches to penal sanctioning in the name of conservatism or of vindictiveness will not be so powerful in the future as to sweep aside programs or alternatives that, by scientific research, prove as effective as incarceration. The demand that prisons be the last resort as a treatment device for offenders takes its place among the criticisms of imprisonment and prisons, the "giant errors"[25] of human efforts to solve social and individual conflicts. I have tried to show that less repression does not necessarily mean a defenseless society. Critical criminology should be operated in order to show further possibilities of escaping the dialectic process of regressive action and reaction attached to crime and punishment as a structural element. We must strive to do everything possible to avoid a "pendulum" approach to crime and penal sanctioning, from a humanistic approach to a vengeful approach. We must attempt to correct criminal behavior in a more satisfactory way than has been developed to date. The appropriate and expanded use of fine system is but one approach; there are many more to be unveiled in progressive society in the future.

Notes

1. Parts of the penal traffic law were decriminalized through the enactment of regulations of minor offenses against public order (Gestz Uber Ordnungswidrigkeiten) a Bill numbered BGBI.I, 481 and passed May 24, 1968, as well as the enactment of the 4th Statute to the Penal Law Reform (4th Gesetz zur Reform des Strafrech, BGBI.I, 1725, passed November 27, 1973). This is a revision of the sexual penal laws for moral-offenses, (Sittlichkeitsdelikte) suggesting that moral offenses should no longer be punishable because of immorality; the punishability should be limited to such cases in which rational menace (that is, socially endangering) took place.

2. Deutscher Juristentag, *Sanktionen für Kleinkriminalitat* [Sanctions for Petty Criminality] (Munich, 1976). Includes a detailed discussion of petty property criminality in West Germany.

3. H. Popitz, *Uber die Praventivwirkung des Nichtwissens* [On the Deterrent Effect of Being Unaware] (Tubingen: University of Tubingen, F.R. Germany, 1968). See especially Popitz' comments about penal sanctioning: "If the norm is no longer punished, or not often enough, then it loses its bite; . . .if the norm is always having to bite, its bite loses its sharpness. However, not only does the punishment lose its effect when the neighbors are punished right and left [indiscriminately] but it also becomes very obvious, in a very direct way, that the neighbor does not conform to the legal norm, either." (p. 16.)

4. Max Weber, *Wirtschaft und Gesellschaft* [Economy and Society] (Cologne, Berlin, 1964). See M. Weber, *Economy and Society* (New York: Bedminster Press, 1968).

5. G. Kaiser, *Strategien und Prozesse stratfrechtlicher sozialkontrolle, [Strategies and Processes of Penal Law Social control] (Frankfurt an Main, F.R. Germany, 1972) pp. 71-99, p. 56. Also see G. Kaiser, "Recent Developments in German Penal Policy," International Journal of Criminology and Penology* 4, 2 (May 1976):193-206.

6. Erstes Strafrechtsreformgesetz [First Penal Law Reform Statute], (Bonn, F.R. Germany: Government Printer, June 25, 1969).

7. B. Huber, "Die Geldstrafe in England und Wales" [The Fine in England and Wales], in H.H. Jescheck and G. Grebing, eds., *Die*

Geldstrafe im Deutschen und Ausländisch en Recht, [The Fine within the German and Foreign Law], (Baden-Baden, F.R. Germany, 1978), pp. 341, 395.

8. F. Exner, *Studien Uber die Strafzumessungspraxis der Deutschen Gerichte*, [Studies of the Penal Measures Practice in German Courts], (Leipzig, F.R. Germany, 1931).

9. A. Blumstein and J. Cohen, "A Theory of the Stability of Punishment," *Journal of Criminal Law and Criminology* 64 (1973):204.

10. This study was carried out by staff members of the Criminal Research Unit, Max Planck Institute, Freiburg, F.R. Germany. Of those surveyed, only 5 percent of the judges and public prosecutors interviewed criticized the fine in favor of prison sentencing or claimed that there was any loss of deterrence in the use of the fine as a sanction.

11. See note 10; 95 percent of those surveyed agreed.

12. N. Walker, *Sentencing in a Rational Society* (New York: Basic Books, 1969), especially p.3ff.

13. H. Janiszewski, "Bietet unser Strafrecht noch ausreichende Moglichkeiten zur Wiksamen Bekampfung der Alkoholdelikte im Strassenverkehr?" [Does Our Penal Law Yet Supply Sufficient Possibilities for an Effective Attack of Alcohol Offenses in Traffic?] Blutalkohol 8, (1971): 179-206, especially 179. "Of the concern which, for many, results from the fact that on the one hand since about the beginning of 1970, we were alarmed about a partly considerable increase in alcohol offenses while, on the other hand, at about the same time, the legislators within the range of penal law reform instituted regulations which, by quite a few people, is perceived as a softening of sanction possibilities or, as it was often called, as an introduction of a 'soft wave' " (p. 179).

14. The study was limited to Baden-Württemberg in West Germany and included the offenses of traffic [violations], property, [theft or damage], physical injury, and certain tax rule infractions (that is, Nebenstrafrecht).

15. Regarding the relation and the effect of normative and pragmatic action control, see the following: E. Blankenburg, K. Sessar and W. Steffen, *Die Stattsanwaltschaft im Prozee strafrechtlicher Sozialkontrolle* [The Prosecutor's Office Within the Process of Penal Law Social Control], (Berlin, 1978) 119-143.

16. D.A. Westen, "Fines, Imprisonment and the Poor: 'Thirty Dollars or Thirty Days' " *California Law Review* 57 (1969):778, 821. See also: R.G. Fox, "The Fine, Restitution and Reparation as Effective Sentencing Measures," and "Modern Developments in Sentencing" *in Australian Institute of Criminology* (Canberra, 1974):217-238. The adjustment of the fine amount to the ability of the offender to pay presents the biggest problem (p. 221).

17. Petty Misdemeanors (Ordnungswidrigkeiten), mainly traffic violations, are prosecuted by local administrative offices, and they are sanctioned with so-called penance money, the amount of which is regulated by the "Penance Money Catalogue" (Bussgeldkatalog). A West German traffic violator who receives a ticket for a minor traffic law infraction, for example, can go to the local bank in his own community or in any other community and pay the fine. The bank clerk or teller will stamp the ticket paid.

18. Here, for example, I am thinking of the differentiated jurisdiction in regard to the question, "What obligations have to be considered (by the judge and court) while calculating the amount of the day fine?" See: H.H. Jescheck and G. Grebing, eds., *Die Gelstrafe im Deutschen und ausländischen Recht* [The Fine Within the German and Foreign Law], (Baden-Baden, F.R. Germany, 1978), pp. 13-164, especially 98ff., 111ff., Regarding the written penal order, Schmitt created the clear phrase "Penal procedure second class"; see R. Schmitt, "Das Strafverfahren 2. Klass" [*Penal Procedure Second Class*] Public law ZStW 89 (1977), pp. 639-648.

19. Those who must serve a substitute prison sentence can be paroled only after having served two-thirds of the sentence according to the legal system statutes.

20. Similar results were found by C. Latham, "Enforcement of Fines," *Criminal Law Review* (London, 1973):552-559; and P. Loftley, "A Survey of Fine Enforcement," *Criminal Law Review* (London, 1973).

21. E. Dreher, *Strafgesetzbuch* [Penal Code] (Bavaria, Munich, F.R. Germany 1978), especially footnote 2 concerning public law § StGB; in regard to the theoretic construction of "want of competence of action. See also: R. Bohnsack, *Handlungskompetenz und Jugendkriminalitat* [Competence of Action and Juvenile Criminality] (Berlin: Neuwied and Co., 1973); W. Steffen, *Analyse polizeilicher Ermittlungstatigkeit aus der Sicht des spateren Strafverfahrens* [Analysis of Investigational Police Activity from the viewpoint of Subsequent Legal Proceedings] (Wiesbaden, F.R. Germany 1976), pp. 201-202. These works relate to juveniles and their limited ability to cope with certain social situations with the aim of enforcing their own acting concepts and to be able to 'see through' certain definitions and consequences of control instances. They, therefore, get caught more easily as well as indicted [more often] than adults. The ability to cope with situations that require on the one hand the knowledge of normative regulations and their consequences and, on the other hand, the possibilities to guide and intervene in concrete interactions in order to be able to have a voice in the matter is being requested for adult penal procedures as well as for the process of the collection of fines. The court has the chance during main proceedings with compensatory intents to inform the convicted person about payment of fine by installment, how to request for this procedure, and so on. In the case of a written penal order, however, it is required that

the sentenced person himself take the initiative. Regarding problems of the ability to observe rights, see also; H. Giehring, "Rechte des Beschuldigten, Handlungskompetenz und kompensatorische Strafverfolgung" [Rights of the Accused, Competence of Action, and Compensatory Penal Prosecution], in W. Hessemer and K. Luderssen, eds., *Socialwissenschaften im Studium des Rechts* [Social Science within the Study of the Law] 1 (Munich, 1978), pp. 281, 314. Concerning legal-political problems, see also; G. Baumgartl, *"Zugang zum Gericht für Unterpriviligierte: Rechtshilfe und Rechtsberatung"* [Entrance to Court for the Underprivileged: Legal Help and Legal Counsel] *Humane Justiz 1 (1977): 17-28.* S.L. Albrecht, and M. Green, *"Cognitive Barriers to Equal Justice before the Law," 14 Journal of Research in Crime and Delinquency* (1977): 206-221. Especially the comment that "Our preliminary analysis suggests the presence of a very basic lack of knowledge of important legal and constitutional rights among our population. This is especially true of persons characterized as having lower social economic backgrounds in terms of education and income" (p.218).

22. Because of the operationalization of legal behavior by way of the entrances in the Federal Central register, naturally, next to the dimension "behavior of the proband" is recorded the dimension, "behavior of instances."

23. S.L. Albrecht, and M. Greene, "Cognitive Barriers to Equal Justice before the Law," 14 *Journal of Research in Crime and Delinquency* (1977): 206-221.

24. C.R. Dodge, "A Nation without Prisons: Dream or Reality," in C.R. Dodge, *A Nation without Prisons* (Lexington, Mass., Lexington Books, D.C. Heath and Co., 1975), pp. 233-249, especially p. 247.

25. E. Schmidt, *Zuchthauser und Gefangnisse* [Penitentiaries and Prisons] (Gottingen, F.R. Germany, 1960).

9 Japan

Japan has developed a rather sophisticated and modern prison system and has recently expanded its alternative programs. Legislation known as the *Kangokusoku,* or prison rules, were developed in 1872. In this period there were two types of prisons. One was under the jurisdiction of the central government, and the other was managed under local municipal control. The Japanese Ministry of Justice supervised both types of prisons as a central administration agency. In 1874 prison administration and supervision were placed in the hands of the Ministry of Home Affairs; in 1903 they were placed under the jurisdiction of the Ministry of Justice and have remained there ever since. In 1949 the system was reorganized into the Correction and Rehabilitation Bureau, and at this time juvenile training schools and juvenile classification centers became a part of the network. Additional reorganization came in 1952 and in 1958 when the women's guidance homes were established. Japan has 7 central detention homes and 107 smaller units. It also has 57 prisons with 9 additional branches. There are 62 juvenile training schools, including 2 branches. There are 52 juvenile classification centers and 3 women's guidance homes in Japan. While the actual capacity of Japan's detention houses, prisons and juvenile prisons is over sixty-three thousand, the actual number of prisoners amounts to about fifty thousand.[1] Juvenile training schools have a capacity of about ten thousand but at present house only about four thousand. Juvenile classification homes have a capacity of twenty-six hundred but at present hold only about nine hundred. While crime caused by the younger generation is on the increase, its rate is somewhat less than in other countries especially in the Western world. In addition, Japan is taking steps to improve the alternative approaches. The Ministry of Justice in Japan has become somewhat westernized, and has been adopting practices and administrative procedures somewhat similar to those of U.S. police, courts and other phases of western systems of justice. Japan is concerned about any increase in its crime rates. In 1978, however, the crime rate in Japan was generally decreasing. Japan's theft, fraud, embezzlement, dealing in stolen property, and other property crimes amounted to only 73 percent of the 1948 total while homicide and murder amounted to only 31 percent of the 1948 figure. Sex offenses had also dropped from slightly over fifteen thousand in 1967 to about eleven thousand in 1974. In contrast to the United States, Japan has an enviable record.

We can only attribute this exemplary improvement in the crime picture to the crime preventive measures of the Japanese. With great public backing Japan has retained its concept of small neighborhood units even while it grew into an extremely complex society of considerable industrial magnitude. This subdivision has allowed Japan to retain the traditional artifacts that seem to emerge as the key to the prevention of crime. These are, very briefly, the neighborhood walking policeman, the family group concept, community policing with everybody involved, confidence in local government, confidence in the court and police systems and a network of communication between various agencies and the public. The Japanese people have a philosophy that permits them to retain the principle of obedience to others and trust in this obedient interaction. Most people have a sense of belonging in Japan because of their cultural ideas. Extreme individuality is frowned on, and this concept of the Japanese culture reduces misbehavior, deviancy and crime, in that the more group-oriented a society is, the less the chances for deviance. Obedience to authority is not a state control, as it was under Generalissimo Franco. The Japanese are free and unhampered in the legal sense of obedience. Japanese law imposes fewer controls than American law. Socially, however, the Japanese are less free and are deeply interested in the behavior of their family members, neighbors, and friends. The behavior of others is looked on as either contributing to or detracting from close family relationships. The Japanese people are reminded, in many ways, which course they are to follow. Freedom-loving Americans may see these restrictions as infringements on the individualistic way of life. But the positive side to the coin is that there is less anomie in Japan. As crowded as Japan is, it does not live the life of impersonal urbanism. Densely crowded Tokyo, for example, has small neighborhoods with all the attributes of the family concept in living. This community cohesion leaves little room for feelings of isolation or alienation. Most Japanese have a purpose in life and have a good feeling about direction and support. Apparently the Japanese culture prevents crime to a much greater extent than the millions of dollars spent by the United States to prevent crime.

Even Japan's prisons carry over the concept of the subunit family. That is, each small group of prisoners is allotted radios, televisions, games, a library of a few books, and a daily newspaper. These diversions and a program in which small groups of prisoners work together, participate in group discussion, meditation, religious ceremony, and so on appears to be a way of preserving the family or neighborhood idea of close interrelationships as a system of social control.

Noninstitutional Treatment of Offenders

Noninstitutional care of criminal offenders in Japan began recently with the enactment by the Japanese Diet beginning in 1949, of several laws that deal with noncustodial care:

1. The Offenders Rehabilitation Law (1949) was designed to provide principles and procedures for the organization of juvenile probation as well as juvenile and adult parole.
2. The Law for Probationary Supervision of Persons under Suspension of Execution of Sentence (1954) provided for adult probation.
3. The Law for Aftercare of Discharged Offenders (1950) prescribes categories of criminal offenders who may be qualified to apply for rehabilitation aid. This law was also the first legislative act that created principles and procedures for opening and administering halfway houses managed by voluntary organizations to accommodate offenders not placed in prison. It also gives the government the authority to provide aftercare for discharged offenders who voluntarily seek help.
4. The Volunteer Probation Officer Law (1950) developed from such programs as the Volunteer Probation Officer's Program, established by the U.S. Boulder County Juvenile Court in Colorado in 1963, which has now spread to many nations. The law in Japan, consisting of some fourteen articles, describes the qualifications, selection and duties, of the volunteer probation officer who acts as a government agent in the rehabilitation service.
5. The Amnesty Law (1947), with its fifteen articles, describes the kinds of effects a variety of pardons should have for offenders. It includes definitions of general amnesty, special amnesty, commutation of sentence, remission or pardon of execution, and restoration of rights. This law is probably Japan's best support for alternative programs placed under legal definition. It appears to be ushering in the age of alternatives to prison in Japan.

Crime Prevention as a Legitimate Alternative

In chapter 7 I discussed the nature of the community programs in The Netherlands and suggested that these programs help prevent criminal activity. Japan has an approach that appears to approach this community care concept in an even more meaningful way. For this reason these activities will be described as alternatives. Japan's efforts to prevent crime and delinquency may generally be classified into two types. First, an effort is made to prevent illegal conduct through an approach to the individual who has been identified as prone to deviance. Members of several Japanese neighborhood groups are organized to study the problems and to solve them by working with the individuals. The members of these groups cooperate with local probation officers in helping to befriend predelinquents. Referrals may come from the family court, for example, after a sudden and unexpected death of father or mother in which trauma may be registered by delinquent acts, from Child Guidance Centers, or from the school. Often it is the parents who seek help from members of these groups. The probation offices in Japan sponsor a movement each year which, literally translated, means the movement to enlighten the society.[2] The general purpose of these yearly campaigns is to get people interested in preventing crime and in volunteering to participate in these programs to help predelinquents.

These two efforts, the individual approach with predelinquents and the community campaigns made by the probation department, aim to obtain more cooperation from the family and the individual in helping youths in trouble. As a result of these programs a substantial number of Japanese citizens are involved in volunteer work with delinquents, predelinquents, and adult offenders. Like other nations, Japan has its share of prejudice and resentment toward law offenders. The Crime Prevention Campaign and other public educational programs attempt to alleviate this problem by involving citizens. Great effort is made to convince people to accept and help predelinquents, delinquents, and convicted offenders. Emphasis is continually placed on the development of programs in the local neighborhood. Japan, like the Netherlands, spends a good deal of money and television, and radio time on this effort. Over 400 programs were aired on television in Japan in one year, 273 programs were aired over the radio, and some 3,517 reports were published in Japanese newspapers in the same year. Some 531,000 posters concerned with these preventive programs were posted during one year.[3]

Prison Pardons

The pardon in Japan has existed in the form of an exclusive right of the emperor, but in 1949 the pardon became an official part of the program for corrections and rehabilitation. It was at this time that the Offender's Rehabilitation Law was enacted. Since this time the pardon has become an alternative to imprisonment and has been used more widely.

There are two classes of pardons in Japan. One is the general pardon, which is provided in the form of a cabinet-level ordinance in commemoration of some occasion of national significance. The ordinance, when issued, classifies offenders in terms of the offense, length of offense, and other offender descriptions. Every offender falling within these general classifications is granted pardon. The general pardon may be compared with the American amnesty programs following the Vietnam War in which special pardons were given to certain persons who defied the American government (draft evaders, for example). To date Japan has issued only eight general pardon ordinances.

The individual pardon is the second type of pardon and is the more significant in terms of alternatives for criminal offenders. A person who is placed on probation, for example, may receive a pardon from further supervision after a certain period of time. Pardons, in these cases, are the only means by which the offender may be released from justice department control. Pardons also include special amnesty and commutation of sentence. An important part of the pardon system of Japan is the restoration of civil rights to the offender. A person who has completed a specified prison sentence may have his civil rights restored, including access to certain occupations and the right to vote. This restoration of rights help relieve the stigma of prison both socially and psychologically. After release from the jurisdiction of the justice department, such as in an act of prison release, pardon, or commutation of sentence, the criminal records are destroyed after several years if there are no further convictions. At one time Japanese prison records restricted offenders from becoming medical practitioners, school teachers, lawyers, real estate dealers, and many other occupations, this is no longer the case except when the crime involves drug abuse or is of a heinous nature (murder, rape, etc.).

Pardons may be executed through probation and parole departments, or they may be developed by the warden of a prison. They may also be applied for by the public prosecutor, who has authority to initiate the procedure of pardon for an offender who has been sentenced to a fine or a sentence, and it is primarily in this case that the pardon truly serves as an alternative.[4]

The Aftercare Program

While the Japanese aftercare program cannot be called an alternative, it is unique. Many other countries discharge a person from prison with little concern for his welfare, but the Japanese are concerned for the welfare of the ex-convict. The Japanese have concluded that the absence of adequate concern and support for ex-offenders may easily jeopardize his chances of remaining within the law and may endanger society as well. With this in mind, Japan has passed the Law for Aftercare of Discharged Offenders, which states that it is the responsibility of the state to aid offenders in their efforts at resocialization. The law affects the following types of persons:

1. Any person who has been released without parole supervision.
2. Any person who has received a suspended sentence without supervision or whose suspended sentence with probation has not begun.
3. Any offender whose parole has ended.
4. Any person who has been released because prosecution was suspended or whose sentence was remitted.

This special aid is usually limited to six months. Suspects or defendants who have not been detained are not officially entitled to this type of aid. Discharged prisoners who apply for the aid five months after release may expect this aftercare service only for the balance of their eligibility, which would be one month. The service is also given only to offenders and ex-offenders who officially apply for it through the probation office. Each case is screened in order to provide aid according to the urgency and type of need and the person's willingness to try to help himself.

The types of aid provided in this program include provision of meals, clothing, medical care, recreation, travel fare, lodging, and referral to public agencies for employment and welfare assistance. The probation department may give some of this aid or enlist the aid of other agencies. When lodging is necessary, the probation officer generally refers the case to a halfway house managed by voluntary organizations. Expenses for lodging and board are reimbursed from the national budget. In the halfway house counseling, employment services, and other help are given. Japan has been expanding its system of halfway houses, and at present it is estimated that some ten thousand persons coming into contact with the law may have been helped by them in any one year.

Probation

Japan has made considerable use of its probationary powers to provide the means for alternatives to incarceration. The probation department operates very much like the probation departments in other countries. There are two types of probation. One is for juveniles and the other is for adults. In some cases an adult may fall under the juvenile category and a juvenile may be handled with the stipulations of adult parole. Adult probation is used in Japan as a complementary measure to a suspended sentence. Cases to receive probationary services are selected from offenders eligible for suspended sentences. Eligibility for this type of probation consists of these three requirements:

1. The sentence must be under three years, or the fine must be less than 200,000 yen.
2. The offender must not have been sentenced to imprisonment in the previous five years.
3. The offense being considered, must not have been committed during a probation period previously authorized by the court.[5]

In Japan probation may be given even for the most serious offenses, including murder, if some special circumstances justify this action. Probation is rarely applied in connection with a fine. In 1972 Japan had about seventy-five thousand convictions resulting in imprisonment, while suspended sentences accounted for forty-five thousand cases. Probation with a probation order accounted for seven thousand of these forty-five thousand cases. The balance of the suspended sentences were accounted for without probation orders. Of some fifty-five thousand probationers accounted for in 1972 only about forty-seven hundred had their probation revoked. Since probation may be considered an alternative to imprisonment, this record is excellent; the country probably saved several millions of dollars in costs associated with imprisonment. In Japan there are fifty central probation offices and twenty-one branches.[6] About eight hundred probation officers are employed, including administrative officers. Case loads per officer are extremely high. About 270 probationers are assigned each probation officer. This alone would practically nullify any services the officer could provide. The volunteer probation officer in Japan, instead of simply being a record keeper provides much of the services that offenders need.

The Volunteer Probation Officer

After Japan reorganized its noninstitutional treatment system in 1949 the trust in volunteers to serve the rehabilitation program was manifested by the development of the Volunteer Probation Officer Program. By 1950 some fifty thousand Japanese were involved in the program.[7] The activities of the volunteer probation officer cover a wide spectrum of services for the probationer and include assistance in finding accommodations, admission to halfway houses, assistance in the application for welfare, visitation to homes of offenders, assistance to the offender's family, and collaboration with public and private organizations to find a variety of resources to assist the probationer in resocializing himself. The volunteer probation officer is very active in public programs to eradicate poor housing and to improve crime-prone run-down neighborhoods.

The volunteer probation officer is a nonpermanent official of the Japanese National Government and is entitled to certain benefits such as insurance against bodily injury and incidental expenses incurred by him in working as a volunteer. The volunteer is not paid, but when he takes time off from a job in order to participate in a training program, some compensation is made for this loss of salary. Since the main benefit derived from the job is helping others, volunteer probation officers tend to be dedicated and gratified by their work. Public recognition of the volunteer and meritorious service awards may provide some incentive, since these give a degree of social prestige to the volunteer probation officer. Volunteer probation officers are carefully selected. They must be financially stable, of good health, enthusiastic, and have a background of work and social life that demonstrates an ability to get things accomplished. Of the fifty thousand volunteer probation officers some, 17 percent are female. Ages of volunteer probation officers tend to be between forty and sixty-five. There are also over eight thousand volunteer probation officers in Japan who are aged sixty-five to eighty-five, in contrast to volunteer probation officers in the United States who average around twenty-five. Their occupations range from fisherman to physician.

The Halfway House

Originally, in the 1880's Japan had established many halfway houses for its discharged war prisoners. These hostels were operated by voluntary individuals and various organizations. At that time juvenile institutions, which included hostels, were also operated under a voluntary system. Today in Japan there are about two hundred halfway houses for adult and juvenile offenders operated by volunteer groups under the authorization of the Minister of Justice. About one hundred have been in operation since before World War II, including a few of the juvenile homes.

In 1950 the Law for Aftercare of Discharged Offenders strengthened the halfway house program in terms of financial support. Today private organizations planning to develop a halfway house are required to meet certain operational standards and to be approved by the Ministry of Justice. Qualified persons, usually under some form of probation, may be assigned to a halfway house, and the halfway house may then receive reimbursement from national budget funds for such service. If the halfway house staff chooses to give aid to other individuals, they do so at their own expense and must depend on other sources of funding. Usually, as in the United States, the services offered in this program include room and board, counseling, job referral, and similar types of aid. Assignment to a halfway house may not be made by the court, as is possible in some other countries. But if a person is on probation, he may seek out or be referred to the halfway house for help. About four thousand Japanese offenders are involved in halfway houses. Accommodations range from rooms for nine to hostels for one hundred persons. Average per house in 1978 was about twenty-three people. Persons living in halfway houses usually work in the community. Some halfway houses have their own workshops and provide work especially for persons not yet ready or able to work in the community. One halfway house is attached to a psychiatric hospital and accommodates mentally disturbed ex-offenders. While the volunteer probation program offers some help in the services Japan renders to its offenders and ex-offenders, this program has had its problems in the area of recruitment and training of volunteer workers. Recently Japan has recognized the need for analyzing its total program for persons convicted of crimes, and it will probably begin to broaden its approach, following patterns that may have worked in the United States and in other countries.

Korea, Japan's neighbor, has innovated some programs that may be labeled alternatives, but, in general, my research in the Orient during 1976 and 1977 suggests that innovative alternatives to imprisonment or a community approach toward working with convicted criminals are developing slowly in Korea.

Notes

1. Japanese Correction Bureau, *Correctional Institution in Japan* (Tokyo Ministry of Justice, 1973), pp. 1-2.
2. Rehabilitation Bureau, *Noninstitutional Treatment of Offenders in Japan* (Tokyo Ministry of Justice, 1974), p. 57.
3. Ibid., p. 59.
4. Ibid., p. 55.
5. Ibid., p. 28.
6. Ibid., pp. 36, 11.
7. Ibid., p. 12.

References

William Clifford. "Criminologist on Crime and Community in Japan." *Japan Times,* July 4, 1976, p. 9.

Takashi Fujino. "The Attitude of Juvenile Probationers towards the Volunteer." *Koseihogo to Hanzaiyobo* [Rehabilitation and Prevention] 4 (1969), pp. 118-126.

Albert G. Hess. "Volunteers in Probation and Parole in Japan." (New York: National Council on Crime and Delinquency, 1969), 25 pages.

Japan Rehabilitation Aid Association, *Koseihogo Rehabilitation,* Journal issued monthly, Tokyo, Japan.

Japan Rehabilitation Aid Association, *Koseihogo To Hanzaiyobo* [Rehabilitation and Prevention], issued quarterly, Tokyo, Japan.

Ministry of Justice. *Correctional Institutions in Japan.* Pamphlet (Tokyo: Correction Bureau, 1973).

Ministry of Justice. *Criminal Justice in Japan.* Pamphlet Undated, 41 pages.

Tsuyoshi Murai. "Public Gets Peek at Prison Life." *Japan Times*, June 27, 1976, p. 9.

Atsushi Nagashima. "The Responsibility of Voluntary Agencies to Support and to Question the Government Correctional Program." Mimeographed. Tokyo: Ministry of Justice, 1968, 11 pages.

Yasuyoshi Shiono. "Use of Volunteers in the Noninstitutional Treatment of Offenders in Japan." *International Journal of Criminal Policy* 27 (1969):46-47.

Youth Rehabilitation Welfare Center, *Hanzai to Hiko* [Crime and Delinquency], issued quarterly, Tokyo, Japan.

10 Sweden

On July 1, 1974, Sweden enacted the Correctional Care Reform Act that revised its approach to correctional treatment and ushered in a new era in the progress of noninstitutional care.[1] The act resulted from a series of events in Swedish corrections which included a national hunger strike of prisoners in thirty-five prisons in 1970.[2] Before this development of a new corrections code there had been a decade of developments that were leading Sweden toward much tighter controls. Sweden had been developing a system of corrections including large maximum security prisons that were more commonplace in larger European, American, and Asian countries. The Swedish people had been experiencing many difficulties with the corrections branch of their government. Public charges of administrative laxity in prison management, a series of convict escapes, public demands for greater public safety, and a war on rising crime rates in Sweden contributed to this popular demand for a tougher attitude toward lawbreakers.[3] Plans were being made for the construction of twenty-five new, more secure prisons by 1990.

The situation has changed considerably since the 1960s. Political and economic events influenced Swedish methods of correcting its law offenders, resulting in a move away from the construction of bigger and more secure prisons. The punitive attitude of the Swedes toward offenders changed to an attitude of care and concern. A corrections reform movement had been gaining momentum during the 1960s alongside a public clamor for harsher penalties. The reform movement greatly influenced the move toward humane care and resocialization of prisoners supported by the Swedes in the 1970s. This movement arose from two different sources. Outside the prison walls it was initially developed in an informal manner through the efforts of several reform groups. Inside Swedish prisons it developed through the efforts of several small groups of prisoners and later through a more formal union of convicts whose members included prisoners and paroled or released offenders.

Sweden's reform movement, usually known as KRUM (literal English translation—Organization for Humanization of Treatment of Criminals) became formalized with the founding of the National Association for Penal Reform. This organization started with about fifteen hundred members in a nation of 8 million people.[4] KRUM was founded late in 1966.[5] Early in the history of the organization's development its members determined that it would be a political organization rather than a social welfare body. Its membership in 1979 exceeded 7,500. The long-range objective of KRUM was to abolish a major part of the prison system in Sweden, beginning with the dissolution of the youth prison system and a sharp reduction in the use of remand prisons. Much planning and groundwork has been accomplished by the organization's membership in achieving short-term goals that helped to answer the prisoner's immediate needs and complaints. Data collected by the group have been accumulated and utilized in the media and with efforts by legislators to do away with a major part of the prison system and prison practices. KRUM enlisted the aid of public officials, the press, radio, and television in a hard-hitting public campaign to demonstrate the uselessness of most forms of incarceration in Sweden.

The reform movement inside the prisons began when prisoners joined together to protest inadequacies of the corrections system. This became the foundation for a Swedish prisoner's union in 1970 and helped to ignite national efforts such as a prisoner's hunger strike that involved about half of the prisoners in Sweden. One of the many reasons for the strike was a protest against the newly developing Swedish factory prison which included electronic security devices, underground passageways by which prisoners were to be moved from one building to another, and other methods reminiscent of the days of the development of the Auburn prison in New York in the early 1800s. Behavior modification, adverse conditioning, and other involuntary methods were to be used in these maximum security prisons according to some who witnessed this stage in the history of Sweden's prison development.

The activities and actions of prison reform groups inside and outside the prisons were welded into an influence strong enough to help change the course of the Swedish corrections system. As Sweden enters the decade of the 1980s with slower-growing but still rising crime rates combined with a still vociferous demand for tougher measures, it continues to approach corrections and resocialization of social deviants from a humanistic viewpoint. Only the passing of time will disclose which attitude will be most useful for Sweden and its own future in terms of crime deterrence.

The combination of these efforts resulted in the enactment by the Swedish Parliament of Public Law SFS 203. This Correctional Care Reform Act, which became effective in July, 1974, may be summarized as follows:

1. There must be an effort toward a minimum of intervention into the lives of offenders. The principle behind this attitude is that noninstitutional care is the most natural form of resocialization.
2. Whatever institutional care is found necessary in the corrective process must be closely coordinated with noninsitutional programs of care. All Swedish corrective programs must be coordinated.
3. Care of offenders (often called clients in Sweden) must be in facilities or

programs as close to the offender's place of residence as possible, providing that such placement does not interfere with public safety.

4. Organizations outside the corrections system must be used as far as possible in the resocialization process. Dependency of the formal or closed system of corrections must be minimized.

System of Sanctions

Sweden launched its corrections reformation program in 1974, but much of the reform movement had to be developed within the existing penal code, which was established in 1965. The penal code consisted of general rules, descriptions of offenses, and terms of punishment. Sanctions were divided into general punishments, which included fines and imprisonment, disciplinary punishments aimed at the armed forces, conditional sentences, probation, youth prison confinement, internment prison, and commitment for special care. These various sanctions provide the courts with a variety of sanctions, including considerable freedom in expanding probation, thus allowing for alternative methods of resocialization.

Fines

The day fine is the most common type of fine in Sweden, but courts may also impose monetary fines and standard fines. The day fine may vary from 1 day to 120 days. A unique feature of this fine is that the court considers the economic resources of the offender before determining the fine, but the number of days is determined independently based on the seriousness of the offense. The total financial worth of the offender is considered, and the days fine is multiplied by 0.1 percent of the client's annual income. These day fines may be imposed by judges, but public prosecutors may also impose the fine according to a specific set of restrictions. Monetary fines are for a predetermined amount of money. For example, a monetary fine for speeding is equal to $500 in American currency. In some cases fines may be given in combination with other sanctions.[6] For example, a suspended sentence might be combined with a day fine.

Imprisonment

Imprisonment laws in Sweden are somewhat similar to those of most Western nations in that they usually specify a term ranging from one month to ten years, but the court may exceed this limit in cases of murder or when consecutive punishments are called for. Parole is usually possible after an offender has served two-thirds of his sentence and can be granted only after the prisoner has served at least six months of his term. In some cases prisoners may be released on parole halfway through their sentence.[7] The effects of deprivation on the prisoner's family, his potential for adjustment, and his employment and housing possibilities are considered in early release programming. For release at the halfway point of a prisoner's sentence, additional criteria on which to base such release may include the prisoner's age and term. If a life sentence is imposed, the prisoner cannot be paroled unless the government reduces the sentence through a pardon. Sweden has both local parole boards, called local probation boards, and a National Probation Board. Local probation boards handle cases in which the client is serving less than a year. Usually grants of parole include the stipulation that parole include supervision for as long as five years, but there is a strong tendency in Sweden to reduce this length of time considerably, for most reformers see a lengthy parole period with supervision as a hindrance rather than a help in the resocialization process.

In 1976 about ten thousand persons were admitted to prisons. Sixty-nine percent of these were sentenced to less than four monhts in prison. Twenty percent of this total were sentenced to between four and twelve months of imprisonment. Eleven percent of this total received sentences amounting to at least one year in prison.[8] Sweden's imprisonment sentences were given for drunken driving in 32 percent of all the cases, while unlawful appropriation sentences were given to 17 percent of the ten thousand persons receiving prison sentences. Cases in which crimes of violence resulted in a prison sentence amounted to 12 percent, while insubordination including the refusal to bear arms amounted to 9 percent of the cases. In 3 percent of the total population sentenced to prison, drug offenses were the reason for conviction. The average number of prisoners was 3,632 in 1975 and 3,415 in 1976, while in January 1977 Swedish prison population had continued to decrease to 2,644.[9] This downward trend continued in 1978.

Conditional sentences are another form of penal sanction in Sweden. These are given when, in the opinion of the judge the client committed a crime unlikely to occur again and the chances for recidivism are extremely low. No supervision is involved, and the condition is that no incarceration will be given, providing the client does not commit another offense during a two-year trial period. This sentence may not be combined with any special instructions except the time and manner in which payment for any damage done by the offender is to be made. In 1975 some forty-four hundred Swedish offenders were given conditional sentences.[10]

Probation can replace imprisonment for any offense that would ordinarily be punishable by imprisonment. Usually probation is for a three-year period, and supervision is involved during the first two years or even less in many cases, especially where the probation department feels that supervision is not necessary. Probation in Sweden, as in many other countries, may be combined with court orders for special types of programs or the opportunity for the offender to voluntarily enter special programs ranging from alcohol and drug detoxification programs and to other programs for resocialization and rehabilitation. Probation may also be combined with day fines. If the offender is eighteen years old or older, he may also be given a directive to some institution for special care, for example, to a mental health facility. These institutional programs are limited by probation board regulations to at least one month but not more than two months. This care usually begins when the probationer begins his probation period. If the sentence for this time is to a more closed institution, the purpose is usually to provide a shock type of imprisonment to the offender in an attempt to interrupt the offender's criminal activity or remove him from a detrimental environment. If the probationer fails to adhere to rules of probation to which he agreed, then probation may be terminated and the court may impose some other sanction. In 1975 some 5,500 persons were sentenced to probation and in only 370 cases was some institutional sentence involved.

Youth prison is a sanction given for offenses that are punishable by imprisonment. The period of confinement to a youth prison is usually indeterminate, and it may continue for as long as three years. Usually this type of sentence involves the assistance of several outside care agencies including social welfare, mental health, and others. Usually the youth (eighteen to twenty) enters an institution for a year before being sent to less restrictive forms of resocialization. If considerable time is spent in programs outside the insitution, the combination of institutional care and additional noninstitutional care may last as long as five years. In 1976 some 150 persons were sentenced to youth prison, and 60 of these cases were readmissions.[11]

Youth prison may be abolished in Sweden, since various inquiry commissions have found that it is not an effective means of resocialization and that replacements to it must be found. A replacement for youth prison will probably emphasize community care.

In Sweden the age of criminal responsibility is fifteen years, and youths of this age or older may stand trial for a crime. Youths under fifteen who commit crimes are apprehended but sanctions are not penal. Instead the corrective measure will involve a commitment to a public welfare agency for assistance and resocialization procedures. The Swedish Department of Social Welfare is responsible for such facilities as reformatories and orphanages as well as for the placement of youths in acceptable private homes. For youths between the ages of fifteen and eighteen penal sanctions may be given, but it is up to the prosecutor to recommend a route. A penal sanction may be recommended for one person, while the assistance of public welfare may fit another case. In many cases, the court may choose to use measures under the Swedish Child Welfare Act to assist the offender rather than to impose penal sanction. Persons who are between eighteen and twenty-one may be sentenced to imprisonment only if deprivation of liberty is called for in the interests of public safety or when incarceration is thought to be the only alternative for a particular offender.

Internment is still another form of incarceration, and this sanction involves a sentence of indeterminate time and may be imposed when the offender has committed some offense that would ordinarily be punishable by imprisonment for two years or more. This particular sanction is intended for the recidivist who, in the eyes of the court, cannot be deterred from a criminal career at that time in his life. Internment involves care both inside and outside institutions. The emphasis, however, is on institutional care. Usually the internment involves a period of at least one year but not more than twelve years in an institution. When the minimum period of time in the institution is completed, noninstitutional care continues in cases where, in the opinion of the internment board, there is a high risk of recidivism. The local probation board usually oversees the client's noninstitutional care and can recommend to the internment board that the client be recommitted. In 1976 Sweden sentenced 220 persons to internment, and, of these, 197 were readmissions.[12]

Offenders may also be committed to closed or open psychiatric care facilities for participation in special alcohol, drug, or mental health programs.

Modernization of Penal Sanctions

In the late 1960s penal sanctions and the correctional system in Sweden began to change. There were a number of inquiries, and a Committee on Institutional Correctional Treatment drafted a law to replace the old Act of Treatment in Correctional Institutions. At the same time another investigation was made to develop a plan for the needs and organization of noninstitutional care.[13] By 1971 there was enough evidence and demand to indicate the urgency with which an overhaul of the correctional system was needed. The greatest need appeared to be the need for coordinating and establishing priorities among reform proposals. The minister of justice appointed a special committee for the drafting of reform measures which could be submitted to Parliament. There was a general consensus among committee members representing the four major parties and the Ministry of Finance that deprivation of liberty does not work and does not improve the individual's chances of adjusting to a life of freedom.[14] It was also generally agreed that prevention results from efforts at the individual level and from correctional-care programs conducted outside institutions. Noninstitutional care, it was also emphasized, was less expensive, more humane, and more effective. A strong effort was made to assure the public that its confidence in noninstitutional-care programs should be increased. The programs of noninstitutional care were to be brought to a level that substantiated, without any doubt, that such care could be an adequate alternative to sanctions involving deprivation of liberty and that the public safety would not be jeopardized in the process.

Sweden's noninstitutional-care programs began to develop and expand as a result of these efforts. Hundreds of new positions in noninstitutional-care programs were created, and new and broader functions for the use of these programs were developed. The investigation of each case was transferred from the courts to the noninstitutional-care organization as of April 1, 1974.[15] The move to give case-study investigation to noninstitutional-care agencies was made to assure that the defendant's own views were properly recorded and to improve the case-study system. In addition to these changes, a much greater emphasis was placed on assisting those convicted persons who were suffering from severe social maladjustment, especially as a result of alcohol and narcotics misuse. Provisions were made for the special training of noninstitutional-care personnel to assist these offenders in their reintegration into a normal and satisfactory life. For less severe cases, lay supervisors who were volunteers were to continue in helping the offender become a part of his society again.

The criminal code was also amended so that probation and parole supervision was reduced from three years to two.[16] Grants of money for social work in the noninstitutional program were greatly increased, and such items as housing, field worker training, individual and group therapy, and leisure time activity programs began to be emphasized as aids for improving the client's performance as a social being.

Another important factor related to the series of changes begun in Sweden in the 1970s was the attitude of correctional leaders, court staffs, and others with regard to an offender's home environment. Swedish correctional leaders now believe that there are usually more positive than negative aspects to the home environment. At one time it was believed that to correct an offender he must be removed from his home environment and not be allowed to return until the state felt that he was "cured" of his criminal inclinations. Sweden has launched a program to help the offender by applying the local principle, which means that the offender should be sentenced to a facility, institution or noninstitutional program as near his home as possible so that both institutional and noninstitutional personnel can work together for the client's aid.[17] Institutions in this network are called local institutions, and there are about fifty local institutions in Sweden, each with a capacity of twenty to sixty beds. A building program for the construction and development of local institutions was launched in 1975 to add to those local institutions already operating. These local institutions admit persons who have received sentences of up to one year and prisoners who are completing a longer term at some other prison. An important part of this program is the provision that prisoners of local institutions are given the same rights of social support and care as are other members of free society. The fact that these persons have broken the law and are having difficulty in conforming does not eliminate their privilege, nor does it mean that the community can disclaim responsibility for their care. As a result of this modern view, clients are given the same assistance, as far as possible, in education, training, employment, medical care, and cultural activities as would ordinarily be available for any nonoffender in Sweden.[18] The objective of this combination of efforts is the gradual return of the client to his home community with the ability to cope with and adjust to life among his peers and neighbors.

The efforts toward noninstitutional-care programs also took into account that some offenders require more intensive care, for their own and the public's safety. But even in this concern for secure institutions, the estimated numbers of required beds and cells were reduced during the program planning stages; the number estimated was about two thousand beds as opposed to three thousand beds in the original plans. Length of stay in a closed or medium security institution was also to be shortened as much as possible and the offender transferred to a local institution or noninstitutional-care program, according to Swedish reformists.

By January 1978 a system of regional districts called correctional care regions had developed. A region consists of one or more remand prisons plus a number of local institutions and noninstitutional-care districts. In this system, at present, there are about fifty noninstitutional-care districts in full operation. The Swedish system of national prisons (there are twenty) is separate from this regionalization system. The main task of the regional-care staffs is to monitor the progress of clients and direct-care porocedures in noninstitutional-care programs as well as in programs in remand prisons and local institutions. Regional directors, who are usually professionally trained probation officers, are especially concerned with the offender's placement in an institution. A major task of these directors is to provide whatever resources are available, in an efficient manner, for their clients. They are responsible for initiating and directing local cooperation with welfare, education, and medical organizations. In order to keep correctional care programs within the same jurisdictions of other social welfare agencies, each noninstitutional-care district in Sweden was developed to correspond geographically with one or two counties.[19]

Sweden's revised laws and its new legislation for correctional care as outlined and developed in the Act on Correctional Care in Institutions and in the Act on Calculation of Imprisonment Terms, effective in July 1974, give clear directions for preparing the offender for life outside institutions. Such care, it was stated, should include a well-planned and well-conducted prerelease program and extra-institutional care. The aim of these directives was to enable noninstitutional-care personnel to participate in the institution's programs of rehabilitation as a member of a team working together on behalf of the client. Another important directive emphasized a new responsibility of correctional-care personnel to include all other social agencies deemed necessary for the client's resocialization. The act also specifies that persons sentenced to terms of imprisonment of up to one year shall be placed in local institutions when confinement is necessary. There is also a provision that states that persons under twenty-one years of age are to be separated from other offenders as much as possible. The act does not stipulate separation of men and women, but Sweden's few female criminals are placed in special-care facilities at local institutions.

Other provisions of the new law suggest that, whenever possible, offenders should be placed in open institutions, passes and leaves should be given more generously, and opportunities for participation in work and leisure activities outside prison should be expanded. Rules for furloughs for work, education, and caring for personal matters were made much less restrictive. Preparation for release from prison should include an opportunity for the client to live outside the institution even before the earliest possible time for release from prison.[20] For example, a client may be placed in a boarding school, a treatment home for drug addicts or alcoholics, a particularly excellent private home, or even into military service.

The new law also expanded the probation officer's much wider influence in determining a prisoner's release from an institution. Another provision of the new law provided supervision personnel with much greater powers to help offenders, especially in work programs. The work experiences and remuneration are extremely helpful in raising the offenders' self-esteem.

By 1978 Sweden had fifty-two local institutions with places for 1,974 clients, nineteen independent remand prisons with a total of 1,081 places, and twenty national institutions with a total of 1,842 beds. In 1976 some 42,673 furloughs were granted, an all-time high for the nation. These were granted to a wide variety of offenders serving time in prisons. In 3,402 cases the offender failed to return at the end of the furlough. This amounts to about 7 percent of the total number of furloughed convicts. During 1976 there were also 1,980 escapes from all institutions in Sweden, and of these, 1,054 were from open institutions.[21]

The remand prisons of most of the countries that I have investigated appear to be simply jails for holding persons awaiting appearance in court. Sweden, however, takes a different approach. One result of the Swedish reform movement was a much greater degree of involvement of its noninstitutional-care personnel in the work on behalf of clients in remand prisons. Offenders were given as much assistance and support as possible as their situations warranted. The consent of the detained person is required before this assistance may be rendered. The supervising probation officer of the district in which the remand prison is located is directed by law to visit the offender or client unless the client is already under the supervision of another probation district. An assessment of the client's needs is to be made, and any assistance that does not influence the outcome of the case in court is to be rendered. When a detainee is sentenced, the noninstitutional-care personnel may assist the regional district supervisor in selecting a suitable institution for the client. Noninstitutional-care personnel can be involved on a client's behalf from arrest to discharge.

The purposes of the Swedish reform laws included the development of an interlocking effort by local care agencies. These may include medical, dental, mental health, housing, social welfare, employment, and other community agencies working together on behalf of the client in the corrections process. The idea behind this effort is to minimize confinement and to maximize the chances for a successful and quick return of the client to his family and community. Sweden ranks with the Netherlands in minimizing the length of confinement. Sweden confines about 50 persons per 100,000 population, compared with 250 to 280 in the United States and only 21 persons per 100,000 population in the Netherlanders.[22]

Along with the development of the noninstitutional-care programs, open institutions, and other reform programs, Sweden made considerable changes in its laws relating to inmates in all its institutions for criminal offenders. Liberalization ranged from greatly reduced mail censorship and the expansion of furloughs to the right to form prisoners' councils and the reduction of terms of imprisonment. Sweden had learned from experience that the prison system is useless, and the nation launched an effort on behalf of its incarcerated citizens with the philosophy that they, too, were entitled to the same assistance as other Swedish citizens. Many of the reforms are still in their infancy, many programs are in the experimental stage, and many original plans are being revised. The new open attitude will probably depend, to a great extent, on the efforts made by the probation service, which has considerable authority in the total scheme. Whether this open atmosphere will become ingrained into the culture of Sweden remains to be seen. There is no doubt, however, that it represents a modern and clear attempt to set the goals of penal care in clear-sighted, less emotion-laden terms than in the past.

Experiments in Corrections

In the late 1960s and early 1970s Swedish correctional workers and reformists were engaged in the development of a number of different approaches
to improving its prison, corrections, and noninstitutional corrections programs. One of the essential aims of these efforts was to develop a modified
therapeutic community in keeping with the purposes and directives of the
new acts of Parliament for modernizing the corrections administration and
programs. The task of the planners was to propose modifications in the
system of corrections that would greatly increase the amount of contact between correctional personnel and prisoners. Another task was to revise and
redesign training for prison staffs, probation office staffs, and lay supervisors.

The modified therapeutic community program was applied to several
experiments in selected prisons in Sweden. The core of this effort included
greatly increased opportunities for prisoners to work, play, attend school,
and have home furloughs. The emphasis was on allowing these activities to
take place outside prison walls. These outside contacts ranged from visits to
sporting events, from participation in physical exercise programs to lengthy
furloughs for education, and work, and work-training purposes. Other
changes included the use of civilian clothing within prison walls. Lockup
times were made much more flexible, and greatly increased contact between
social workers and other assisting agents was promoted. The modified
therapeutic community program in these experimental prisons came as a
shock to traditional, custodial prison staffs and administrations who were
accustomed to the system of security and restraint of freedom for inmates.
Training programs for prison staffs were helpful but often did not change
the attitudes of the old guard.

At the beginning of these experiments there emerged the expected problems of differences between prisoners and prison staffs. The group could
not communicate with each other with much trust or empathy. Prisoners
violated many of the new more liberal rules concerning their conduct inside
and outside prison and often disregarded their responsibilities for fulfilling
the conditions of furloughs and leaves. In the mid 1970s the picture began
to change. The Gàvle prison experiment demonstrated these changes.

In Gavle prison, a forty-cell building constructed in 1840 was selected
for an experiment as a modified therapeutic community. An average of
twenty-five prisoners was involved in the experiment. Prisoners were
selected from other institutions after they applied for entrance into the
experimental unit. They were selected on the basis of cooperative

participation. Gävle prison was originally a closed or maximum security prison. Despite the fact that the experiment was designed to provide a more relaxed atmosphere, prisoners and staff were reacting on the basis of their previous roles in a closed prison environment. The prisoners had little trust in the staff, and the staff did not have much confidence in the prisoner's ability to live in an open milieu. When furloughs were given, many prisoners tried to escape. The misuse of alcohol and drugs appeared to underline the probability that furloughs might not be continued as a part of the experiment.[23]

At one point in the Gävle experiment, some staff members wanted to discontinue the use of furloughs. In the spring of 1972 prisoners were requesting much greater leniency in the granting of furloughs while, at this time, the staff felt that the abuses of many privileges by prisoners destined the experiment to failure. The more articulate inmates insisted that contact with free society was a basic element of the experiment as, indeed, it was.

A series of events instigated by certain prisoners was probably responsible for saving the Gävle prison experiment. Several of the more articulate prison leaders began to insist that prisoners who were given furlough or other privileges become fully responsible for adhering to them. These rules had been developed by prisoners and prison staff in a series of meetings and confrontations. Prisoners became more critical of their own misuse of the opportunities that were being provided for them in this experiment. The prison culture began to change as a result of this assumption of responsibility, and a more cooperative attitude was established by the prisoners themselves. The prisoners demanded that their fellow inmates act more responsibly in connection with the changes and the aims of the experiment. Communication between prisoners and staff was beginning to mature and to expand. The staff's anxiety began to lessen when the prisoners demonstrated this new responsibility through their own improved conduct.

The goals of the Gävle prison experiment included increasing communication between staff and prisoners, developing a pleasanter atmosphere within the prison community, developing programs inside and outside prison that would aid prisoner resocialization, improve education, work skills, and relationships of the prisoners. Other goals of the modified therapeutic community plan included a program to assist the prisoner with personal, family, and socialization problems and to greatly increase prisoners' time away from the prison itself. Which of these goals have all been realized through the Gävle prison experiment and other like it remains a moot question since, by the late 1970s, follow-up research was still in the stages of final analysis. At the same time Sweden was in the midst of a far more significant effort in expanding its noninstitutional-care programs.

The Sundsvall Experiment

Another experiment, launched on July 1, 1972, was known as the Sundsvall experiment. This experiment dealt with persons on probation in the Sundsvall probation district and a sample of probationers in the Karlstad probation district who served as the control group. The independent or experimental variables in this experiment included the use of three times as many persons in the treatment staff, which meant an increase from three to nine staff members. The independent variables also included increases in office staff and the development of a special clinic in social medicine manned by a part-time psychiatrist, a psychologist, and a nurse. The experiment also involved the use of a hotel for temporary residence where twenty clients lived until permanent living accommodations were found. There was also a halfway house which accommodated twenty persons who were moved from an institution to spend the last part of their prison sentence in the community. In addition, a representative of the labor exchange was engaged specifically to assist the participants in this experiment in employment matters.[24]

About 300 clients participated in the Sundsvall experiment. The activities of these offenders were researched over a period of two years after their release from probation (noninstitutional) period and compared with the control sample which consisted of about 250 clients. In the various stages of the experiment both clients and supervisors were interviewed to determine the progress of the program and the effectiveness of the independent variables. Data were accumulated with regard to contacts between supervisors and clients, the use of outside resources, medical and labor assistance, and other help. Data gathered from the experiment indicated that both the experimental and the control groups saw the need for certain kinds of help in about the same order of rank. Living accommodations, for example, were ranked as the greatest need followed by education, creation of a better public image, perhaps related to a better self-image, benefits such as unemployment compensation, and assistance in job search. The data also indicated that both groups prefer probation to any other type of penal sanction even though probation means that a much longer period of time would be spent under supervision of correctional system representatives and authorities. Both groups suggested later in the experiment that problems most often discussed with their supervisors for which they were assisted included financial difficulties, employment problems, getting a driver's license, finding a place to stay, economic planning, accumulating money to pay fines or the court costs of their trial, and education and alcohol problems, in that order.

Another important part of the Sundsvall probation experiment was the decision to select lay (volunteer) supervisors over professional probation supervisors to work with clients and the decentralization of this supervision to the client's home neighborhood. Efforts were made to combine the most appropriate lay supervisor with the most compatible client. The client was asked to choose his own supervisor whenever possible. These lay supervisors usually included a workmate, a relative or someone close to the family, or another person who was acquainted with the offender but who could be a positive influence in the resocialization process. Lay supervisors who were chosen were made fully responsible for the communication and treatment segments of the program, and the supervision or interference of professional supervisors was minimized. A list of resources, called a catalog, was given to each lay supervisor during the supervisor's training period. This catalog provided the names and addresses of community agencies who could be of help in the resocialization process. The number of clients for each lay supervisor was limited to three, but most lay supervisors worked with only one client. Paperwork was to be minimized, but some documentation of progress was to be maintained. Lay supervisors began their contacts by recording the subjective needs of their clients. The classification of clients assigned to lay supervisors was based on their risk as potential recidivists, and supervision varied according to the degree of risk. Training of lay supervisors was upgraded so that volunteers had a much better understanding of their role as a caring person rather than a watchman. Contacts between lay supervisors and clients varied and ranged from one or two contacts per month to several contacts per week in some cases.

The Sundsvall experiment began in 1972, and preliminary data from this and similar experiments in Sweden are beginning to underline important and well-researched discoveries. Preliminary findings suggest that probation is no greater a risk than incarceration when recidivism is considered. Data have indicated that intense supervision in numbers of contacts and significance of contacts between supervisor and client may be significantly related to a decrease in recidivism no matter what the subject of communication may be between the two persons. The transactions, however, must relate to one of the several priority needs, and some solutions to problems must be found. Probation appears to be the far wiser choice, especially when compared with recidivism rates of persons sentenced to long terms in prison. Probation is also the far wiser choice for adults and for youths who are placed in the care of child welfare personnel.

The experiment also revealed that with more intense supervision there was a direct and positive correlation between contact with supervisors and job location, location of accommodations, assistance with finances, and mental health assistance. The Sundsvall experiment led to some interesting preliminary suggestions with regard to contacts between clients and supervisors and resulted in the recommendation that there be three types of supervision:

1. Normal supervision, in which the aim is to maintain friendly relations between client and lay supervisor.
2. Crime-prevention supervision, in which frequent and intensive contacts would be maintained to help with problems of a minor or major nature. A lay supervisor with many contacts with social agencies such as a workmate or a job foreman are examples.
3. Intensive supervision, in which an intensive pattern of contact is established between client and supervisor to focus on financial and other social problems of the client. This type of supervision must be carried out by well-trained probation officers or well-qualified and trained lay supervisors.

Critics of the Sundsvall experiment have suggested that too much emphasis had been placed on facilities, manpower and other symbols rather than on specific measures of rehabilitation. This experiment brought to light many deficiencies in the design of experiments, but it did point out problems of contacts between helping agents (such as lay supervisors) and clients.

The Stockholm Experiment

The Stockholm Probation Treatment Center conducted extensive research in its efforts to work closely with probationers.[25] There were 336 clients involved in this experiment. This program was started in 1972 and, like the Sundsvall experiment, demonstrated that close contact between supervisor and client was associated with lower recidivism rates. Only two-fifths of the total sample relapsed into criminal behavior after the first year of the experiment. This was considered significant, for high-risk clients had been selected for inclusion in the program. This experiment included the use of a hotel for persons without accommodations, job location assistance, and the use of community organizations to assist the client. The training of lay supervisors included on-the-job training alongside professional supervisors. The hostel (hotel) could house twelve clients, and special efforts were made to assist those who were not able to cope with their environment. Professional mental health care was frequently involved in efforts to assist clients in this experiment. About twenty-five staff members participated in the program with lay supervisors during the first year of the experiment. Most of the staff members were responsible for the hostel regardless of their grade or function. Staff members took turns working evenings, overnight, and on weekends. Employees such as cooks, secretaries, and others were also involved in direct social work with clients. During the first two weeks of the program, half the staff from social services and half from corrections, worked out many differences in philosophies. These differences continued to be discussed during the first year of the project's operation. Staff members often worked in teams of two, one experienced and one less experienced, to help clients who were extremely upset or who needed intense assistance. Weekly meetings of the entire staff were used to work out differences on a continuous basis. During the first six months of the program, work was uncertain and often disorganized. Roles became clearer after the first year, and then the experiment began to function more smoothly.[26]

Early findings of the Stockholm experiment indicate that high frequencies of contact between helping persons and clients are a signficiant factor in the reduction of the client's use of alcohol and drugs. Within one year after entering the experimental program, one-fifth of the clients were sentenced to sanctions involving deprivation of liberty, and one-fifth of the sample were sentenced to sanctions not involving deprivation of liberty. The remaining three-fifths were not involved in lawbreaking activities, to the court's knowledge. Research of other factors involved in the experiment did not have the significance attached to the frequency of contact, and the researchers found it "difficult to distinguish in a meaningful way the effect of the [other] different measures."

Birch Tree House

Sweden, like other countries, had been experimenting with the halfway house or prerelease centers for several years but had no real research data on the operation or success potential of the halfway house concept. The Birch Tree House experiment was one of the more sophisticated attempts to develop a systematic study of an alternative to prison. The program design and research efforts were a cooperative project of the Pedagogic Institute of Stockholm University and the National Correctional Administration. The study was made in 1972. Study visits were made over a five-week period during the evaluation part of the project.

Birch Tree House, a halfway unit located in Stockholm, was operated for young male prisoners. The home is owned by the welfare society of Sweden and was first opened in 1968 as a halfway house. Clients are sent to the home from the prison on a special type of leave. Most clients are between eighteen and twenty years of age. Most of the youths placed in Birch Tree House have served a considerable portion of their minimum of one year in the youth prison. This usually amounted to a period of about nine months. The program of Birch Tree House is centered on helping the youth reenter his free environment through the development of close relationships for helping with personal problems, job location, financial difficulties, and work-skill training. Birch Tree House has places for an average of fourteen youths. The staff consists of six persons and two alternates, for a total of eight staff members. Since the house is located in an urban neighborhood, many services of local community agencies are used. Birch Tree House, in 1972, was the only one of its kind in Sweden. Youths who apply for transfer to Birch Tree House and are unsuccessful can be returned to the youth prison if they fail at Birch Tree House.[27] The staff consists of the director, social worker, two recreation organizers, a house mother, two deputy house mothers, a work instructor, and usually a practicing student from the Social Work Training School.

Daily and weekly routines at the house are based on the concept that all or most of the residents will work out of the house during the day. Newcomers may work with the work instructor while they are searching for a job. There are two weekly meetings of residents with certain staff members, and two other evenings are used for special recreational activities. The staff use these more formal get-togethers as a means of counteracting any feelings of isolation on the part of the residents. Residents also may use one weekend or more and one night a week to visit their own homes or some other specified place. The residents of Birch Tree House do not want to return to prison, and for this reason they only test the staff and the program of the house within certain limits. Practical help with work, living accommodations, psychological problems, finances, and other needs is given on a continuous basis. An attempt is made to keep the atmosphere as homelike as possible. Staff members try to exemplify, to the residents, a social learning model of an adult individual with which they can identify. Every attempt is made to keep relationships between staff and residents informal and intimate. Family-style meals enable staff to keep in touch with their clients. Conflict situations are used to help teach the youth to deal with their feelings in a more constructive manner. Awareness of these feelings is emphasized in this training effort.

Birch Tree House and others like it in Sweden have every possibility of success. Their records of placing inmates in jobs and conducting successful lives in the free community help to justify their existence. Placement in the house is a slow process, and during the early part of the project it often took two months for the prison administration to make a conclusion concerning a youth's application. As a result, Birch Tree House had less members than it could handle. The researchers suggested, however, that Birch Tree House and others like it limit the number of residents to eight, and the economics of this size are often impractical.

Other Experiments

In addition to these experiments, Sweden has also been researching the potential for using full labor wages for prison inmates who work inside the prison. The Tillberga prison experiment is an example of this type of program. About eighty inmates participate in it. They are involved in building prefabricated homes which are consigned to a marketing firm for resale. One of the main purposes of this experiment is to give the offenders the opportunity, as far as wages and worker requirements are concerned, to do their work under conditions similar to those they would encounter outside prison. Participants in the program are given home leaves every fourteen days, and their wages are at the full-time labor market scale outside prison. These wages are used for self-improvement and to care for family needs. Follow-up studies of the initial participants indicated that recidivism nine months after their release from Tillberga amounted to 38 percent compared with 51 percent of the control group. This was a fairly significant difference. These statistics apply to those subjects in the experiment who had previous prison experience. There was no significant difference between participants in the program and control group members when only first-time prison inmates were considered.[28]

Other data concerning the potential of the Tillberga experiment have encouraged Swedish authorities to continue the experiment, and in 1975 it was extended to another prison in Sweden with differing prison residents and conditions.

These experiments are intended to combine innovative ideas with more sophisticated research methodology in order to test the significance of the various experiments and research projects so that more successful programs may be reproduced in other parts of Sweden.

The Gruvberge Village Experiment

The Gruvberge Village Project is a unique experiment conducted in Sweden. The Swedish authorities purchased a former forestry company village consisting of several houses. The environment was similar to pioneer villages in America's early western movement. The timber area provided ample possibilities for developing job-skill training programs. The houses provided the experiment with typical home settings. Some participants were allowed to move their families into the house to live with them. Job and work-skill training was emphasized, while the semifree environment and special training programs provided the teaching arena for civil rights and responsibility training, family problem solving, and the development of more constructive personal relationships. Data on the success of the program are being gathered to determine the future of such projects.[29]

The Future of Alternatives

From these brief descriptions of the various experiments with prison reform methods and alternatives we may conclude that Sweden is taking its prison reform movement and corrections program seriously. The recent literature concerned with Swedish corrections, emphasizes respect for the offender and the provision of social services. For offenders who receive sentences the goal of Swedish correctional authorities is to cooperate in the efforts to move the offender to noninstitutional-care programs as quickly as possible in view of the risks to the public and to the offender himself. Isolation from the world outside for prisoners or other clients of the state is regarded as a poor method of resocialization or cure. The family and the home neighborhood are considered to be the most therapeutic environments for resocialization.

During the development of these experiments and programs, a demand for systematic evaluation has helped provide data of considerable value which may be used in planning the future of Sweden's corrections process. Many of the experiments are now being evaluated, and their impact on the corrections system and their effectiveness are still a matter of conjecture. At present, even these methods of evaluation are being scientifically improved. Improved methods of experiment design and research methods are being made to help solve problems encountered in the earlier stages of this national effort.

The attitudes of judges and the courts have also been changing in Sweden, and present research indicates that probation, with its wide variety of opportunities for the use of special alternatives to fit individual needs, is clearly superior to long or intermediate prison sentences. Evidence from these research efforts also indicates that probation is a workable alternative even when only minimal supervision of the client is needed. It is at least as successful as prison and much less costly than any form of incarceration.

Sweden is a socialist nation and maintains a concern for all its citizens with respect to their rights to social services. The fact that some citizens have committed crimes and have special adjustment difficulties does not automatically make them second-class citizens. The logical consequence of this attitude, which was expressed in the 1973 Correctional Care Reform Drafting Committee report, exemplifies the prevailing atttitude in Sweden today. This attitude is not confined to correctional care or reformist circles but characterizes the national population. The citizens of Sweden are concerned with crime but also with the offender. The Swedish people feel that they are also partly to blame for their fellow citizen's deviant behavior. This nationwide respect for citizens and the national concern and involvement with criminal law offenders may be one of the most important variables to consider when an appraisal of a nation's corrections or crime picture is made. Criminal activity in Sweden is distinctly different from American criminal activity with regard to violence, for example, and low rates of violent crimes and serious offenses have helped to encourage this national attitude. If Sweden were a melting pot of races and ethnic groups, perhaps the story would be different. If Sweden had been involved in the war efforts and changes that America has witnessed, perhaps the story would be different. Nevertheless, this national attitude must be seen as an enviable one from the standpoint of corrections, at least, and something that other nations may emulate in an attempt to improve their corrections systems. In 1975 and 1976 the prison population was decreasing faster than anticipated, and it has now become clear that Sweden's plans for building will have to be drastically changed. It appears that alternatives are working and that criminal offenders are not being sent to prisons. Prisons will be useless in the future in Sweden if the present decreases in demand continue.

Whether all the reforms in prisons and in the noninstitutional-care programs can create a more open atmosphere within Sweden's prison system or whether they are simply dreams remains to be seen. The world's penal reformists and abolitionists will be watching to see whether Sweden has paved the way for other nations to follow in the 1980s in the evolution of the corrections systems.

Notes

1. National Correctional Administration, *The 1973 Correctional Care Reform Report,* Pub. No. 2-003, (Stockholm, 1973), p. 2.

2. Desmond Smith, *Opening Up the Prisons,* Pub. No. 2-010, (Stockholm: National Correctional Administration, undated), p. 7. See also Thomas Mathiesen, *The Prison Movement in Scandinavia,* (Copenhagen: undated), p. 47.

3. The National Prison and Probation Administration of Sweden, *The Prison and Probation System,* Pub. No. 2-001, (Stockholm, 1975), p. 2.

4. Mathiesen. *The Prison Movement in Scandinavia* (London: Halstead Press, 1974) and T. Mathiesen, *The Politics of Abolition in Political Action Theory,* (Oslo: University Press, 1974). See also Louis Bultena, *Deviant Behavior in Sweden,* (New York: Exposition Press, 1977), chap. 3.

5. The Swedish Institute, *Facts: The Correctional Care Fact Sheet, Correctional Care in Sweden* (Swedish Institute: Stockholm, 1977).

6. Ibid., p. 3.

7. Ibid.

8. Ibid.

9. Ibid.

10. Ibid.

11. Ibid., p. 4.

12. Ibid., p. 5.

13. National Correctional Administration, *The 1973 Correctional Care Reform,* p. 1.

14. Ibid., p. 2.

15. Ibid.

16. Ibid., p. 3.

17. Ibid.

18. Ibid.

19. Ibid., p. 7.

20. Ibid., p. 12.

21. Swedish Institute, *Fact Sheet,* p. 2.; See also National Correctional Administration; and *Swedish National Prison and Probation Administration, Information Unit,* Pub. No. 2-016 (SFS 1974:248) *Swedish Code of Statutes;* (Stockholm: Government Printer, 1974); Pub. No. 2-016 (SFS 1976:16) *Swedish Code of Statutes;* (Stockholm: Government Printer, 1976); Pub. No. 2-015 (SFS 1976:506) *Swedish Code of Statutes;* (Stockholm: Government Printer, 1976); Pub. No. 2-001, The Prison and Probation System, Sweden; (Stockholm: Government Printer, 1976); and Lennart Geijer, Act on Correctional Treatment in Institutions Given the 19th of April, 1974 (SFS 1974:203) (Stockholm: Government Printer, 1974).

22. Hans v. Hofer, *Dutch Prison Population,* Mimeographed, University of Stockholm, Institute of Criminology, Department of Sociology, Stockholm, 1975, p. 4.

23. National Prison Association, *The Gävle Prison Experiment,* Stockholm, p. 169.

24. Ekart Kuhlhorn, *Noninstitutional Treatment: A Preliminary Evaluation of the Sundsvall Experiment,* National Swedish Council for Crime Prevention, Research and Development Section (Stockholm: 1976) Report No. 4, p. 15.

25. Bengt Warren, *Kriminalvardsstyresen, Utvecklingsenheten; Frivardens Behandlingscentral,* Report No. 20, December 1976. The English translation of a summary of this project, The Stockholm Probation Treatment Center, may be found on pp. 2-6.

26. The Stockholm Probation Treatment Center, p. VI.

27. Anita Castberg and Gumilla Nirman, *Björkahemmet: En Studie av ett Övergangghem,* Report No. 5, Stockholm University, Stockholm, September 1973, pp. 6-11. The English translation of a summary of the Birch Tree House experiment is given on pp. 6-11.

28. Borje Olsson, *Efter Tillberga, En Uppfoljningsstudie,* Report No. 14, Stockholm, September 1973, Kriminalvardsstgrelsen. (The English summary of the Tillberga Prison Experiment may be found on pp. 5-9.)

29. National Prison and Probation Administration, *The Prison and Probation System,* Pub. No. 2-001, 1975 (Norrkoping: 1976).

References

Lars Krantz, Lars Bagge, and Norman Bishop, *Vilkorligt Frigivna 1973: En Uppföljning med Avseende på Återfall,* No. 18, (Stockholm, November 1976).

Christer Krohn, Bo G. Peterson, and Anders Rossell, *Rymmare i Östra Räjongen-Egenskaper och Farlighet* (English summary), (Government Printer, Stockholm, May 1973).

Ann-Charlotte Landeholm-Ek, *On Change in Prison,* abridged version of the Final Report on an Experiment, Report No. 17, (Stockholm National Prison and Probation Administration, Research and Development Unit, January 1976).

Norval Morris, "Lessons from the Adult Correctional System of Sweden," in *Corrections Problems and Prospects,* ed. David Petersen and Charles W. Thomas (Englewood Cliffs, N.J.: Prentice-Hall, 1975), p. 298.

Borje Olsson, Lars Bagge and Norman Bishop, *Skyddstillsynsdömda 1971, -en Återfallsstudie.,* No. 19, (November 1976).

Part III
Conclusions

11

Some Criticism of Community Treatment Projects and Other Alternatives Examined

Jerry Bergman

A number of recent writers in corrections have inferred, on various grounds that nothing works and that the money and effort expended on the various nonprison treatment programs is largely wasted. This research has lent support to those in the law-and-order movement who are encouraging increased use of incarceration and decreased use of programs that work with offenders in the community. The rally cry that nothing works refers to the belief that efforts to rehabilitate especially in the community do not work, and that we should therefore focus solely on punishment and not delude ourselves into thinking that offenders can be rehabilitated. It is believed that services such as those designed to help the offender find a job, to secure mental and physical health services or counseling, and other features normally part of alternatives should be optional, and while they may help the person become more employable and happier, they do not rehabilitate him. We shall now examine some of these criticisms.

One of the most controversial articles published in the last few years in corrections (which gave us the expression nothing works) was published by Robert Martinson in 1974.[1] Martinson completed what appears to be a much needed and thorough review of all research studies in corrections published from 1945 to 1967 and concluded, from this review, that everything we have tried in corrections has either proved not to work or has not demonstrated clear evidence of success.

A major problem of his work is that the cutoff date for inclusion in his review was 1967. Many important studies have been completed since then or are currently in progress. Even among several well-known studies, such as the California Community Treatment Program, much important information was released after 1967. California's Community Treatment Program intake continued into mid 1969, and the follow-up period continued well into 1973, greatly increasing the earlier sample size and parole follow-up period. The experimental group was then found to have committed offenses at a significantly lower rate than their experimental control group.[2]

Another problem is that studies were selected from "all those studies whose findings were interpretable—that is, whose design and execution met

Jerry Bergman is a professor at Bowling Green State University, Bowling Green, Ohio.

the conventional standards of social science research," according to Martinson's opinion.[3] That a majority of the studies consulted were rejected raises several questions relative to any conclusions one can make from Martinson's review. If nothing else, it indicates that it is difficult to do good research in corrections. This is true because it is difficult to obtain a control group, especially if the treatment being withheld is perceived as effective. There are ethical problems, and, typically, clear objections to withholding help for research reasons. More important, studies that met Martinson's "rigorous but hardly esoteric" requirements are likely to be measuring factors different from those measured by studies that were "not as rigorous." Thus it could be that many of the studies selected would be those that tend to produce a given result, not that a particular result is commonly found in all programs. Some of the criteria used to reject many studies had little to do with the study itself but were factors such as space limitations or publishers' requirements and problems such as the point that the research report only presented preliminary conclusions or that treatment descriptions were vague or that the statistical tests were inappropriate and "did not provide information so the reader could recompute the data." The results of many excellent programs probably were not included for reasons that had nothing to do with the quality of the project. Even the 231 studies that Martinson found acceptable contain major problems that make it very difficult to draw firm conclusions for the following reasons:

1. There are numerous methodology complications that make it difficult to understand the findings. When comparing projects, we find each deals with a different staff, philosophy, goal, and type of offenders. It is very difficult to control for many factors, although some of the more blatant factors, such as the size of the project city, can sometimes be controlled.

2. Martinson used primarily recidivist rates in his conclusions. Some of the major problems of this technique include the following:

   a. Usually only convicted offenders are included; excluded are offenders who were not apprehended, not charged, not prosecuted, or not convicted.

   b. The rate of apprehension and conviction for experienced criminals is not known, but several estimates indicate that it is quite low. Younger inexperienced criminals are more likely to be caught.

   c. Many other factors aside from recidivist rates are important (such as community, adjustment, gaining employable skills, changing one's attitude), and in the long run these factors may be more important. Many of these factors cannot be measured or can be measured only with difficulty. Problems with court records alone make it difficult to adequately assess recidivism, let alone other, less tangible factors.

3. There is no established criteria for determining recidivist rates. Whether a person has become a recidivist depends on the offender, the probation officer, the court, the community, the judge, and, more important how the offender feels about his probation officer in terms of abiding by his rules and so on. Criteria for a guilty verdict vary, and whether or not a person is violated for an offense depends on many situational factors. For this reason recidivist rates normally vary tremendously—from 2.8 percent to 74 percent even for very similar programs. Although the rate for prison cases tends to be around 50 percent and for probation cases around 20 percent, within these two groups there is tremendous variation. Thus the recidivist rate depends on many chance factors.[4]

Much of the criticism of correctional research, particularly alternatives to prison research, tends to focus on problems of research in corrections more than the effectiveness of the various correctional techniques. Martinson states:

> Despite our efforts, a pattern has run through much of this discussion—of studies which "found" effects without making any truly rigorous attempt to exclude competing hypotheses, of extraneous factors permitted to intrude upon the measurements, of recidivism measures which are not all measuring the same thing, of "follow-up" periods which vary enormously and rarely extend beyond the period of legal supervision, of experiments never replicated, of "system effects" not taken into account, of categories drawn up without any theory to guide the enterprise.[5]

These comments apply equally to studies in which no significant differences were found between prison and the alternative being compared, as well as to studies that supposedly found a significant difference. Martinson concluded, that "It is possible that some of our treatment programs are working to some extent, but that our research is so bad that it is incapable of telling."[6] This is a conclusion made on the basis of hundreds of studies that, according to Martinson, are the best available. The important question is, Can we, by means of the research method and given the resistance of the public, correctional workers, and judges, use the research method to determine what does work?

Critics of alternatives tend to accept the results of programs that produce no significant difference almost without question, but for studies that do produce significant positive results, such as Schnur (1948) and Saden (1962), a number of questions about the validity of the research are raised. Studies that produced no significant differences also should be critically examined. We must insure that factors are not present which cause us to find no significant difference when there actually is a significant difference. One could proceed from either assumption when analyzing a set of studies. This is not to say that studies that found positive results should not be examined with a high level of scrutiny; but that regardless of the results, all studies should be equally scrutinized. The implication is that if negative results are found, the study must be valid, and thus few details need to be supplied about these studies. Possible problems were not usually examined.

This bias is rather blatant in such statements as: "One can be reasonably sure that, so far, educational and vocational programs have not worked."[7] Aside from the difficulty of not knowing what is referred to as "worked," and the problems of making statistical comparisons, the critics of the Community Treatment Program or other alternatives rarely deal with the problem that it is difficult to demonstrate that a program such as fines or half-way houses and so on works, whether or not it actually does. Demonstrating that a program works and proving that it does are two different things. Many correctional workers with whom I have worked will vouch strongly for the fact that, for them, a certain program has worked even though some study (an artificial attachment to any program) has not proved it successful. For example, Martinson stated that "education and skill development have not reduced recidivism by rehabilitating criminals."[8] What he may have said is that it has not yet been demonstrated, in reference to the criteria that he has set up, that these programs reduce recidivism. The total worth of any program requires years of intensive follow-up, a procedure that few programs have had the benefit of using. An offender may return to crime several times after completing a program, but the effects of even the better programs tend not to show up until the recipient has had the benefit of years of maturity. Because one has a relapse does not mean the medicine has not helped.

We also have the problem of contradictory results. For example, in Martinson's discussion of the effect of individual counseling, one of the few significant results found, according to his selection criteria, was with individual psychotherapy with juveniles. Yet numerous studies have demonstrated that psychotherapy cure rates are close to spontaneous remission rates in adults. On further examination we find that the contradicting results can be accounted for if we control for relevant factors.

Of eight studies that researched juveniles in treatment, six found significant improvement for the experimental group. This is commensurate with several of Martinson's statements which indicate that the younger the offender the more amenable he is to treatment. Relative to the first statement, Palmer, who did most of the research for the California Community Treatment Program, agrees, but as to the latter statement he points out that it "holds up only if one has included, in the overall analysis, offenses which are of a minor nature—more specifically, technical violations . . ."[9] Thus as many factors as possible must be examined in addition to the rate of recidivism.

Palmer stated that Martinson's research produced certain significant positive findings from which several relatively optimistic conclusions can be drawn, in spite of Martinson's rather sweeping, negative conclusions.[10] Palmer reviewed the twenty studies, which, according to Martinson had significant positive results, in an attempt to find common elements and found, among other things, support for his thesis that the therapist's motivation and skill (and especially matching) is a factor found to be instrumental in the success of most successful programs. Martinson's conclusions were partly justified because, according to Palmer, Martinson was looking for "treatment methods that could be recommended on an across-the-board basis—i.e., for the offender population as a whole."[11] As in all other behavorial sciences as well as in medicine, there is simply no one treatment method that works in every case.[12] Treatment has to be individualized. The wonder drug, penicillin, is effective for almost all patients, but it has also killed some patients. A teacher ideally should assess each student's individual cognitive style to find which way of teaching will work best for each student. There simply is no across-the-board mode of treatment in the behavorial sciences; therefore, why should we expect one in corrections?

To illustrate why we find conflicting results in various studies, Palmer uses two hypothetical counseling studies where the experimental group of one study contained primarily offenders of personality type A and the experimental group of a second study was made up primarily of personality type B. If the counseling is beneficial to personality type A but not personality type B, the first study would "succeed" where the second would "fail," producing contradictory results. If the researcher controlled for this personality factor, the contradictory results would be understood.[13] Palmer stressed that

> . . . taken together, the various factors and conditions that have been described make it very difficult for any one treatment method to avoid being associated with a number of conflicting results. Given these practical and methodological "realities," only an unusually powerful and flexible mode of intervention would have been able to satisfy, even figuratively, Dr. Martinson's criteria of success for methods of treatment as a whole.[14]

The Oakland County Community Treatment Program (OCCTP) also found this factor to be very important.

Martinson almost consistently found positive results when the therapists were "specially chosen for their 'empathy' and 'non-possessive warmth.' In other words, it may well have been the therapist's special personal gifts rather than the fact of treatment itself that produced the favorable result."[15] In support of this Dodge found that a competent parole agent produced relative improvement in his charges whether he had a small or large case load, but an incompetent agent was more likely to produce a higher percentage of failures when he was given a small case load rather than a large case load.[16] Evidently the quality of supervision is more important than most other factors. Success, then, rests in the person doing the supervising. An inadequate supervisor is not going to help his charges by spending more time with them. Palmer has repeatedly stressed that many of the things we have looked at are irrelevant. The important factor is the personality of the probation officer. The fact that most other factors are somewhat irrelevant helps us to understand our failure to obtain significant results when these various factors are studied. For example, Martinson, in summarizing his review of numerous studies stated:

> These programs are especially hard to summarize because of their variety; they differ, for example, in how "supportive" or "permissive" they are designed to be, in the extent to which they are combined with other treatment methods such as individual therapy, group counseling, or skill development, and in how completely the program is able to control all the relevant aspects of the institutional environment.[17]

This finding is understandable when we consider Palmer's conclusions. Likewise, many other studies that concluded that there was no significant difference, when examined, may produce significant results.

One of the studies that found positive results and is used in the United States as an example of a successful alternative is the California Community Treatment Program. This program was criticized on grounds that are equally valid for studies that concluded that no significant differences exist. The California Community Treatment Program found lower recidivist rates for the experimental group at twelve and thirty-six months, but not at twenty-four and sixty months. The twelve- and thirty-six-month results were quoted to prove success, while the twenty-four- and sixty-month figures were ignored. A longer follow-up for studies with negative conclusions could result in positive results. Ideally, to draw *any* conclusions, we should use much longer follow-up periods, at least five years and preferably seven to ten years. The fact that the populations of the study were not fully comparable and that different organizations were used for each population (a probation agency for the experimental group and a parole agency for the control group) could also apply to many studies that found no significant positive differences. Further examination of many negative studies could find that the two groups are not fully comparable on other grounds as well. Often there are elements involved in the control group that clearly could be seen as treatment, reducing the difference between the two groups. This was an important factor in the California Community Treatment Program's results.

Many critics of prison alternatives imply that the number of recorded violations is the number of real violations. Often actual, reported, and convicted violations are three different numbers. More intensive treatment in any program tends to place the offender in the limelight more often and therefore it is commonly believed, tends to cause the officer to become more aware of violations. Consequently, with more intensive treatment, there may be a tendency for more reported violations. The number of actual violations may not be much different or may possibly be fewer than the control group.

The Effectiveness of Prisons

Martinson summarizes the effects of the general type of prison on the level of recidivism: "In short, we know very little about the recidivism effects of various degrees of security in existing institutions."[18] This could be extended to, relative to prison treatment, that we know very little about what works and what doesn't work. Individuals are infinitely complex, and an endless number of elements probably influences one's propensity to crime, although undoubtedly, there are several major factors. This argument concerning which treatment program is best or most successful seems to come up again and again in most of the studies done in corrections. For instance, Martinson quoted a study done by Garrity which found that when offenders were divided into three categories, prosocial, antisocial, and manipulative, the prosocial category had a low recidivist rate regardless of the length of their sentence, the antisocial group did better with short sentences, and the manipulative group did better with longer sentences. Palmer and other researchers have found this same factor.[19] Yet a study in Britain found that previous offenders, but not first offenders, had a lower rate of recidivism when they served longer sentences,[20] while another British study found the reverse to be true with juveniles.[21] All of this clearly stresses that many factors are involved in achieving success. The handful of studies completed so far has not even begun to control for the many factors that obviously influence length of sentence. The majority of the completed studies that Martinson examined (including, ironically, several of his own studies) did not meet his criteria, criteria that he terms "minimally acceptable."

Critics of alternatives use much space criticizing studies that work but merely accept without question the studies that do not work. This does not mean that criticism of the studies that work is not necessary. In many cases excellent, cogent criticism of successful studies is presented. Often the criticism does not negate the results but could be understood to do so by an uncritical reader. For instance, Martinson quotes five studies that conclude that intensive supervision does work. He then states

> . . . yet these studies left some important questions unanswered. For instance, was this improved performance a function merely of the number of contacts a youngster had with his probation officer? Did it also depend upon the length of time in treatment? Or was it the quality of supervision that was making the difference, rather than the quantity?[22]

These are all excellent questions, but they do not negate the positive results of the studies under discussion, although it is implied that these qualifications do bring the results into question.

Another criticism leveled against successful programs is that the program could have succeeded because of the enthusiasm of the staff and the newness of the program, not because of the effectiveness of the program. This effect, commonly known as the Hawthorne effect, is extremely important and should be examined, but it is present in almost all new programs dealing with human beings. This criticism simply stresses that it takes time before we can determine the effectiveness of any new program. A program must function for a while before we can assess its effectiveness. This reality certainly should not discourage us from doing social science research but should encourage us to do more longitudinal studies.

Occasionally, researchers make unsupported statements such as the following:

> It was claimed, the higher reported offense rate was primarily an artifact of the more intense surveillance that the experimental youth received. But the data show that this is not a sufficient explanation of the low failure rate among the experimental youth; the difference in "tolerance" of offenses between experimental officials and control officials was much greater than the difference in the rates at which these two systems detected youths committing new offenses.[23]

No research data was given to back up this statement, and it is difficult to determine the effects of more intense surveillance, although it would be ideal if this factor could be isolated. Until it is, we must rely on the limited research available which supports the belief that intense surveillance uncovers more offenses, producing an artificially higher rate.

In spite of the attempts to be objective, researchers often make a number of clearly subjective statements. For instance, Martinson says, one cannot ignore the fact that the *punishment* of offenders *is the major means we have of* deterring incipient offenders.[24] Then he goes on to admit that it is not known whether punishment is, in fact, a deterrent. "We know almost nothing about the 'deterrent effect' [of punishment] largely because 'treatment' theories have been relegated to the status of a historical curiosity."[25] This cogent statement contradicts the previous assertion. In another place Martinson stated, "By and large, intensive supervision does work,"[26] and then in his summary, stated, "No single treatment method consistently works."[27] Many other examples could be cited.

Martinson concludes that "with few and isolated exceptions the rehabilitative effects that have been reported so far have had no appreciable effect on recidivism,"[28] but a statistical tabulation done by Palmer reveals that 48 percent of the total number of cases selected by Martinson have yielded positive or partly positive results.[29] A breakdown of this total is rather impressive, but, more important, only published results were used. We have no idea how most programs turned out, but only those that were researched and that managed to publish the results. It would seem more difficult to publish a study that found negative results, possibly biasing the results of Martinson's study in the direction of his conclusion.

A factor rarely considered is that because of the nature of research, studies that produce negative results quite possibly are easier to carry out (thus there are more of them) than studies that will produce positive results. The only way to eliminate this problem is to systematically examine every project, using the same evaluation criteria for each. It is also unsound to base conclusions about what works on published studies because there are many factors that determine whether or not a study is published; not the least important is the identification, prominence, reputation, or fame of the author or researcher. Well-known researchers are in a position to publish their findings, but other researchers, whether they find results that are positive or negative, may have a more difficult time.

For a more complete evaluation an examination should be made of all studies completed. For example, Martinson reviewed but excluded a large number of studies. Palmer's evaluation of Martinson's research concludes that many were rejected because the evaluation focused on "educational achievement, personality and attitude change, general adjustment to the outside community" as opposed to purely criminal recidivism.[30] Palmer notes that of the studies rejected there were "a large number of favorable" compared with "unfavorable" or "ambiguous" studies and many that examined probation in lieu of prison. Also, small case loads and intensive supervision were not used in many studies.

Palmer concludes, in his sumamry of works critical of the Community Treatment Program, that instead of asking What works? we should ask, "Which method works best for which type of offenders, and under what conditions or in what types of settings?"[31] The field of education, where this problem has been more thoroughly explored, has validated the contention that Palmer's question is more appropriate. Since correctional rehabilitation is primarily adult education, studies done in the field of education shed some light on the problems of rehabilitation. Much of the research done in education is superior to research done in corrections. Since it has long been recognized that the research done in education tends to be somewhat less scientific than that of the physical sciences and even many of the behavioral sciences (especially experimental psychology), the corrections field has a long way to go before credence can be placed in the results of its research.

After reflecting on the gloomy conclusions of various correctional researchers, an examination of other studies helps to give a proper perspective. Eysenck concluded that his research fails to support the hypothesis that psychotherapy facilitates recovery from neurotic disorder, finding essentially no difference in the speed and quality of recovery between those receiving therapy and those not receiving therapy.[32] Peel has concluded from his review of several studies that there is no difference in longevity rates between individuals who regularly receive medical care and individuals who avoid all medical care for religious reasons and that some studies even indicate that those who refuse medical treatment have the advantage.[33] He states that this research data is impressive enough that "special provision is made for Christian Scientists by an increasing number of insurance companies," because, statistically, not using medical treatment does not shorten their life span or make them less healthy. In other words, medical treatment confers no advantage on the population compared with Christian Scientists whose religion forbids them to receive medical care. Long-term studies by Theodore Newcomb in answer to the question, What does college do for a person? concluded that it does very little.[34] Thus if modern psychotherapy, modern medicine, and modern education have essentially no effect on people, why do we spend billions of dollars on education, medicine, and mental health care? We would expect to find differences between countries who have these advantages and those who do not. Clearly there are differences. The problem is that it is hard to prove scientifically that these institutions have an effect on those who receive their services. The problem seems to be demonstrating the effect that we believe to be there. One who has worked in these correctional programs and is clearly seeing results cannot say that the program does not work. There is little doubt that the Oakland County Community Treatment Program worked at least for some offenders for the duration of the project, but proving that it did is an entirely different matter.

Some researchers seem to conclude that every program designed to help offenders should be abolished unless they can be proved to be successful in every case. Criminals and the public are often dichotomized with the conclusion that criminals should be dealt with, but few feasible methods are suggested. Researchers often spend more time criticizing persons holding the opposing view than they do attacking the issues.

This does not mean that the results of programs should not be criticized. It is imperative that valid criticisms be developed in order for correctional research to move forward. For example, a valid criticism leveled against many programs was given by Martinson, namely, if a "program works and research uncovered an 'invention' which could 'significantly reduce' recidivism, the public would want to know by how much. 5 percentage points, 10? 15?' "[35] These questions are very significant.

A common problem is that people do not recognize that crime is a social problem, and the public produces criminals as much as it is victimized by them. Labeling does not solve problems, especially complex social problems. A program may be successful but may not reduce the crime rate, which depends much more on social conditions than programs dealing with convicted offenders. Many researchers want to develop radical methods of crime control that will drastically reduce the crime rate, yet few ideas are produced. I have read of few innovative programs. Most are variations on existing ones. They are always faced with the problem of demonstrating scientifically that a program is successful—one of our main difficulties.

Researchers are finding that some programs are successful. Community Treatment Programs, for example, when compared with prison, work. Palmer found that, for the California Community Treatment Program, "more than 93 percent of the eligibles appear to have been handled at least as effectively within the community located program as in the prison program, and . . . 50 percent have been handled more effectively."[36] In another paper Martinson states that "we are not apologists or . . . advocates of those who incarcerate all or most offenders,"[37] and in yet another paper Martinson states, "those placed on probation almost inevitably perform better relative to recidivism than do those of similar background and criminal history who are placed in prison."[38]

Martinson, although somewhat pessimistic regarding treatment as a whole, supports prison alternatives compared with prison, stating, "Our research indicates that the mere placement on probation or parole may be more important in the reduction of recidivism than are treatment elements, such as group counseling, prevocational training, job placement, and psychological testing which have been pasted onto probation and parole."[39] [Assuming that these things produce better-adjusted individuals, we might be producing better-adjusted criminals instead of better-adjusted persons less likely to continue as criminals.] As Martinson states, ". . . why [would we] expect group counseling, or learning to read, or being taught how to fill out a job application would transform most violent offenders into law abiding citizens?"[40] The treatment model is based on the plausible theory, that teaching a person to read will help him get a better job, thus helping him to achieve satisfaction in a noncriminal life, which in turn reduces his need to pursue a criminal life once criminal behavior has become part of his lifestyle. But teaching him to read may simply result in a criminal who can read as opposed to a criminal who cannot read. Thus, in theory, reading may be highly instrumental in reducing involvement in crime, but the offender probably must know how to read first, then successfully achieve in noncriminal areas before he is less likely to become involved in criminal behavior. It is difficult to demonstrate what specific effect learning to read has on crime without an adequate number of good studies, and, therefore, at this point, we cannot say that teaching an offender how to read does not help until these studies are done.

Martinson advocates removing the criminal justice system from the treatment business, assuming that the state and local governments could provide the existing services to the offender population. Actually, most of the state and local services are available to the offender population at the present time. The problem is that few offenders avail themselves of these services without some type of coercion. Martinson's main substitute for treatment is what he terms "restraining" in which, in essence, a private policeman is assigned daily to follow each offender, without the offender's knowing it. The restrainee is not to know who his agent is, and the agents will be periodically shifted to different restrainees to guard against corruption. The restrainer could be a paraprofessional and could include ex-offenders, unemployed teenagers, and the like. His only job would be to catch the restrainee in the act of crime. When this occurs, he is to call the police and either testify or produce evidence (photographs, fingerprints, and so forth).

Other Criticisms of Alternatives and of the Community Treatment Programs

Conclusions in the published literature sometimes show lack of research, especially in blanket condemnatory statements, such as Robison's, ". . . there is, as of yet, almost no evidence that available correctional alternatives have any impact on . . . [the likelihood of recidivism]".[41] In his review Robison does not consider the importance of using established criteria in interpreting an event as a violation. While it is true that uniform standards are seldom agreed on, this certainly does not justify the generalization that "no evidence was found to support claims of superior rehabilitative efficacy of one correctional alternative over another."[42] There are a number of studies that indicate the reverse. For example, Davidson concludes that in the attempt to rehabilitate chronic juvenile offenders through community-based treatment "behavior modification techniques can be successfully used with hard-core delinquents . . . [and] . . . many of the negative effects of institutionalization can be avoided by community treatment."[43] The evaluation of the Provo experiment concluded that with "persistent delinquent offenders" community treatment was more effective than incarceration and was more humanitarian and far less costly. Although even these examples may be criticized, statements such as Robison's indicate either ignorance of the field or inside information that few researchers possess.

Probably one of the most reasonable criticisms of both community corrections and the prison system has been made by David F. Greenberg. After restating the evidence for the belief that prisons deter crime, Greenberg cited the several studies which indicated that "length of sentence for adult male prisoners appears to have no measurable effect on outcome after release, as one might expect if prisons were truly criminogenic."[44] Still other studies also show that success rates of probationers and released prisoners are substantially the same when the background variables of offenders are controlled. Recidivist rates are often much higher for those institutionalized compared with those on probation, but rarely are the great background differences between the two groups controlled for.

One important factor rarely dealt with when looking at the Community Treatment Program is the problem of working with an offender in the community where temptations, including pressure from the environment and his peers to resume a former life-style, abound. Community treatment programs could be located in the community but as far as possible from high crime incidence areas. Ideally offenders should be removed from their old environment and placed into a new community environment to reduce criminal contact and to develop beneficial community contacts. Another serious problem is that in theory the offender has many opportunities in the community that he does not have in prison, but realistically many opportunities, including employment, training, and so forth, are severely limited. If good schools, adequate housing, and good jobs reduce crime, what good does it do to live in a community that lacks them? The offender in the community program is still working with professional personnel; thus the conflict between the offender and most authority figures is still present.

Another valid criticism of the community treatment programs include is its expense.[45] Many of the costs involved in institutional care are fixed, and a reduced number of inmates does not usually mean a lower cost, but simply a higher per capita cost for those still incarcerated. Greenberg "knows of no Department of Corrections . . . where extensive decarceration has taken place that has reduced its overall budget."[46] More important, Greenberg stresses that the effect of substituting community alternatives for imprisonment on crime rates (instead of recidivism rates) has not been fully assessed. Going to prison may not change the offender's chance of recidivism, but it may affect the would-be offenders in the community. Another important point is that community correctional programs would probably vary widely in quality. Small towns without a crime problem are unlikely to invest much money in specialized programs. This possibility would call for a community correctional system to be set up by the state or another large agency.

Robison and Smith summarize the studies done on California's alternatives, concluding "variations in recidivism rates among these alternatives are, for the most part, attributable to initial differences among the types of offender processed, and that the remaining differences in violation rates between programs may be accounted for by differences in interpreting an event as a violation, or in officially designating it as such. No evidence was found to support claims of superior rehabilitative efficacy of one correctional alternative over another."[47] Robison stresses that the effectiveness of many programs was not studied rigorously until recently and gives two reasons for this lack of research.

1. The effectiveness of various correctional programs is difficult to evaluate because adequate measures of performance have not been established.

2. Attempts to measure behavior are made more difficult by variances in systems of reporting and recordkeeping.[48]

Unfortunately, these are still serious problems in correctional research, and there are at present, few concerted efforts to overcome them. Robison are still serious problems in correctional research, and there are, at present, few concerted efforts to overcome them. Robison stresses that efforts to work with offenders in the community have not been studied until recently; thus there has not been enough time to establish the degree of effectiveness (or ineffectiveness) of the various types of community treatment and that current trends away from the therapeutic approach to treatment are premature. By any standards though, the community treatment concept has not been adequately evaluated. Robison stresses that even with the sophistication of multivariate analysis, it is still difficult to separate all the influences—both known and unknown—on the measuring instruments.

Robison states that California's Community Treatment Program has not consistently demonstrated statistically significant differences in favor of community treatment as compared with the control group. In terms of actual offenses it appears that the experimentals committed more known offenses than the controls (2.81 per experimental compared with 1.61 per control). Robison concludes that this higher incidence of crime commitment by the experimental group is probably an effect of increased supervision and hypothesizes that if the controls had been watched as carefully, there probably would have been few differences. But like many other researchers, he is stressing the recidivist rate and is not looking at the many other factors of community treatment. We may have only better-adjusted criminals, but the long-term effect of increased help is rarely examined. It is quite possible that although the number of delinquent acts may remain high while the offender is in his youth, his behavior twenty or thirty years later may be drastically different. Early experiences tend to be cumulative, that is, the benefits of high school compared with a sixth-grade education are cumulative. The person makes more money, is able to afford better medical care, and is better adjusted, which in turn enables him to work more, earn more money, and receive better medical care, and so on. Even the short-term effect is such that Robison concludes "One might, however, still argue in favor of 'community treatment' on humanitarian and economic grounds."[49]

Robison quotes a study by Jaman which indicates that keeping men in prison longer increases the probability of recidivism.[50] This is in direct contrast to several other studies which indicate that there are no differences. Berecochea reviewed six studies, all of which found no relationship between prison time and recidivism. Obviously Robison is either selecting studies that support his thesis or is unaware of many studies. Contradictory studies must be carefully compared to discover the contradictions in them. Even in expository writing it is a poor practice to conclude anything from a single study, especially when contrary evidence exists.[51]

Robison's discussion of group counseling brings out an important point: "Only infrequently are treatment programs subject to the types of experimental testing necessary for valid evaluation."[52] Unfortunately, as stressed in this chapter, much of the published research in corrections deals with simple descriptions of the program: narratives, theoretical justifications, or, in Robison's words, "shoddy evaluations without adequate control group and random assignment of cases."[53]

The prison offers an ideal situation for research, and it is difficult to understand why there is not a large amount of adequate research done. Robison then concludes on the basis of studies that he previously described as "shoddy" that "participation in group counseling and community living did not lessen even the limited endorsement of the inmate code, nor did it result in a demonstrable decrease in frequency of prison discipline problems."[54]

In correctional literature it is common to read of extensive criticisms of a research study and then to find overgeneralizations from this poor research and the conclusion that some program is unsuccessful. Clearly, larger studies are needed, controlling for many more factors. But until we have these larger studies, and some firm conclusions, let us not disseminate generalizations.

There are, however, elements that have been consistently found to be instrumental in success (for example, the personality of the correctional worker). Therefore, the limited follow-up studies that looked at a limited number of factors (such as recidivism) could not support sweeping generalizations such as, "There are still no treatment techniques which have unequivocally demonstrated themselves capable of reducing recidivism."[55] In the same way that Robison applies this quote to corrections it could be applied to most therapeutic techniques used in psychology including psychotherapy and general counseling, as well as to most educational programs. What teaching techniques has "unequivocally demonstrated itself capable of" teaching all students? Correction programs are not the only factor to be considered. It is not only the inability of corrections to change the behavior of those under its care, but also the inability of the schools, therapists, counselors, and the church and family. But there are obvious techniques that are effective even though it is difficult to prove that they are effective in every case.

In summary, Robison's criticism of treatment consists of a review of a limited amount of literature which indicates that many treatment programs have not worked. He endeavors to reduce the commonly used treatment dichotomy concept realizing that treatment is not the antithesis of punishment and that punishment itself can be a type of treatment. He concludes, "Will the clients act differently if we lock them up, or keep them locked up longer, or do something with them inside, or watch them more closely afterward, or cut them loose officially?—Probably not."[56]

Some alternatives work for some offenders; in other cases a stint in jail or prison may work best. Jail can and does motivate many offenders to lead noncriminal lives, but it does not affect others, and it makes still others bitter and more likely to relapse. The words and actions of the offenders themselves commonly bear this out. If there was some balance among these three groups, and the experience of many probation and parole officers indicates that there is, then we would expect that for an aggregate number of offenders imprisonment would make little difference while still making a positive difference for many other offenders. Certainly Robison's cursory examination of the literature does not warrant the conclusion, "Since the more unpleasant or punishing alternatives tend also to be more expensive, the choice of appropriate disposition for offenders should be determined by the amount of punishment we want to impose and the amount of money we are prepared to spend in imposing it; it should not be obscured by illusions of differential rehabilitative efficacy."[57] Possibly the vantage point of a person involved primarily in administration or university teaching, as most contributors to correctional research tend to be, differs from that of a caseworker who spends a great deal of time each day in contact with probationers. This difference produces varying opinions.

It is not uncommon to find contradictions even within a single research article which is an indication of the poor research often found in corrections. For instance, Daniel Glasser's article in the January 1971 issue of *Crime and Delinquency* states "all criminal record information will be incomplete . . . since one can know only about the offenses for which a man is caught."[58] Two pages later he forgets this consideration and states, "Considering also the combination of low income, limited resources, accumulated needs, pent up desires, and prior criminality, it is remarkable that at least nine out of ten adult offenders spend at least their first month out of prison trying to solve their problems by legitimate means; in most jurisdictions for which data are available, a majority seem to persist indefinitely."[59] It is doubtful that nine out of ten try to solve their problems by legitimate means. Even five out of ten may be an overoptimistic estimation. It can only be said that at least nine out of ten adult offenders are *not convicted* of an offense they commited in their first month out of prison. Garabedian states another problem:

A . . . problem with controlled experiments is the necessity of maintaining integrity of the research design throughout the experimental period. The history of controlled experimental research in corrections clearly reveals that it is impossible to maintain the required level of rigor. There is not a single instance of controlled experimentation in corrections that has maintained complete integrity of the research design so that observed changes in dependent variables can be attributed indisputably to the independent variable. The difficulties involved in random selection, the attrition in numbers of experimental and control subjects, deliberate or unintentional changes in the program, and the difficulties of clearly defining the program (the independent variable) are fundamental reasons for the failure of the controlled experiment as an unambiguous evaluative method of correctional research.[60]

The constant problem of different violation standards (especially more lenient violation standards with the treatment group) caused Garabedian to state that it is "difficult to keep faith in the concept of controlled experimentation as a method of correctional research."[61] Even if a study were to maintain full integrity, outside researchers would probably be somewhat skeptical due to the lack of rigor of most past research.

Garabedian proposes several excellent reasons for the difficulty that many programs have had in demonstrating success. He stresses the advantage of controlled experimentation where a two-group, randomly assigned, experimental control group is measured in a before-and-after sequence model, and "while the controlled experiment represents the most powerful theoretical model for deriving reliable knowledge . . . especially in social control systems, [it] is fraught with difficulties."[62] These difficulties include the serious ethical problems of programs which utilize involuntary subjects or subjects who do not fully comprehend the purpose of the program. Garabedian states "we can predict that future decisions by the Supreme Court will make it increasingly difficult to conduct controlled experiments with offenders."[63]

Another problem that Garabedian mentions is that "correctional institutions exist to perpetuate themselves."[64] For this reason decisions are made from the perspective of organizational maintenance. This tends to make the prison structure so rigid that it is very difficult for research on community treatment programs to be carried out properly. Garabedian feels that " 'treatment-oriented' institutions are really not radically different in their form of organization for 'custody-oriented' institutions," stressing that the experimental group is often not much different from the control group as far as the actual treatment received is concerned.[65] This explains why recidivist rates of offenders released from treatment institutions tend to be similar to those of offenders released from so-called custody-oriented institutions. He also stresses that there is strong resistance to change by the "existing correctional organizations . . . and . . . petrified bureaucracies." High-quality research is rare, partially because the prisons and most treatment centers tend to be responsive to developing conditions and make system change in order to meet them, contaminating the research design. As was the problem in Oakland County's Community Treatment Program, most correctional personnel seem to be unaware of the necessity for many of the elements necessary for good research design.

Many recent programs have been established with the goal of working with offenders in the community. This is obviously threatening to prison administrations and personnel alike. Especially within the prison we find the paradox that prisons are increasingly willing to play host for projects designed to bring about change yet have so far remained "virtually untouched by them."[66] As the newness of a project wears off, Garabedian states, these projects "becomes a thorn in the side of the prison's administration. Occasionally, overt conflict erupts. Thus, despite the usual publicity given to a project when it begins, prison administrators and project staff alike are generally relieved to see it end. When the demonstration period is completed and the foundation grant used up, prison and project personnel shake hands, congratulate each other on a job well done, and part company, probably never to see or hear from one another again."[67] This summary of Garabedian's experience is similar to mine; once the project has been finished, there is little attempt to fully assess what has happened and there is even less attempt to apply the implications of the program to correctional practice. The ending of a program probably has a negative effect on the inmates. As Garabedian states, "Within hours the program, where the inmate perhaps for the first time in years was allowed to speak his piece on matters that directly affected him, becomes a thing of the past. The inmate again is a number doing time. This dramatic reversal of status serves to reaffirm what the inmate knew all along: that prison authorities only pay lip service to the ideal of rehabilitation."[68] It is obviously difficult for innovate programs to work, because, as Garabedian says, "at best, research-demonstration projects have been successful in bringing about limited change temporarily."[69]

Another reason for the limited success of research projects is the lack of commitment of many of the administrators and supervisory staff. The project ideally needs to be initiated from the top administrators down. The project supervisor, who is typically responsible for planning and implementing the research, is often viewed by administrators and staff alike as simply another administrator, an associate superintendent. This is probably true in correctional institutions and parole and probation facilities as well. The project director may be fully convinced of the value of his program, and, armed with a lot of academic information and innovative ideas, may leave the impression on the prison, probation, or parole staff that he is there to fix or change the program and help the poorly equipped staff who appear not to know what they are doing in the project director's view. There is deep resentment against these reformers who are often seen as having little practical experience to solve long-standing problems. The project director is seen as an outsider, having little practical experience, and lacking a long-range commitment to the agency. In addition to being suspicious of him, they are likely to feel he is naive and impractical. Antagonism is especially strong between project director and the top administrators. In many ways the project director, not the administrator, is the man with knowledge. Administrators thus often react negatively to the project, sometimes even overtly sabotaging the project. As Garabedian says "the top administrative staff can literally make or break the project."[70] It is all too easy for administrators to project any problems, which may or may not have anything to do with the project, onto the project. An innovative project is an easy scapegoat for administrators and staff alike, especially if the project increases the workload and the number of problems for the staff or administrators.

In summary, there is a lack of good research on alternatives to prison (as well as lack of good research on the effect of prison) and much of the completed research evidences methodological problems. Whether an offender is rehabilitated depends on so many factors that sorting them out would require more research than has so far been undertaken. And there is clearly a need to integrate this research, to coordinate projects, and to make sense out of what has been produced in a rational, unbiased manner, much as was attempted by Martinson.

There is much evidence for the efficacy of the alternatives or community treatment approach, but many questions still have to be answered. It is also clear that most agencies are not willing to expend the funds and energy necessary to effectively evaluate their programs.

In the past few years attacks from many quarters have been directed at any approach that does not involve uniform punishment. Thus we have seen both justifiable and unjustifiable attacks on most alternatives to prison. Many are valid and should be carefully considered, but many amount to little more than stacking the cards, selective perception, and playing with statistics. It is clear that there are many effective, feasible alternatives to prison, many alternatives that have not been tried or have been tried only to a limited extent. Much of the research indicating that nothing works has been examined, and while it has raised many important questions, it is partially the product of the disappointing results of many projects, and, more important, of the current mood of the public. Tragically, it has actually exacerbated the situation; many agencies, including most of the large government funding sources, are unwilling to fund programs or research dealing with the community treatment program. This has resulted in an extremely discouraging state of affairs. I have been repeatedly turned down for grants to complete a five-year follow-up study on the highly successful community treatment program of Oakland County. The battle cry that nothing works is considered gospel by many, at least in the case of community alternatives approaches. Community treatment has been condemned even though the evidence points to the fact that it does work in spite of the limited and haphazard attempts to make it work.

There are some signs that the negative feelings toward prison alternatives are changing. For most offenders the community treatment approach may not achieve all of the desired results, but its shortcomings are fewer than in the prison system. The examination in this chapter is an attempt to honestly appraise the situation and not to sell any one approach. I hope that this discussion will facilitate honest inquiry into what does work, and especially what works best with whom, an important question all too often left unasked.

Notes

1. Robert Martinson, "What Works? Questions and Answers about Prison Reform," *Public Interest* (1974):24. Reprinted with permission.

2. Ted Palmer, "Martinson Revisited," *Journal of Research in Crime and Delinquency* 12 (July 1976):133-152.

3. Martinson, "What Works?" p. 24.

4. Palmer, "Martinson Revisited," pp. 133-152.

5. Martinson, "What Works?" p. 27.

6. Ibid., p. 49.

7. Ibid., p. 28.

8. Ibid.,

9. Palmer, "Martinson Revisited," p. 145.

10. Ibid., p. 138.

11. Matinson, "What Works?" p. 27.

12. John M. Reed, *The Murderer and His Victim* (Springfield, Ill.: Charles C. Thomas, 1961), p. 39.

13. Palmer, "Martinson Revisited," p. 140.

14. Ibid., p. 141.

15. Martinson, "What Works?" p. 32.

16. C. Dodge, "Training Parole and Probation Officers To Use Community Resources for Their Clients" mimeographed (Louisville, Ky.: The Kentucky Manpower Commission, 1973) pp. 25.

17. Martinson, "What Works?" p. 33.

18. Ibid., p. 36.

19. Palmer, "Martinson Revisited," p. 145-146.

20. Ibid., p. 146.

21. See Richard Neville, "Inside Britain's Jails," *Punch* (February 25, 1976):309-311. See also "A British View: Certainty of Punishment 'Is Best Deterrent to Crime,' " *U.S. News and World Report* (May, 1976):41-42.

22. Martinson, "What Works?" p. 42.

23. Ibid., p. 44.

24. Ibid., p. 50.

25. Ibid.

26. Ibid., 24.

27. Ibid.

28. Ibid., p. 25.

29. Palmer, "Martinson Revisited," p. 142.

30. T.B. Palmer, "The Youth Authority's Community Treatment Project," *Federal Probation* 37 (1974):142.

31. Ibid., p. 143.

32. Hans J. Eysenck, *The Effects of Psychotherapy* (New York: International Science Press, 1966), pp. 5-42.

33. Robert Peel, *Christian Science: Its Encounter with American Culture* (New York: Henry Holt and Company, 1958), pp. 151-152.

34. Carol Tavris, "The Art of Staying Optimistic: A Sketch of Theodore Newcomb," *Psychology Today* (September, 1974):73.

35. Robert Martinson, "California's Research at the Crossroads," *Crime and Delinquency* 22 (1976):190.

36. Palmer, "Martinson Revisited," p. 144.

37. Judith Wilks and Robert Martinson, "Is the Treatment of Criminal Offenders Really Necessary?" *Federal Probation* 2 (March, 1976):3.

38. Ibid.

39. Ibid., p. 4.

40. Ibid.

41. James Robison and Gerald Smith, "The Effectiveness of Correctional Programs," *Crime and Delinquency* 17 (1971):67-80.

42. Ibid., p. 67.

43. William S. Davidson, *Kentfield's Rehabilitation Program: An Alternative to Institutionalization*, mimeographed (Grand Rapids, Mich.: Kent County Juvenile Court, 1971), pp. 16.

44. John E. Berecochea, Dorothy R. Jaman, and Welton A. Jones, "Time Served in Prison and Parole Outcome: An Experimental Study," Report No. 1, Sacramento, Calif.: California Department of Corrections, p. 3.

45. David F. Greenberg, "Problems in Community Corrections," *Issues in Criminology* 10 (1975):1-33.

46. Ibid., p. 6.

47. Robison and Smith, "Effectiveness of Correctional Programs," p. 76.

48. Ibid., p. 77.

49. Ibid., p. 78.

50. Ibid., p. 79.

51. Berecochea, Jaman, and Jones, "Time Served in Prison," p. 5.

52. Robison and Smith, "Effectiveness of Correctional Programs," p. 72.

53. Ibid.

54. Ibid., p. 74.

55. Ibid.

56. Ibid., p. 80.

57. Ibid.

58. Daniel Glasser, "Five Practical Research Suggestions for Correctional Administrators," *Crime and Delinquency* 17 (1971):33-35.

59. Ibid., p. 35.

60. Peter G. Garabedian, Research and Practice in Planning Correctional Change," *Crime and Delinquency* 17 (1971):46-54.

61. Ibid., p. 47.

62. Ibid., p. 45.

63. Ibid., p. 46.

64. Ibid., p. 49.

65. Ibid.

66. Ibid., p. 51.

67. Ibid., p. 52.

68. Ibid.

69. Ibid., p. 53.

70. Ibid., p. 54.

12 A World without Prisons: Dream or Reality

This book has presented descriptions of a sample of the alternatives to prison that are currently being used in several nations. To some, these alternatives may suggest that the world is on the brink of a major breakthrough with respect to significant, workable, and empirically researched methods to correct social deviants. There is, indeed, evidence from certain countries that a modern sophisticated and workable approach to corrections is taking effect. Correction systems in most countries are only beginning the long journey toward this modern approach. Old traditions, values, beliefs, and fears are deeply ingrained in the social fabric of societies, and changes are slow in developing. Most corrections systems, especially systems of incarceration, produce little success, and yet they are maintained, expanded, and defended. These systems of locking up law offenders are outmoded, ex-, pensive, inadequately administered, ailing bureaucracies. They adhere to older styles and philosophies of corrections and often succeed in maintaining their antiquated status quo with public support. Their capital investments continue to grow far beyond any original intent and purpose outlined by the legislative bodies that created them. They demand much money and manpower often in the face of questionable data regarding their worth.

In this chapter we shall examine some aspects of this system as it exists today, the forces that are often responsible for resisting change, and some concepts that may hasten a change. Our conclusions will focus on the question, Is it possible to have a world without prisons?

Penal Systems Today

According to a recent United Nations survey of member nations, data indicate that about two-thirds of the member nations responding to the survey are maintaining adequate and humane prison systems and are treating their inmates according to a recommended standard of rules. These rules include the provision for adequate medical services, adequate clothing and bedding, a healthy diet, education and recreation services, certain opportunity for resocialization, and other items. The responses to the survey by member nations does not tell us much about successful work programs, vocational training, work or leave programs, or any alternatives to prison that may be supported by the prison system. These are difficult to find and in many cases do not exist. I visited along with several other investigators a sample of these prison systems in the Orient, North America, Europe, and the Middle East and found that most prison systems have made little progress toward modernization, treatment, resocialization or any significant justification for their existence per se. Prison abolishment and prison alternatives continue to be exciting concepts supported in only a few nations. The success of present prison systems according to all the data accumulated is highly questionable, and prisons are no more successful by almost any set of criteria than they were twenty or fifty years ago. Innovation of resocialization programs is lacking in most of the world's prison programs, and there appears to be little evidence that any great change will take place in the next twenty-five years unless some radically different philosophy of social deviance and its correction develops in these nations. The obstacles to the implementation of even basic rules as recommended by the United Nations is caused by legislative inaction, lack of adequate funding, shortages of facilities, and insufficient numbers of qualified personnel. In many countries the slowness and complexity of the legal machinery prevent implementation of furloughs and work release programs, temporary home leave, programs of increased compensation for prison labor, and programs of parole or probation with concurrent alternatives applied. Overcrowding of prison systems and institutions is now becoming a more serious problem than it has ever been in the history of the modern prison system. Prison programs continue to depreciate in many countries because inadequate funding necessitates the hiring of unqualified personnel, even after training, to work in the system. Low wages earned by prison staffs discourage qualified persons from even applying for the many jobs that need to be filled. Specialists such as psychiatrists, psychologists, medical doctors, and social workers are almost nonexistent in many prisons.[1]

This is a partial picture of prisons systems as we visited them. While this picture is rather bleak, reformists must not be discouraged. This picture only underlines the need for a stronger demand for alternatives. A complex set of forces must be dealt with before change can be suggested. These forces are discussed in this chapter.

The Forces in a Changing Society

Prison systems or their alternatives are basically a means by which societies attempt to correct social deviants. These individuals are so labeled because it appears that they have internalized an incorrect set of norms of their society or culture. In most societies, prevailing standards, values, beliefs, and norms are used to lable and define deviants. The method of resocialization for deviants who become entangled in the legal system is a period of time in a prison or other closed institution where supposedly they will be resocialized to accept the norms of society. This approach, according to sociologists, is the approach of social order theory. It is questionable, and yet it is the prevailing theory of society. Several societies have taken a different view of this perspective of social order. Focusing on deviants, according to the philosophy of these societies, is to focus on the symptom and not on the disease. In other words, individual deviants are simply indicators of the failure of society to meet the needs of the individual citizens. Mental illness, for example, is the result of a poor quality of social life. School dropouts are not the problem of certain students, but a sign of the inadequacy of the educational system itself. Sources of crime, drug addiction, poverty, and racism are but a reflection of social ills and not of particular individuals whose ability to cope with the cause is done through deviant activity. With this focus, by some nations, on the inadequacies and social diseases rather than on individual deviants, there is room for entertaining a new concept in social control. Sweden and The Netherlands, for example, have taken a view of deviancy that may best illustrate this approach.[2]

In nations where the focus of social problems is on society rather than on individuals, there appears to be substance to the concept of prison abolishment and a rapid growth of alternatives for incarceration. There also appears to be wide public support for a humanistic approach to the treatment of citizens who have strayed from normal patterns of behaviors. Swedish citizens, for example, are credited with knowing more about their prison system and its operations than most other populations. The Swedes take pride in the fact that this knowledge has aided them in reducing the number of prisons in Sweden, developing pragmatic programs for offender resocialization, and maintaining the prisoners' civil rights during the process of resocialization.

Another factor to be considered in any discussion of social change is that morality, mores, and norms of societies are rapidly changing. Laws are no longer currently applicable and are no longer coupled with the social normality. This among several reasons has created a whole new school of radical criminologists including Richard Quinney, David Matza, and Anthony Platt who devoted considerable effort to underlining the proposition that crime can no longer be considered deviant behavior but that society itself is the deviant.[3]

Whether the cause is society or the individual, deviancy has its relationship to these norms, mores, and morality. These bulwarks of normality for any given society are becoming fragmented and separated with a disorder that cannot yet be comprehended or dealt with in any realistic manner. As comprehension is increased, society may cope with the problem and provide the mechanisms of legal and social adjustment appropriate for some new order. It is this transition period that is particularly disturbing. Corrections systems are caught between what was and what should be and find it difficult to make any advances with their particular institution of incarceration. There are many social conditions in the world today responsible for a confusion of social values and social conduct, energy and fuel crisis, population explosion, environmental deterioration, threat of nuclear war. This confusion of values helps create anomie or normlessness.

The result of this anomie in society contributes enormously to the problem of the perplexing crime picture. Whatever the cause, the problem is growing. Crime in most countries is increasing at an alarming rate. Methods of punishment or prevention are simply not working. Between 1980 and 2000 the judicial systems in many nations will be so overloaded that they will be at a point of collapse.[4] Law itself is the reactor rather than the anticipator, and it will continue to fall behind in providing definitions and appropriate measures for coping with the rapidly changing norms in the next decade. With this changing picture some societies may choose to maintain the status quo with regard to the handling of deviants and the maintenance of an incarceration type of sanctioning. Other nations may have enough evidence and motivation to usher in a new era of corrections in keeping with a new era of social life. Some countries have already begun to develop this new model of corrections. The recent conference of the European Ministers of Justice on the subject of alternatives to short-term imprisonment held in Zurich, Switzerland, and other similar meetings suggest that the concept of alternatives to prison has come into its own and is no longer simply a theory presented by reformists.[5] The forces of a changing society must be considered as the case for abolishment is presented. There are other forces that we must also consider. These forces can best be described as the forces of resistance to change.

Resistance to Change

In each society there are certain forces that tend to resist changes in the corrections systems of the society. Foremost of these are the political and philosophical outlooks of each society. What are the forces that resist change that must be dealt with in terms of prison abolishment or reform?

The Legal System

We have suggested that the law itself resists change in the corrections system. The United Nations Congress on the Prevention of Crime and

Treatment of Offenders suggested that it is often antiquated laws that prevent action by any and all of the various organized offices responsible for fulfilling the directives of the law.[6] Some nations are at an important turning point with regard to the use of the law in our changing society. It is the end of ten thousand years of juridic development.[7] This lengthy period of legal history was characterized by attempts to have the social behavior of a society, in all its subtle forms, controlled by the law. The law can perhaps be compared with a computer that was programmed to serve man but became so sophisticated that it reprogrammed itself and made man the slave. The law is often blamed for committing the injustices to man. It is argued that we cannot entertain any thoughts of prison abolition because the law says it cannot be done because it would be illegal. However, the law created the penal sanctions and the corrections system. When a citizen becomes involved in the legal system, he is no longer an individual citizen but merely a manila folder or a number that must be processed through the system. It is this unquestioned adherence to the machine-like system by many that has become a major resistance to change in corrections today.

Some nations that have recognized this gross error in which law is viewed as an uncontrollable mechanization of society which can not be changed but must be blindly adhered to and have begun making the law subordinate to the social order of society. Interestingly, the Peoples Republic of China has developed this concept in a clear form.[8] There the administration of justice is a neighborhood, communal affair. It is personalized and humanized in this respect. The family of the accused, his relatives, friends, fellow workers, and others are intensely involved in the fair and just use of law. The law is not the master nor does the law intrude where self-help or help from neighbors and friends is deemed a more pragmatic approach to help the offender.

The court, presided over by a trial judge, is a powerful arm of the law. He holds, perhaps, the most powerful position in the entire judicial and corrections network. Law interpretation, case examination, discretionary powers, and final disposition including sentences to prison or to a choice of alternatives are all within the powers of the judges of many nations. As Richard A. McGee suggests, the judge is The Man.[9] The power of the judge, like the power of the law, may resist change in the corrections system. In some nations the judges themselves have joined the public in making changes which makes the law less a mechanical monster. This should be encouraged. In these nations the judges have maintained their own humanitarian outlook as have many of the judges in The Netherlands. Perhaps their experiences, in many instances, of dehumanization in Nazi prison camps has helped them to maintain this perspective. Judges attending a law conference in Las Vegas, Nevada, recently spent an afternoon or an evening behind bars as a part of their training. A few hours behind bars in a training program may not create an entirely new attitude or significantly greater number of humanistic judges but it appears to be a step in a positive direction. The thread of rehumanization was woven throughout this training. Despite these significant inroads into rehumanizing the justice system and the law, many present laws and many judges remain forces resistant to changing the corrections system today.

The Corrections System

Today we have an inventory of fortresslike antiquated prisons and corrections institutions in almost every society of the world. Billions of dollars are invested in these too often poorly designed and poorly constructed masses of concrete and steel. They stand, in nations all over the world today, as monuments to man's failure to correct his fellow man by the lock-up method. In these prisons there are thousands of administrators, guards, supervisors, and other employees who not concerned with alternatives but only with defending their own institutions. There is a heirarchy of "keepers", "users," and "providers of services to criminals" in the prison complexes of the world.[10] Studies have shown that these groups of employees not only resist changes from prisons to alternatives but also resist changes in the prison system itself. Innovations that may be suggested by one group of prison employees are often quashed by the resistive forces of another group within the same prison. Often this resistance emerges in the form of seemingly objective research proving the worth of one method over another. Established prison systems are often considered to be the private property of their owners, the governor, the warden, legislative bodies, and others in power. With this status, prison systems become pawns of the political system. This factor is so important in many instances that even legislators who have campaigned for prison reform or for alternatives may be powerless when they assume their duties in state and national legislatures.

Prisoners

Strangely enough prisoners themselves may form a strong resistive force to changes in the correction system. Trust in any corrections system is usually low, and prisoners are traditionally suspicious of change. Punishment and resocialization efforts are often confused in the minds of prisoners. In Sweden, for example, experiments with prisoners that involved extended furloughs, greater flexibility of prison rules, and programs of staff and prisoner interactions almost failed until the staff and prisoners began to trust each other more. Fortunately the prisoners themselves discovered the reason for the failure of the experiment and took it upon themselves to cooperate responsibly in order to benefit from the program without destroying it.[11] It is extremely difficult to convince law offenders that any program of resocialization, either operating at present or planned for the future, is needed. Most of the cooperation of prisoners with staff is a part of the game to convince parole boards and prison administration that the offender is responding to the program. Greater resistance may occur when the innovation in the resocialization process appears to be some form of brainwashing such as behavior modification that would tamper with the prisoner's only personal property, the self.[12]

The Public

The people of most societies usually desire social order. While this may be considered elementary, it is a factor that is at the root of public resistance to changing prison systems. Alternatives and talk of abolishment tend to upset the public, who may consider them to be greater evils than the present and established prison system. Empirical evidence to the contrary goes unheard and unheeded if the public feels that their security is endangered. The concept of imprisoning society's felons tends to make the public feel more secure.[13] It is difficult to change this concept. The citizens may fear giving up the established prison system for something that may be viewed as a shaky step toward resocialization of the law offender. In some cases the cure may be more disasterous than the disease; alternatives may turn out to be worse than incarceration. Six years of limited detention, as one example, may be a poor alternative to one year in prison.[14]

These forces of resistance to change must be dealt with before reasonable progress can be made in establishing a new era of penology where the possibility of prison abolishment may exist. Resisting forces can be diluted and change can be fostered so that growth of the new system of corrections may be accelerated.

Changes toward the Abolition of Prisons

We now have enough evidence to support the assumption that prisons may not be needed in the future. Alternative methods of resocialization and changing penal sanctions have accomplished a move toward prison abolishment in several countries. These systems were described in other parts of this volume. Alternatives have already been quite successful in The Netherlands, Sweden, Canada, and in some states in America. Reductions of prison population in the Netherlands and in Sweden have not upset the national order, and public support has not been withdrawn even when crime rates in these countries increase. In order to usher in a new era in corrections, each society must approach the procedure from its own viewpoint.

A process of demythologizing present views of prison should be encouraged. One myth is that prisons deter crime. Incarceration has not discouraged many law offenders from criminal conduct nor has the threat of prison deterred potential criminals from their acts. Another myth is that prisons resocialize or rehabilitate. The records of the world's prisons in this instance are pitiful. Another myth is that prisons are worth their cost. Prisons are the most bankrupt of all public institutions; they fail in their avowed purpose. Still another myth is that prisons protect society.[15] This concept of public safety has been used continually to support prison construction. If security for a small number of dangerous criminals is needed, it can be obtained for much less cost with smaller units. There is also the myth that punishment will deter crime. The evidence contradicts this notion. Harsh punishment can create a motivation for revenge in the prisoner's mind. These myths must be examined, developed, researched, and publicly disseminated so that the general population may arrive at more sophisticated views of the corrections process than are now widely accepted. Established institutions or branches of these institutions must also have the full benefit of this demythologizing process.

It was suggested earlier in this discussion that the law was a resisting force. Laws are manmade and may be changed. Laws are not the master of men; men are the master of laws. Once this concept is made a viable part of the legislative process we may be able to make laws more useful for society. The question of morality and law is quite complex and cannot be properly discussed in the context of this discussion, but there are certain aspects of this morality question that we must touch. The enforcement of morality through public law is difficult and arbitrary. Offenses such as drunkenness, drug abuse, consensual sexual acts including homosexuality, abortion, and other so-called victimless crimes must be removed from the control of the courts.[16] Victimless crimes, crimes which do not result in anyone's feeling that they have been injured, cost the public $20 billion of the total U.S. expenditure for crime control including judicial enforcement, prosecution, and penal sanctioning. The total expenditure amounts to about $51 billion in the United States each year for law enforcement, losses from drug-related thefts, illicit gains from gambling, narcotics, and prostitution. Victimless crimes encourage extensive use of discretionary power in law enforcement efforts. Since there is no complainant, police resort to deviant means of enforcement. The investigations, themselves, are often immoral and illegal. Police tactics such as entrapment, use of informers, wiretapping and infringement of constitutional rights such as illegal search and seizure, invasion of privacy, and tactics to gain self-incrimination are notorious among U.S. police departments.[17]

Nations that have attempted to deal with morality issues in their laws now have many laws that cannot be enforced because of the expense involved. About 95 percent of all the prisoners in American jails for short periods of time are there because they were convicted of acts that could have been decriminalized. The cases of 2 million persons arrested for drunkenness in the United States alone now clog the courts each year. Another million persons are in jail charged with loitering or vagrancy. These are but a few of the problems faced by any nation in the use of morality laws.

A nation with the desire to improve its system of corrections must take inventory of its social and political system with regard to its philosophy of human rights. My research found that several nations adhere to the philosophy and behavior of citizen treating citizen with respect. When this attitude was observed and when the attitude was deeply ingrained in the social fabric of the nation a significant difference exists in the resocialization process. This attitude is woven into both the word of the law and the activity of the law enforcers, police, judges, and corrections personnel. There appears to be a correlation between low prison populations and encouraging attitudes toward abolishing prisons. This occurs when a humanitarian and egalitarian attitude is the core of the philosophy of corrections administration. I found this attitude most predominant in Sweden.[18] The judicial system, the police, the Parliament, and the general public operate in what Norval Morris calls "a very polite" social manner, and the state treats its citizens with respect.[19] In order for any nation to develop this attitude, it must create and support a system of sentencing policies in its courts that promote this egalitarian approach. In reality, however, offenders do not always receive the same sentence for the same crime in court systems throughout the world today. This points to the fact that the sanction policies and procedures in many courts should be reexamined and overhauled. Penal codes should be reconstructed, and state and national legislative bodies must be made aware, perhaps through efforts of the media, that new social and legal controls should be written and old laws expunged. In keeping with this new attitude and effort, prisoners' constitutional rights must be preserved. The equivalent to the European surveillance judge who oversees the offender's sentence should be included in every nation's judicial system. The surveillance judge's task is to make sure the offender receives the prescribed penal sanction, treatment, or resocialization help, and that the prison staff is doing its job accordingly. His surveillance may include visits to the prison and other actions.

This attitude of respect for all citizens must also be maintained in the matter of social rights for prisoners. This means that the right of all citizens to education, medical aid, work training, and welfare must not be stripped from the law offender.[20]

If this attitude of egalitarianism is to prevail in any nation, prisons must be, in fact, the very last resort. Any other viewpoint simply contributes to the myth that prisons are of value in the resocialization process. Gerhard O.W. Mueller, in establishing his ten recommendations for changes in correctional practice, suggests that "a meaningful sentencing hearing [must be exercised], in which the prosecutor has the burden of proving that imprisonment is required. . . ."[21] The use of incarceration as a sanction of the criminal justice system must be restricted as far as possible since it is the least effective sanction.

The value of short-term sentencing is becoming increasingly evident. The United States experimented with programs of short-term incarceration several years ago and found them to aid in terms of deterring crime. In addition, short-time sentencing of six months or less has reduced prison populations and also the disabilities that longer sentences promote. These disabilties include loss of job, family disruption, and other handicaps that contribute, to psychological disorientation and often promote additional, more severe, deviant behavior.

Another important part of this new attitude toward prisoner resocialization is the establishment of resocialization programs in the offender's home community. Even when incarceration is found to be necessary, the offender's place of incarceration should be near his home. At one time penologists believed that placing the prisoner a long distance from his home neighborhood was a correlate to the prisoner's rehabilitation. This is no longer the prevailing view. Instead it has been found that the use of neighborhood welfare, health, educational, and work programs, and the help of relatives, fellow workers, and neighbors are important in the resocialization of prisoners. The Scandinavian countries, The Netherlands, and other nations have found this to be the case. By the same token, however, when this concept is used in the Eastern Communist nations, the application of the home-area principle may be detrimental to the prisoner's life. The Comradeship Courts of Eastern Europe are an example of this negative approach. In this system a guilty person may be returned to his home area in the care of a public organization or working peoples' collective. This system is very efficient. The offender may find, however, that he is processed through unjustifiable interventions in his life, unnecessary sanctions, and personal harassment which make the local resocialization process all but intolerable.[22]

Diversion Programs

If a nation changes its attitude with regard to penal sanction and adopts the attitude that the deviate is a citizen in need of help, then diversion programs can be supported to a much greater extent. Diversion programs and alternatives are not new, and they are not used in many countries. Our examination of the Canadian experiments found several types of diversion programs:

1. Alternatives to prison included absolute or conditional discharges, restitution, fines, suspended sentences, probation, services to the community, partial detention in community-based facilities or programs of parole or release.[23]
2. Pretrial diversion includes the process of referring a case for handling at a pretrial level (through settlement or mediation procedures) instead of proceeding with the charges in the criminal court.
3. Screening is a process by which police refer an incident back to the family or community or simply drop the case rather than press criminal charges.[24]
4. Community absorption exists when individuals or particular interest groups deal with problems in their own area. This is done privately and outside the sphere of police or court intervention although, in some cases, the police or court may have been alerted to the incident.

With any of these diversions, the policies of the community and the police and courts must be publicly proclaimed and observed in every case. Asking the police and prosecutors to screen cases and to divert them from trial according to stated policies and guidelines can open up a whole new system of handling social deviation without challenging the community's prevailing sense of justice.[25] According to the Canadian Law Reform Commission these policies include the following:

1. There must be some rational basis on which to make the decision to indict or not to indict. On the police level these policies must apply so that they identify situations that call for an indictment rather than for screening. They should include criteria for filing charges rather than for screening them. Screening may be applied to many areas. Examples include incidents between juveniles and the elderly, family disputes, drunkenness and misuse of drugs, incidents where the culprit was mentally or physically disabled, and nuisance types of incidents.[26]
2. The following elements might be considered when deciding whether or not a charge should be filed:
   a. The offenses may be less serious than one that would require a trial according to the public interest.
   b. The resources necessary for dealing with the offender under the concept of the screening process must be reasonably available in the community.
   c. The alternative means of dealing with the incident must show the probability of success and should be effective in preventing further

incidents by the offender in the light of the offender's record and other evidence.

   d. The impact of arrest or prosecution on the accused or his family may be excessive in relation to the harm done.

   e. There may be a preexisting interrelationship between the victim and the offender in which both are open to a settlement outside the court.[27]

Diversion with any case that is considered for court hearing and that goes beyond the area of sound police screening practices requires that a role be given to both the victim and community interests in the disposition of the case. Police and prosecutors may be very actively involved in this process. If the circumstances are serious enough to warrant prosecution and the facts of the case are not in dispute, then the offender and victim may be asked to accept some type of pretrial settlement as an alternative to the prosecution and trial. Naturally the needs and interests of the larger society must be considered, but often these needs may be served better by some pretrial alternative than by conviction and sentence.

The growth of pretrial diversion programs has been most significant in the United States, but Canada and several other countries are making progress in this area. It is when these programs receive official or formal encouragement through parliaments and legislative bodies that they benefit the larger society. These programs usually tend to be more curative than punitive, and they are more humanitarian than is incarceration. When they are measured against incarceration in terms of control of crime rates and the correction of offenders, they at least equaled the effect of incarceration and have been many times more economical. They are less expensive universally than traditional programs. Restitutional programs have an added advantage in that both the victim and the offender receive almost immediate feedback which helps them feel that justice has been done and that resocialization may be successful. While the offender works to repay his victim, he receives on-the-job training, counseling, or education in life skills that so many offenders do not at present receive. At the same time, the victim may keep in touch with the rehabilitation of his offender, and in some cases, victims take such an interest in the case that they actually involve themselves in the offender's rehabilitation. The victim also receives compensation for the harm done. This may be a procedure whereby the court includes a restitution of damaged property or payment for the property by the offender by meeting with the victim and working out some form of restitution such as going to work for the victim to pay for the damage done. Under these circumstances, a wide variety of citizens, professionals, semiprofessionals, lay citizens, victims, and offenders are involved in a joint effort that appears to succeed in some communities and is far superior to incarceration methods in other communities.

Diversion programs do create certain risks but if all participants are informed of possible risks and are also informed of the ultimate right to trial, this risk is lessened. It also should be kept in mind that diversion programs are usually applicable only to those who would normally plead guilty or who expect conviction.

If an offender must be processed through the court trial procedure, then the responsibility for resocialization should be transferred back to the offender's own community and not to distant penal institutions.

When the community becomes more involved with the process of corrections, indifference and apathy are lessened. In addition, community involvement usually means that the offender will not be rejected. Apathy, indifference, and rejection by the members of the community are often responsible for the lack of progress in correction reform noted in some countries. The need for community involvement in the prison system can be demonstrated by reports in the media, especially television, on the inadequacies of present penal institutions. Citizen advisory groups can make a significant contribution by gathering data and enlisting the aid of the media in this effort. While direct participation of citizens in the development of correctional policy and programs involves certain risks with regard to conflict of purposes and philosophy with courts and correction programs, these risks can be reduced through a sincere and continued interaction between the various public groups. Prison staffs and prison officials must be involved in making changes so that resistance to change may be lessened. Each nation's bureaucracy and public has its own level of tolerance for change, but these levels should be continually tested by the reformer and supporter of reforms in order to achieve change.

The Present Climate for Change

Throughout this book we have focused on programs that may help move us from an age of penology in which society's deviants are punished to an age in which communities assume the major responsibility for assisting law offenders in a humanistic manner, to become useful, law-abiding members of the community. We have noted the high level of success of the Japanese in providing volunteer assistance for parolees or persons on probation.[28] Many other systems of alternatives exist in which both volunteers and professionals work together to provide a strong argument for the success of the community-based alternative or treatment programs for offenders.

Research for this volume also revealed many programs that were not discussed in these chapters. In Italy, for example, labor performed in prison or under a suspended sentence is combined with an obligation to make restitution from the prisoners' earnings. This procedure has opened the way for a new era in the use of alternatives in that country. Restitution has been made mandatory in Argentina, Norway, Sweden, Columbia, and several other countries. This expansion of the use of restitution is significant in that it paves the way for the development of means other than incarceration. In certain South African societies an offender who has physically harmed his victim is, by tradition, sentenced to nurse his victim back to health. In Poland the new penal code provides for a method of restricted liberty in which work and leisure time constraints open the way for resocialization without incarceration. The use of small villages where an offender and his family may live in the same house and where the entire family is involved in learning new work and life skills is a concept being developed in certain Scandinavian countries. This unique and hopeful concept needs to be explored to a much greater extent. The system of day fines in the Federal Republic of Germany and Sweden, where it originated, has now been incorporated in the Latin American penal code.[29] In the next few years it will be interesting to see whether this new viewpoint expands into a system of alternatives involving the community to a much greater extent than in the past. In Eastern Europe and the Union of Soviet Socialist Republics, community participation in the corrections process has developed into a variety of forms. While some of these alternatives may be more detrimental to the offender than incarceration, many of these programs show significant possibilities for succeeding, if developed with a more democratic philosophy in mind and with a much higher regard for a more progressive approach. These programs need to be explored in considerable detail by members of the democratic world communities.

Empirical research on the effectiveness of community-based treatment programs is scarce. The development of a new era in corrections needs objective research and wide publication of the results of such research.

Conclusions

In the book *A Nation without Prisons* I suggested that prisons serve two legitimate functions. One of these functions is the protection of people and property, and the other is punishment.[30] I suggested that prisons should probably exist for the so-called dangerous offender. This viewpoint was based on available data concerning incarceration in one nation, the United States. My studies of Sweden indicate that this original concept of incarceration is applicable in other countries as well as in the United States. In addition, I discovered that Swedish citizens took great pride in their social welfare system and could express this pride in everday conversation with considerable knowledge of their prison system. Such pride is universal, which is not the case in many other nations. In other nations the prison systems appears to be operating almost with the same philosophies that were in evidence when prisons were places in which prisoners were severely punished, kept in solitary cells most of the time, and treated inhumanely. During my research I found materials that suggest that certain societies may have come half-circle from a time when a more constructive attitude toward prison reformation is replaced recently by a much narrower view. In Madrid, Spain, for example, while I was investigating the Spanish prison system, I learned about the ambush and death of the director general of Spanish prisons because of his do-nothing attitude concerning prison reforms. It seems that in this age of efforts for Spanish democratization by King Juan Carlos, the director general was operating under the old philosophies of Franco. The incident recalled to mind the life of another prison director in that same country, Manuel Montesinos.

During the twenty years of his work as prison reformer and especially as director of the presidio at Valencia from September 2, 1837, until his retirement March 31, 1857, Montesinos was a modern idealist's picture of a reformer. As a boy, Montesinos had fought in the war against Napoleon, spent five years in a prison himself, had been active in the Spanish civil war between 1833 and 1840 and had been a war refugee in France on several occasions.

When Montesinos began to climb the administrative ladder in Spain's penal system, his performance was that of a modern prison reformer. His humanitarian treatment of prisoners at the presidio of Valencia, for example, included the following:

1. He instituted a self-contained military unit at his prison in order to combat the popular trend in those days by politicians and army officers of taking over presidios in order to enlist convicts for their own purposes.
2. He developed forty different workshops and instituted a training or apprenticeship worker program for each shop which included the ranks apprentice, skilled craftsman, and master craftsman.
.3. For youths below the age of eighteen he built a special youth section where chains and fetters were abolished and primary and secondary school subjects were taught along with vocational training.
.4. He provided an improved diet (which included vegetables grown in the prison garden), an emergency infirmary, a well-equipped pharmacy, and a small hospital.
5. He cleared his presidio, a former convent, of useless structures and had a small zoo and a bird sanctuary constructed and enlarged the garden for prisoners to use and enjoy.
6. He instituted furlough or leave programs and provided a program by which good conduct earned early release.
7. He provided a program of remuneration in which prisoners kept one-

fourth of their salary for purchasing personal items and put one-fourth of their wages into a savings account.
8. He deemphasized the vindictive and public-use concept so that almost all work done by convicts was for their own rehabilitation rather than for the pleasure of the state.

Montesinos was doing all this in an atmosphere of trust and respect for the individual in the 1830s and 1840s, a period of world history in which most of the world was barely emerging from feudal philosophies of rights of criminals. Even the present modern concept of work release was a part of Montesinos' routine. He provided programs whereby prisoners left the prison confines without guards, did their work, and returned to the presidio in good faith. His rehabilitation efforts were successful. Spain at that time had a 45 percent recidivist rate. The presidio of Valencia under Montesinos' direction had a recidivist rate of only about 1 percent. Montesinos' innovations including work-skill development in decent jobs, a work remuneration program, abolition of corporal punishment and prisoner harassment, sincere respect for humans including prisoners, exit and work release programs, and the absence of bars, locks, and high walls were truly innovative for his time. He did this at a time when the trend was for the construction of prisons of maximum security, sometimes patterned after the Philadelphia or Auburn prison models in America.

After 1850 Spain regressed to the philosophy that prisoners were simply pawns of the state to be used at the whim and of individual prison directors. Treatment once again often became cruel and inhuman.[31]

Montesinos' efforts at prison reform suggest that reformation of prison systems in any nation mirrors that nation's attitude toward humankind. Humane treatment of criminals is seen as a weakness by the people of some nations. For this reason, the difficulties in establishing universal prison reformation, rapid growth of prison alternatives, or the abolishment of prisons must be viewed much more realistically. While I was completing this chapter, conflict in China, Vietnam, Iran, and Africa reminded me that social changes are rapidly being made throughout the world. The energy crisis alone will change much of the behavior of the people of the world. These social, political, and environmental events will also change the public philosophies of nations with regard to deviance and control. Often correction reform is put aside while a nation concentrates on other seemingly more serious problems.

There are however, a significant number of people in many nations today who take the view that any effort to redirect people's lives within prison is futile and that the effort must be abandoned. This position may be summarized as follows:

1. The institution embodying the concept of incarceration, the prison, has failed consistently to change the behavior of people. No treatment model in these walled environments applied thus far in prison history has made a demonstrable effect on prisoners.
2. The modern medical model of treatment of prisoners is ineffective in resocialization.
3. The fundamental conflict of goals between the various competing groups in prisons is insoluble.
4. The stigma of imprisonment cannot be erased through parole or release, and the attendant labels hinder the offender's remaining years and efforts at reintegration into society. Once the label "convict" is affixed to a citizen, the consequence is that the label becomes indelibly attached to his efforts to become a free citizen.
5. The incarceration of offenders is self-defeating. It is, most often, the informal inmate society of the institution that is the socialization mechanism and shapes the prisoner's reaction to confinement. Prison staff efforts to counteract this socialization process among inmates have always been nonproductive. As a result, the prison or correction institution serves to dehumanize the offender and to reinforce negative social values rather than to modify offender's behavior to some social norm.[32]

From this position, we may conclude that in our world today the problem of prisons is the prison itself. The role of the prison must be limited to a place of confinement only for the most dangerous of our social deviants. Even in this role, prisoners subjected to prison confinement should be sentenced to determinate sentences at the end of which he is released. Prisons cannot serve as treatment centers. Treatment is beyond most prison administrations and the orientation and training of their staff. Programs of work, education, and treatment if provided in prisons should be offered on a voluntary basis. Pragmatic treatment programs should remain a part of the community approach to prisoner resocialization.

In the light of present changes in nations throughout the world, especially those changes related to oil and other fuel and energy shortages, the economic structures of many nations will be affected. These drastic changes will be reflected in the crime picture and in the penal sanctions of each nation. The liberal reform movements of the past, according to Richard Quinney, are unsatisfactory for prison reform since they treat social deviants as the problem rather than society. If economic revolution is the key to change in our corrections systems, as Quinney suggests, then we will have the chance to see a revolution in some nations in the next few years. The swing from prosperity to recession will occur more often in the next few years, and this erratic economic picture will be reflected in the crime, law, and corrections systems of many nations.

Correctional systems of nations are only mirrors of their social and economic systems. The development and progress of corrections systems is limited by the social and political attitudes of any particular population and its leaders. Fortunately certain nations such as Sweden, the Netherlands, and Canada, and perhaps other nations have demonstrated that public attitude can be changed. Public support for the elimination of prisons or for the desire to continually improve methods of treatment of law offenders can be insured when the efforts of reformers become a cooperative endeavor with the media supporting the effort. Denmark has demonstrated an excellent and progressive method of dealing with the psychologically disturbed criminal, and Canada has excelled in certain provinces in the use of the day fine system and Community Work Service Orders. We must make every effort to grasp these concepts, research them, and apply the meaningful methodologies as quickly as possible. The law offender, after all, is a human being and a citizen, and goals for his resocialization should concentrate on creating a lifelong sense of self-esteem and worth. This self-image must be coupled with identification with an anticriminal behavior. If incarceration is necessary, the main goal of such imprisonment should be to enhance the client's chances for achieving satisfaction in legitimate activities after release from incarceration.

If these goals are sought, then the need for prisons in the future may be minimized and prospects for a world without prisons may be realized.

Notes

1. United Nations, "The Treatment of Offenders, in Custody or in the Community, with Special Reference to the Implementation of the Standard Minimum Rules for the Treatment of Prisoners Adopted by the United Nations," Working Paper of the Secretariat, Fifth United Nations Congress on the Prevention of Crime and Treatment of Offenders, Toronto, Canada, September 1975, Document 75-99964, pp. 60-61.

2. D. Stanley Eitzen, *Social Structure and Social Problems in America,* (Boston: Allyn and Bacon, 1974), p. 11.

3. Richard Quinney, *Crime and Justice in Society* (Boston: Little, Brown, 1969) p. 20. See also R. Quinney, *Class, State and Crimes,* (New York: Longman, 1977).

4. Denis Szabo, "Crime, Deviance, and Law in Post-Industrial Society: Profile of Future Trends" in *Criminology between the Rule of Law and the Outlaws,* ed. C.W.G. Jasperse et al. (Deventer: Netherlands Kluwer-Co., 1976), p. 192.

5. P.W. Haesler, ed., "Alternatives to Short-Term Imprisonment," Comité National Suisse de la Santé Mentale, Group de Travail de Criminologie, mimeographed, March 1978, Zurich, 25 pp.

6. United Nations, "Treatment of Offenders," p. 60.

7. Szabo, "Crime, Deviance, and Law," p. 192.

8. J.M. Van Bemmelen, "The Achilles Heel of the Criminal Justice System," in *Criminology between the Rule of Law and the Outlaws*, p. 154.

9. Donald R. Cressey, "Sources of Resistance to Innovation in Corrections," in *Offenders as a Correctional Manpower Resource,* (Washington, D.C.: Joint Commission on Correctional Manpower and Training, June 1968), pp. 31-49; reprinted in *Correctional Institutions,* ed. Robert M. Carter, (New York: J.B. Lippincott, 1972), p. 445.

10. Ibid., p. 444.

11. See chap. 10 *A World without Prisons.*

12. Cressey, "Sources of Resistance to Innovation in Corrections," pp. 456-457.

13. Mark Morris (Pseud. Mark B. Schnapper) with F.H. Knopp, eds., *Instead of Prisons, A Handbook for Abolitionists* (Syracuse, N.Y.: Prison Research Education Action Project, 1976), chap. 2.

14. Dodge, C., ed. *A Nation without Prisons* (Lexington, Mass.: Lexington Books, D.C. Heath, 1975), p. 235.

15. Morris, *Instead of Prisons*, chap. 2.

16. Norval Morris, "Impediments to Penal Reform," *Law Review*, University of Chicago Press, 33 (1966):627-656.

17. N. Morris, *Instead of Prisons*, chap. 2, p. 103.

18. David M. Peterson and Charles W. Thomas, *Corrections: Problems and Prospects,* (Englewood Cliffs, N.J.: Prentice-Hall, 1975), p. 283; see also Dodge, *A Nation without Prisons,* and this volume, chap. 10.

19. Norval Morris, "Lessons from the Adult Correctional System in Sweden," in Peterson and Thomas, *Corrections: Problems and Prospects,* p. 283.

20. Dodge, *A Nation without Prisons,* p. 238.

21. Dodge, *A Nation without Prisons,* p. 237

22. Hans H. Brydensholt and Ole Ingstrup, Involvement of the Community as Volunteers, A Strategy for the Involvement of Members of the Public in the Treatment of Offenders, mimeographed, Ministry of Justice, Kragskouhede, Denmark, 1976; see also United Nations, "Treatment of Offenders."

23. United Nations, "Criminal Legislation, Judicial Procedures, and Other Forms of Social Control in the Prevention of Crime," Fifth United Nations Congress on the Prevention of Crime and Treatment of Offenders, Toronto, Canada, September 1975, Document 75-100028, p. 22. See also Amy A. Wilson, et al., *Deviance and Control in Chinese Society* (New York: Praeger, 1977).

24. Law Reform Commission of Canada, *Studies of Diversion*, Ottawa, Information Department, 1975, p. 4.

25. United Nations, "Criminal Legislation," p. 22.

26. Ibid., p. 23.

27. Ibid., p. 23.

28. Ministry of Justice, Information Bureau, *Noninstitutional Treatment of Offenders in Japan* (Tokyo, 1970).

29. United Nations, "Treatment of Offenders," p. 9.

30. Dodge, *A Nation without Prisons*, chap. 12.

31. Francisco Franco de Blas, "Formación Penitenciaria del Coronel Montesinos y su Celebre Sistema," *Revista Journal de Estudios Pentenciaros*, Madrid, Dirección General de Prisonea, año, 18, no. 159, (October-December, 1962):97-122. See also: Marvin E. Wolfgang, ed., *Crime and Culture: Essays in Honor of Thorsten Sellin* (New York: John Wiley, 1968).

32. United Nations, "Treatment of Offenders," p. 23.

Appendix 12A
Prison Population

Table 12A-1

**Average Prison Population per 100,000 Population in Various Nations:
A Comparison of 1972 and 1974 Census Figures**

Nation or State	1972	1974	Trend[a]
1 Cambodia	*	9	o
2 The Netherlands	22	21	−
3 Cyprus	31	*	o
4 Ireland	35	*	o
5 India	*	36	o
6 Malaysia	25	37	+
7 Norway	*	39	o
8 Spain	*	40	o
9 Nigeria	*	42	o
10 Japan	46	43	−
11 Sweden	54	44	−
12 Portugal	*	44	o
13 Italy	*	51	o
14 France	61	52	−
15 Philippines	*	53	o
16 Denmark	69	54	−
17 Dahomey	*	55	o
18 Belgium	63	58	−
19 Ecquador	58	*	o
20 Iraq	59	*	o
21 Syrian Arab Republic	35	69	+
22 Australia	83	70	−
23 United Kingdom	82	75	−
24 Federal Republic of Germany	86	81	−
25 Mexico	*	83	o
26 New Zealand	*	85	o
27 Trinidad and Tobago	106	86	−
28 Sierra Leone	*	88	o
29 Sri Lanka	64	98	+
30 Canada	90	95	+
31 Finland	102	101	−
32 Tunisia	103	*	o
33 Chile	108	*	o
34 Austria	109	104	−
35 Morocco	96	108	+
36 Argentina	109	*	o
37 Lebanon	120	*	o
38 Panama	120	*	o
39 Jamaica	121	121	±
40 Fiji	*	124	o
41 Ivory Coast	130	*	o
42 Thailand	124	133	+
43 Israel	134	137	+
44 Venezuela	127	151	+
45 Kenya	165	*	o
46 El Salvador	*	175	o
47 Columbia	186	178	−
48 United States	189	250**	+

Source: Various nations' census figures and United Nations' census figures of member nations.

[a]− = downward, + = upward, o = no trend indicated.

*Figures not available.

**Estimated.

Table 12A-2

Average Prison Population per 100,000 Population in Several European Nations, Daily Averages of Total Prison Population and Total Staff

Nation	Year	Average Prison Population per 100,000	(Total) Prison Population	Staff Members[a] Population (includes administrators)	Number of Staff Members per Client[b]
The Netherlands	1974-1978	21	2,950	3,189	1.3
Norway	1975	45	2,250	1,100	0.4
France	1975	55	28,770	11,000	0.4
Belgium	1974	58	5,700	3,074	0.5
Denmark	1975	54	3,283	3,400	1.1
United Kingdom (England and Wales)	1973	75	36,774	18,869	0.5

Source: Census figures of prisons for nations listed and United Nations' census figures.

[a]Total staff populations include administrators.

[b]Number of staff members per client is based on number of staff members who actually come in contact with clients. It does not include administrators.

Table 12A-3

A Comparison of International Prison Populations per 100,000 Populations of Selected Nations

Rank	Nation	Year	Prison Population per 100,000 Population
1	Iceland	1973	19
2	The Netherlands	1971	22
3	Norway	1971	37
4	Spain	1972	40
5	Japan	1972	46
6	Italy	1972	51
7	Belgium	1971	60
8	France	1972	61
9	Sweden	1971	61
10	Luxembourg	1971	64
11	Denmark	1971	70
12	United Kingdom (England and Wales)	1971	81
13	West Germany	1971	84
14	Canada	1972	90
15	New Zealand	1972	93
16	Finland	1972	107
17	Australia	1972	128
18	Poland	1972	190
19	United States	1972	208
20	East Germany	1972	222

Source: The Netherlands Ministry of Justice reports of 1974 and Alfred Heijder, "The Recent Trend toward Reducing the Prison Population in The Netherlands," *International Journal of Offender Therapy and Comparative Criminology* 18 (1974). Reprinted with permission.

Indexes

Name Index

Subject Index

About the Author

Calvert R. Dodge is a lecturer for the University of Maryland and has lived in Korea, Japan, Okinawa, Turkey, Spain, England, and Germany during the last four years where he investigated prison systems firsthand. He received the M.A. in sociology from the University of Wyoming in 1957 and the Ph.D. in communication from the University of Denver in 1971. He was director of the Colorado Youth Workers Training Center and served as vice-president of the American Society for Training and Development from 1969-1971. Dr. Dodge presently conducts classes in criminology, sociology, and communication in the Washington, D.C. area, and is headquartered at College Park, Maryland.